Library of
Davidson College

MILLENARIANISM AND MESSIANISM
IN ENGLISH LITERATURE AND THOUGHT
1650–1800

Publications from the Clark Library Professorship, UCLA

Volumes 1–9 of this Series have been published by the University of California Press

10.
Millenarianism and Messianism in English Literature and Thought 1650–1880. Edited with an Introduction, by Richard H. Popkin.

MILLENARIANISM AND MESSIANISM IN ENGLISH LITERATURE AND THOUGHT 1650–1800

CLARK LIBRARY LECTURES 1981–1982

EDITED BY

RICHARD H. POPKIN
Clark Library Professor, 1981–1982

E.J. BRILL
LEIDEN · NEW YORK · KØBENHAVN · KÖLN
1988

LIBRARY OF CONGRESS
Library of Congress Cataloging-in-Publication Data

Millenarianism and messianism in English literature and thought, 1650–1800 : Clark Library lectures, 1981–1982 / edited by Richard H. Popkin.
    p.   cm. -- (Publications from the Clark Library professorship, UCLA ; 10)
    ISBN 9004085130
    1. Millenarianism--Great Britain--History. 2. Messianism.
3. English literature--18th century--History and criticism.
4. Millenarianism in literature. 5. Messianism in literature.
6. English literature--Early modern, 1500–1700--History and criticism. 7. Utopias. I. Popkin, Richard Henry, 1923-
II. Series.
BR757.M45 1988
236'. 0942--dc 19   88-4284
                                                                                                       CIP

ISBN 90 04 08513 0

© *Copyright 1988 by E.J. Brill, Leiden, The Netherlands*

All rights reserved. No part of this book may be reproduced or translated in any form, by print, photoprint, microfilm, microfiche or any other means without written permission from the publisher

PRINTED IN THE NETHERLANDS BY E.J. BRILL

CONTENTS

List of Contributors	VII
Introduction R.H. POPKIN	1
I. 'Till the Conversion of the Jews' CHRISTOPHER HILL	12
II. England, Israel and the Triumph of Roman Virtue STEVEN N. ZWICKER	37
III. Bishop Berkeley's Messianism HARRY M. BRACKEN	65
IV. Mysticism and Millenarianism: 'Immortal Dr. Cheyne' GEORGE S. ROUSSEAU	81
V. Freemasonry and the Utopian Impulse MARGARET C. JACOB	127
VI. The Body of God in the 17th Century Theology and Science AMOS FUNKENSTEIN	149
VII. On Reading Newton Apocalyptically ARTHUR QUINN	176
VIII. The Voice of the Text HENRY LEWIS GATES	193

LIST OF CONTRIBUTORS

Harry M. Bracken, Department of Philosophy, McGill University, Montreal, Canada

Amos Funkenstein, Department of History, University of California, Los Angeles, California

Henry Louis Gates, Department of Afro-American Studies, Cornell University, Ithaca, New York

Christopher Hill, Master of Balliol College, Oxford, retired

Margaret Jacob, Provost, New School for Social Research, New York, New York

Richard H. Popkin, Professor Emeritus, Washington University, St. Louis; Adjunct Professor, Departments of History and Philosophy, University of California, Los Angeles, California

Arthur Quinn, Department of Rhetoric, University of California Berkeley

George S. Rousseau, Department of English, University of California, Los Angeles

Steven N. Zwicker, Department of English, Washington University, St. Louis

RICHARD H. POPKIN

INTRODUCTION

Millenarianism and Messianism in English Literature and Thought

The idea for this series of seminars derived from a talk I gave at the Clark Library in 1975, when Perez Zagorin, then Clark Library Professor, invited me to participate in his program on "Culture and Politics from Puritanism to the Enlightenment." I presented a paper on material I was working on called "Jewish Messianism and Christian Millenarianism." The Clark Library, through its former director, Professor Robert Vosper, invited me to expand on this theme, by making it the program for the academic year 1981–82. By this time I had become immersed in various aspects of the topic from the Renaissance and Reformation up to the 19th century, and was (and still am) projecting a large study on the Christian roots of Zionism. I was delighted to have the opportunity to organize the series of seminars on aspects of the theme of Millenarianism and Messianism. In view of the Clark Library's special holdings, its rich collection of English materials from the 17th and 18th centuries, the topic was mainly focused on relevant developments in English literature, philosophy, politics, science, and theology from 1650–1800 (though, of course, speakers sometimes stretched these boundaries in terms of their own special interests and to explain the developments in England and their importance).

In the last few decades there has been a growing interest in the history and influence of Jewish, Christian and Moslem movements which have been guided by an intense conviction that the "end of days" was approaching, when the climax of Providential history, as forecast in the Old Testament, the New Testament or the Koran, will occur. In each tradition there is a vision of Divine intervention in human history that will transform the human scene into some kind of paradise on earth. Although such movements in Judaism go back into pre-Christian times, in Christianity to the second or third centuries, and in Mohammedanism to the seventh century, there has been little interest or concern to understand the motivations and influence of such groups. They were usually regarded as irrational or prerational expressions that no longer were of any importance.

It was perhaps the enormous impact of two secular Millenarian movements of the twentieth century that made the study of Millenarianism significant. Both Nazism, preparing for a thousand year state ruled by the Aryan elite, and Communism, preparing for an endless, happy, classless society, transformed modern world history. Attempts to understand the force of these views led to looking at earlier examples. Hence, works like Norman Cohn's *Pursuit of the Millennium* sought to find antecedents for what had transpired in the mid-20th century, in late medieval European revolutionary Millenarian movements. Research into earlier revolutionary movements with egalitarian aims revealed that religious forces and ideas were usually involved in such developments as the Puritan Revolution and even the French Revolution. Great expectations of the imminent reentry of God into history were involved in the Jewish Kabbalistic ideas that emerged in the 16th and 17th centuries, and culminated in the most important and disastrous Messianic movement in Jewish history. Humane groups such as the Quakers, the abolitionists, the Mennonites, and the Unitarians had arisen out of new Millenarian interpretations of the message of Christianity.

Previous generations of scholars were content, by and large, to ignore the antiquated and incredible (to enlightened minds) interpretations of Scripture, and assume that these views did not have to be seriously examined. They thought the interpreters of Biblical prophecies, like the astrologers and alchemists, had little to offer to the modern mind. Studies such as Ernest Tuveson's *Millennium and Utopia* and *Redeemer Nation* indicated, however, that the enlightened world issued from some of these unenlightened views. The work of Gershom Scholem, Frances Yates, D.P. Walker and Walter Pagel, among others, showed that one had to recognize the role of the so-called irrational mind in the making of the modern mind. Possibly because the modern world is turning out to have so many forceful, irrational elements that do not disappear with the growth of scientific knowledge, there has been an interest in understanding the irrational elements of the past. Movements and ideas that would have been dismissed or ignored by earlier scholars have recently become the focus of new studies, to be understood as vital features of the human scene. Developments in the Middle East from Israel to Iran have made us realize the latent force of Millenarian and Messianic movements today, and how they can make the most stubborn secular humanists take note that religious people's ideas of religious events to come can transcend *realpolitik*, economic advantage, or anything else. And we have begun to see how these can affect the very world in which we live and its future.

The turn to the scholarly exploration of Millenarian and Messianic movements has been very rewarding in elucidating many interesting and intriguing texts in the history of science, philosophy, politics, religion and literature. Political and social historians, literary scholars, anthropologists, political scientists, sociologists, students of religion, psychologists and psychiatrists have been examining the nature and importance of beliefs about forthcoming events that would transform the quality of human life, and associated beliefs about the nature and destiny of man. Such views appear in many cultures and traditions from the cargo cults in New Guinea to various ancient, Near Eastern religions, to traditional Judaism, radical Christianity, certain Islamic groups, as well as post enlightenment nationalist and socialist movements. This has led to a great deal of reexamination of various parts of our history.

The period covered by the holdings of the William Andrews Clark Memorial Library, English publications, 1640–1750, has been one of those that has been especially rewarding, interpreted in terms of Millenarian and Messianic movements. Studies of the Puritan Revolution, the Restoration, the impact of the Revocation of the Edict of Nantes in bringing Huguenot Millenarians and Millenarian thought to England, the rise of science in England and the role of the Royal Society, the interpretation of Jewish and Christian ideas from the early Puritans onward, the development of deism, and secular Millenarianism, the theological impact of Newton's scientific and religious ideas, and many other cases, have revealed hitherto neglected or misunderstood aspects of both major and minor streams of English thought in the period. And the lessons learned from re-evaluating this material have often turned out to be extremely fruitful in providing further understanding of our intellectual history.

When I was invited to be the Clark Professor in 1981–82, I felt this would be an opportunity to make the scholarly world more aware of the kinds of research being done about Millenarianism in the 17th and 18th centuries, and some of the applications of this research in various areas. Still, with the vast range of research going on concerning almost every topic of intellectual interest in the period, the nine lectures by specialists in various disciplines could naturally give only a partial picture of what we are now learning about an aspect of our past, and what could be applied to understanding the present. By bringing to the fore what is usually considered the under side of history, it is hoped that people will realize the range of new insights and interpretations that are being developed in political, religious, cultural and intellectual history when it is seen in relation to the Millenarian and Messianic currents of the time.

A decade ago, I gave a seminar on Millenarian and Messianic thought. As I presented to the class the apocalyptic religious elements in various intellectual movements from the Reformation and Renaissance to the Enlightenment and the French and American Revolutions, a student asked me in amazement if I really believed that the "nuts" who were interpreting obscure texts in Scripture as predictions of what was going to happen, really have had any influence in the important developments from 1500–1800. I told him plainly that not only did I think that one had to appreciate how much the Millenarians and Messianists influenced history then, but also, how much they influenced it before and after that period. The student was sure I was joking. By now, he and other scoffers and doubters have had to realize that everything from present day American politics to the secular-religious conflict within Israel, Zionism itself, the re-emergence of Shi'ism as a force in the Moslem world, the imminent revolutionary forces in Poland, Protestant and Catholic nationalism in Northern Ireland, and more, is deeply enmeshed in Millenarian and Messianic ideas.

In the recent past the emergence of a so-called "Moral Majority" in the United States as a powerful political and social force has made us ask when and where did the ideas behind the movement arise. This quickly led us back to Fundamentalism, to the 19th century conflict between religion and science, to the 18th century as both an age of reason and an age of revelation, and to the 17th century as the time when new religious ideas, new scientific ideas, and new political dreams, produced numerous Millenarian theories that interacted with and interpreted the vast changes taking place in the Thirty Years War, the Puritan Revolution, the Turkish invasion of central Europe, and the increasing triumphs of colonialism all over the planet.

These astounding events came after such momentous developments as the Reformation and the Counter-Reformation, the conversion of most Spanish and Portuguese Jews to Christianity, the discovery of America, the re-discovery of the ancient Mediterranean world, and the emergence of national states. Was "all coherence gone," or did these events make sense if seen as the prophesized developments of human history as it approached its climax? Learned theologians, Jewish, Catholic and Protestant, began to offer radical new interpretations of these earth-shaking events. The Jewish Kabbalists studying with Isaac Luria in Palestine saw God re-entering history to bring about its fulfillment. People were living through the birth pangs of the promised Messiah; Catholics such as Luis de Leon in Spain, Antonio de Vieira in Portugal, and Guillaume Postel in France and Italy saw that the restoration of the world was imminent. Protestants in Holland, Germany, Bohemia and England became convinced the Reformation had revealed Antichrist, the Bishop of Rome, and that Christ's reappearance as world ruler was at hand. As John Napier, Thomas Brightman, John Henry Alsted, Jacob Boehme, and Jan Amos Comenius insisted, the turbulent events of the time were those predicted in the book of *Daniel* and the *Revelation of John the Divine*.

The "dean" of English Millenarianism, Joseph Mede, at Cambridge, 1586–1638, found the key to the *Apocalypse* in a system of synchronisms of the events forecast in *Daniel* and *Revelation*, and in a way of identifying present events with the prophetic scenario. At the Clark in 1981–82, going over its large collection of great, good, mediocre, poor and sometimes dreadful theology, I found that the theory of "the very learned and very pious" Joseph Mede of Cambridge emerged from his struggle to overcome his own personal skeptical crisis, engendered when he read Sextus Empiricus as a freshman. He was able to escape from complete doubt only when he found the key to the Apocalypse, a method for interpreting the *Book of Revelation*, and for calculating when the Millennium, the Thousand Year reign of Christ would begin; and when the antecedent events, the fall of Antichrist, and the conversion of the Jews would take place. Mede saw that these events were part of what was taking place before his very eyes in the European history of the time, the Thirty Years' War, the turbulent history of England, and in the development of a purer Christianity there.

Mede and his students and disciples, including John Milton, Henry More, Samuel Hartlib, John Dury, William Twisse and hosts of other Millenarians, took seriously the injunction in *Daniel* that, as the end approaches, knowledge and understanding will increase, the wise will understand, while the wicked will not. They also took seriously the need to prepare, through reform, for the glorious days ahead. Their efforts to gain and encourage scientific knowledge, to build a new educational system, to transform political society, were all part of their Millenarian reading of events. They needed to understand, to construct a new theory of knowledge, a new metaphysics, for the new situation, the Thousand Year reign of Christ on earth, which was to be followed by a new heaven and a new earth. Efforts to accomplish this great end are part of the making of the modern world and of the making of the modern mind. By the focus on Millennial aspects, in this lecture series, it was hoped scholars would see how all pervasive the theme was, and how influential it was, and would better understand subsequent developments in intellectual history. Some of the papers illuminate parts of 17th and 18th century history in terms of the Millennial thinking and activity involved. Others show basic metaphysical changes that took place. And some show how the Millennial model can explain major conceptual views in quite different contexts up to the 20th century.

The series began with Christopher Hill's giving a new exegesis on Marvell's line, "Till the conversion of the Jews," bringing to the fore the forgotten message that the conversion of the Jews is seen as *the* crucial pre-Millennial event, and that important people expected the event to actually take place in the 1650's. Hill's delightfully rich paper showed how the theological calculations and expectations fused with English political and economic interests up to 1656, the predicted year, according to some Millenarians, of the great event of the conversion of the Jews. Then, though the Millennial fervor cooled and was forced down during the Restoration, the colonial empire that grew in part out of the expectations managed to remain and flourish without the conversion of the Jews.

The paper of Stephen Zwicker carefully portrays the contrast between England of the Puritans, seeing itself as the new and true Israel, and the England of the establishment during the Restoration, seeing itself as the new and true Rome. As is only fitting in a seminar series at the Clark Library with its impressive Dryden collection, Zwicker uses Dryden to portray this shift, as he moved from Biblical themes to his translation of the *Aenead*. The difference in metaphor and imagery, and in the value system being conveyed is striking, as the Restoration establishment tried to quiet down, and, if possible, eliminate the force of Millenarian thinking.

The next two papers, those of Harry Bracken and George Rousseau, are significant case studies of the ideas of two major intellectuals of the early 18th century, (when it is often claimed that Millenarianism had disappeared as a view of serious intellectuals, and had been turned over to the rabble to revel in). The philosopher, Bishop George Berkeley, and the leading medical doctor, George Cheyne, each seem to have had a Millenarian vision that changed their lives. In Berkeley's case, Bracken contends, it may have led to the philosopher's decision to go to America to found a college in Bermuda to convert the Indians. Putting Berkeley's educational project in the context of the view of the time that the Indians were Jews, part of the Lost Tribes, puts a new perspective on Berkeley's plan, and makes it less of a peculiar historical oddity.

Dr. Cheyne, as Rousseau points out, was deeply immersed in the vital Millenarian currents of the time, the views of Boehme that were widespread then, their interpretations by Jane Lead and the Philadelphians, the excitement caused by the newly arrived French prophets who were spreading their visions around England, and such active Millenarian Newtonians as Fatio de Duillier and William Whiston, who were combining their Newtonian science, with prophecy, and preparations for the Apocalypse. Dr. Cheyne saw his own bodily development, as he grew to weigh over 400 pounds, then reduced to 130 pounds, and again became enormously fat, as an apocalyptic drama within himself.

Berkeley became a joke among the wits of the time for his philosophy and his failed Bermuda plan, but Cheyne, the mystical doctor, remained a significant figure because he was the physician to so many important people, the author of a crucial interpretation of medicine and Millenarianism, and a friend and associate of important literati.

Another way such powerful ideas were diffused is presented in Margeret Jacob's paper. The Millenarian and Messianic views that were embraced by Newton, his chosen successor, Whiston, and others, were transformed into secular utopian ones, especially by the emerging movement of the Free Masons. In the elite culture, the spokesman for the Masons described a "Masonic paradise", that would exist on earth among the enlightened and the educated. Jacob, using some of her newly found materials about the 18th century Masons, deftly shows how the lodges, both in England and on the Continent, offered a formulation for earthly happiness that no longer required a transformation of the world, a new heaven and a new earth.

But, as Jacob points out, the utopia portrayed by the Masons gave rise to its own revolutionary pressures, that were to have almost as much impact as some of the apocalyptic views.

The Millennial theology that developed in Europe in the 17th century led to reconsidering the nature of God, if God was playing such an active role in human history. One of the most important theoreticians of Millenarian theology was the Cambridge Platonist, Henry More, a student of Joseph Mede's. More went through his own sceptical crisis when a student at Cambridge, and emerged with a spiritual outlook that led to his formulation of a metaphysics for the new theology of the Millenarians and for the new science of Galileo, Descartes and Harvey. Amos Funkenstein shows how the fundamental characterization of the nature of God changed from its totally noncorporeal form in medieval Christian theology, to the spiritual-corporeal view of Henry More and Isaac Newton that provided the basis for the new science and the Millenarian world.

Although More's was not the only new theology offered at the time, it was an important theory, providing a basis for a Christian theology that could encompass spirit and body as features of God. And this, in the metaphysics of the Cambridge Platonists and their student, Isaac Newton, provided the basis for the new science and Millenarianism. Funkenstein, dealing with the inner ideological shift from late medieval theology to the "corporeal" theology of More, throws light on an important perspective of our subject, namely what underlying changes in the history of ideas took place to buttress or justify the historical Millenarian reading of Scripture, and the expectations of those who read it in this fashion. Further study of 17th century metaphysical theories, such as those of Spinoza and Leibniz, may reveal other fundamental shifts in theological concepts related to the Millenarian concerns of the time.

The last two papers develop aspects of Millenarian concerns that began in the 17th and 18th centuries, but become transformed in other contexts. Both show that other kinds of Millenarianism play vital roles in intellectual and social history. In delineating the Millenarian aspects of these transformations Arthur Quinn and Henry-Louis Gates illuminate some striking developments in modern culture.

Quinn starts by provocatively exploring the Millenarian texture in Newton's writings, showing how signs of Newton's great theological interest are interwoven with his scientific concerns and his presentation of them. Further, Quinn shows that this Millenarian impulse, so important and often blatant in the 17th century as a way of overcoming doubts can be found in the most unlikely places in the 20th century, as in the claims made by Bertrand Russell, G.E. Moore and their excited Cambridge disciples at the beginning of this century, about the potential role of the newly formulated analytic philosophy in liberating and transforming mankind.

Anglo-American analytic philosophy began with a fervent Millenarian zeal, expressed in almost the same terms as were used by Henry More and Isaac Newton in the 17th century. This zeal persisted through the joining of logical positivism and the early ideas of Wittgenstein to the original work of Russell and Moore. And the Millenarian impulse suggested this new philosophical method would bring about a secular intellectual Millennium freed of philosophizing. But today the proferred new Millennium appears to show itself as a new wasteland, devoid of intellectual guidance to resolve human problems. In this light, the drama of 20th century philosophy may be seen as a transformed Millenarianism, at first strong and confident, then slowly losing its force as the promised new heaven and new earth, a new earthly Jerusalem of thought, did not appear.

Other secular intellectual movements may well be capable of being analyzed as comic-tragedies of the same kind.

The paper of Henry-Louis Gates forcefully and brilliantly presents a special dimension of Millenarianism. The apocalyptic picture of *Daniel* and *Revelation* has had great appeal to the downtrodden for centuries. But it is not just the hope for a better world for the victims of European colonization, the search for black liberators, that Gates is concerned with. From the 17th to the 20th centuries blacks have seen their situation as that of outcasts to be redeemed through the Millenial transformation of the world. Blacks as victims were suffering for the world's redemption. The blacks were the true Israel.

Gates had focused on another aspect of the quests for liberation developed among the black victims, namely that they will become free and redeemed through achieving intellectual equality with their European and American masters. This will occur through their becoming literate thus becoming verbal and expressive equals. This kind of equality would overcome attempts to cast the blacks below the Biblical world. The notion of redemption through literary achievement, Gates shows, runs from the Renaissance to the 20th century, as blacks sought acceptance as full human beings in a world of European values. This notion of redemption is expressed in the metaphors of Millennial terminology. Hence, the Millennial ideal is shown to be transformed from its historical Judeo-Christian form into a means of liberating peoples through changing them from illiterate, mute victims into great writers and spokesmen for human freedom and human aspirations.

One additional paper was presented, but unfortunately could not be included in this volume. This was the lecture of Mayr Vereté of Hebrew University on "The Idea of the Restoration of Israel in English Thought."

Vereté, a diplomatic historian working in Israel, has been concerned for many years about the roots of the "Zionistic" foreign policy of successive British governments starting early in the 19th century. Going back, he has found that one of the outcomes of the late English Reformation interpretations of the *Book of Revelation* was the realization that one of the Millennial developments, expected shortly, would be the restoration of the Jews to their ancient homeland in Palestine. Vereté traces the way this realization colored thinking about developments in the Near East in the 17th and 18th centuries, culminating with the excitement amongst some English Millenarians about the "Providential" significance of Napoleon's Egyptian campaign. In his paper Vereté also brings out what was to become all-important in British support for the Zionist movement, namely the emergence of a conception of the restoration of the Jews to Palestine as Jews, not as people about to be converted to Christianity. Hence, His and Her Majesty's government could look with favor on the establishment of a Jewish homeland in Palestine.

Vereté has also been concerned about discovering when and why Christian exegetes changed their views about the role of the Jews in the world to come. In this paper and the appendix to it, he has made an exciting and interesting breakthrough in showing that the interpretation of Romans 11.25–26 by Calvinist theologians changed in the mid 16th century, and this change involved the insistence that St. Pauls's reference to "all Israel" meant the historical Jewish people. This may help pinpoint when the theme of the restoration of the Jews entered Millenarian literature, but it still leaves the question, "Why?" Like Vereté, I think it represents some profound element in the development of Reformation theology.

English thinkers during the 17th, 18th, 19th and 20th centuries talked of the restoration of the "mortal" Jews to their homeland. In practical terms, English diplomats, theologians and mystics have played a great role in the development of Zionism, and in the actual achievement of the Jewish state. Vereté's researches show that this goes back to the 16th century Calvinist interpretations of "Jews" as discussed in the New Testament, and leads to the proposal of various Millenarians in the 17th and 18th centuries to rebuild Palestine as a restoration of Israel, a Jewish state. In the 19th century and in the 20th, English figures—missionaries, statesmen, writers—pressed for a return of the Jews to Palestine, supporting new Jewish Zionism and resulting in the Balfour declaration. The interrelationship of the theological, political and diplomatic elements leading to modern Zionism is a fascinating story. Vereté has delineated a vital part of what occurred in England. Due to his poor health he was unable to complete his researches, and present his paper in final form in time for this volume. When he does, though it cannot be included in this volume, it is to be published in another collection.

In closing I should like to thank the Clark Library Committee for appointing me as Clark Library Professor. I was the first philosophy professor to hold the chair, and I hope this added to the broadening character of the Clark Library as a center for 17th and 18th century studies.

I also want to thank those scholars who participated in the series of Clark Library seminars, and who prepared the papers for this volume. In addition I am most grateful to Robert Vosper, former director of the Clark Library who helped arrange the program for the year, to Norman Thrower, the present director, and to Thomas Wright, Librarian, each of whom helped immensely in making this so successful a year. I am also most appreciative of the cooperation, friendliness and assistance of all of the members of the Clark Library staff. My wife and I shall always treasure our inclusion, only too briefly, in the family of the Clark library.

CHRISTOPHER HILL

"TILL THE CONVERSION OF THE JEWS"

I

Some 25 years ago I published a 360-page book on economic problems of the early 17th-century church, which I described, a bit wrily, as a footnote to *Lycidas*. My lecture to-day is a footnote to the familiar opening lines of Marvell's *To his coy mistress*:—

> Had we but world enough, and time,
> This coyness, lady, were no crime.
> We would sit down and think which way
> To walk and pass our long love's day.
> Thou by the Indian Ganges side
> Shouldst rubies find: I by the tide
> Of Humber would complain. I would
> Love you ten years before the Flood:
> And you should, if you please, refuse,
> Till the conversion of the Jews.

If you try just to read the words on Marvell's page, much of his wit will escape you. That happened to John Crowe Ransom, no mean critic in his day, who accused Marvell in this poem of "indeterminacies that would be condemned in the prose of ... College freshmen". He criticized "the tide of Humber", as though Marvell were indulging in mere periphrastic poetic diction. In fact the Humber is the greatest of all English tidal rivers, in which Marvell's father had been drowned in 1641, a few years before the presumed date of the poem. Marvell had reason to complain of Humber's tide.

Ransom also objected to "Indian Ganges", since "Ganges has little need of a defining adjective"; and suggested that it ought to be balanced by "English Humber". No doubt 20th-century American readers know more about the Ganges than about the Humber, but the reverse was true of 17th-century Englishmen, for whom the Ganges must have been incredibly exotic, whilst the Humber was one of the three greatest rivers in England. Slapdash ignorance like this in literary critics encourages readers to underestimate the skills of a great poet.

Of the lines "And you should, if you please, refuse / Till the conversion of the Jews", Ransom said "refuse brings out of the rhyming dictionary the Jews, which it will tax the poet's invention to supply with a context. ... The historical period from the flood to the conversion of the Jews ... is a useless way of saying ten thousand years, or some other length of time".[1]

At first sight indeed Marvell's lines seem merely fanciful. He will love the lady for a long time in the past, she shall refuse him till a long time in the future. The two propositions appear to have no more in common than this. Ransom might indeed have noticed an apparent failure in the parallelism: the Ganges is far distant in space, as Noah's Flood is in time; but the Humber is just round the corner if—as is highly likely—the poem was written either in Hull or in Fairfax's house in Yorkshire where Marvell was tutoring Mary Fairfax in the early sixteen-fifties. The parallel would be more exact if we could think of the conversion of the Jews as imminent—as near as Humber, so to speak.

That, I shall suggest, is exactly what many of Marvell's contemporaries did think. I want to spend a little time looking at 17th-century ideas about the conversion of the Jews.

II

The conversion of the Jews in the 16th and 17th centuries was part of a package of ideas about the approaching end of the world and the millennium. I will not bother you with the detailed calculations, based on Daniel and Revelation, which occupied some of the best mathematicians from Napier in the late 16th century to Newton at the end of the 17th. The ultimately agreed consensus was that 1260 years ("a time, times and half a time") should be added to the date at which Antichrist set up his power. Protestants took Antichrist to be the Pope, and various different but converging calculations pointed to the years 1650–1656 for his destruction, the gathering of the Gentiles, the conversion of the Jews and their return to Palestine. Other estimates gave the year 1666 as an alternative.[2]

The conversion of the Jews and the spreading of Christianity to

---

[1] J.C. Ransom, *The New Criticism* (1941), pp. 311–13.
[2] E. Rogers, *Some Account of the Life and Opinions of a Fifth Monarchy Man* (1867), pp. 12–13, 148–51; B.S. Capp, *The Fifth Monarchy Men* (1972), p. 192.

all nations were necessary conditions without which the millennium could not take place. Another was the destruction of the Turkish Empire, which controlled Palestine and under whose rule most Jews lived. Some thought the Great Turk was Antichrist: Christianity could not spread over the whole globe so long as Turkish power survived (China and India hardly occur in these discussions, so unaware were most Europeans still of the significance of their vast civilizations).

This time-table is particularly associated with Protestantism.[3] Catholics, naturally, did not accept the equation of Antichrist with the Pope. They held that Antichrist had not yet come; when he did come he would be a Jew. This doctrine was proclaimed in England in 1635 by the Laudian Robert Shelford.[4] The Laudian campaign to accept Rome as a true church and to reject the identification of the Pope with Antichrist helped to convince many protestants that Laud was preparing for a restoration of popery in England.

There are mediaeval heretical precedents for these protestant attitudes. Wycliff and Hus both interpreted literally the Biblical texts relating to the return of the Jews to Palestine. 15th-century Hussites had been eager for the conversion of the Jews.[5] Lollards had no doubt that the Pope was Antichrist. But interest developed in England especially after the Reformation; it naturally heightened as the sixteen-fifties approached.

There was an additional pointer to the mid-17th century as the time for the series of events leading up to the millennium. Protestant chronologers generally accepted that the date of Noah's Flood was *anno mundi* 1656. Matthew's Gospel said "as the days of Noah were, so shall also the coming of the Son of Man be".[6] As early as 1548 the English protestant George Joye argued from this analogy that the

---

[3] Martin Bucer and Peter Martyr taught it in England under Edward VI; Béza and the Geneva New Testament of 1557 expressed concern for the conversion of the Jews (B.W. Ball, *A Great Expectation: Eschatological Thought in English Protestantism* (Leiden, 1975), p. 107; A.F. Dallison, "Contemporary Criticism of Millenarianism", in *Puritans, the Millennium and the Future of Israel* (ed. P. Toon, 1970), pp. 104–14.

[4] R. Shelford, *Five Pious Learned Discpurses* (1635), p. 314. For Shelford my *Antichrist in Seventeenth-Century England* (1971), pp. 38, 180.

[5] Ruth Gladstein, "Eschatological Trends in Bohemian Jewry during the Hussite Period", in *Prophecy and Millenarianism: Essays in Honour of Marjorie Reeves* (ed. A. Williams, 1980), p. 248; M. Vérété, "The Restoration of the Jews in English Protestant Thought", *Middle Eastern Studies*, January 1972, p. 14.

[6] Matthew XXIV. 37.

last judgment would come in or soon after 1656 A.D..[7] A century later this had become a commonplace. In 1639 Thomas Goodwin, writing in exile in the Netherlands, gave the parallel with Noah's Flood as a reason for expecting Antichrist's reign to end in 1655 or 1656.[8] In 1651 Samuel Hartlib published a translation of the anonymous *Clavis Apocalyptica* in which the parallel was drawn, though the years were given as 1655 a.m. and 1655 A.D.[9] On Guy Fawkes Day 1651 Peter Sterry, preaching to Parliament, dated the Flood 1656 a.m. and continued "How near is that year 1656. ... A flood of fire is coming upon all the world. The windows of heaven are already open". Luther, like Noah, had foretold the day of doom 120 years before it came.[10] The millenarians John Tillinghast and John Rogers both expected "the flood of God's wrath upon the idolatrous antichristian world" to be poured out in 1656: the redemption of Israel would follow.[11] "As in Noah's Flood, after the doors were shut up, there was no mercy.—Haste—haste—haste" cried Rogers.[12] Robert Gell, in a sermon to the Lord Mayor of London and the Drapers Company, published in 1655, said that the years from Adam to Noah were 1656, and "many believe that the next year [1656 A.D.] will bring with it a notable change in the world; yea, many place the end of the world in that year".[13] William Oughtred, a very serious mathematician indeed, said—also in 1655—that "he had strong apprehensions of some extraordinary event to happen the following year", because of the correspondence with the year of the Flood. Perhaps the Jews would be converted by our Saviour's visible appearance.[14]

Andrew Willet in 1590 seems to have been the first English Biblical

---

[7] G. Joye, *The coniectures of the ende of the worlde* (Antwerp, 1548), Sig. B ii.
[8] T. Goodwin, *Works* (Edinburgh, 1861–63), III, p. 196.
[9] *Op. cit.*, p. 34. John Dury contributed a preface. *Clavis Apocalyptica* was probably written by Abraham von Franckenberg, a great admirer of Jakob Boehme.
[10] P. Sterry, *Englands Deliverance from the Northern Presbytery* (1652), pp. 43–44.
[11] J. Tillinghast, *Knowledge of the Times, Or, The resolution of the Question, how long it shall be unto the end of the wonders* (1654), pp. 41–97, 306. For further examples of parallels between 1656 *a.m.* and 1656 A.D. see Elisabeth Labrousse, *L'Entrée de Saturne en Lion: L'Eclipse de Soleil du 12 Août 1654* (La Haye, 1974), pp. 7–8.
[12] John Rogers, *Sagrir or Doomes-day drawing nigh*, quoted in E. Rogers, *op. cit.*, p. 83. Lady Eleanor Davies also expected a new flood in 1656 (Theodore Spencer, "The History of an Unfortunate Lady", *Harvard Studies and Notes in Philology and Literature*, XX, 1938, p. 58.
[13] R. Gell, *Noah's Flood* (1655), p. 17.
[14] Ed. E.S. de Beer, *The Diary of John Evelyn* (Oxford University Press, 1955).

scholar to devote a whole treatise to the calling of the Jews.[15] But the subject was discussed by William Perkins, Richard Hooker and many others from the turn of the century onwards.[16] Gradually an agreed time-table emerged. The great mathematician John Napier, inventor of logarithms, committed himself to the view that "the day of God's judgment appears to fall" between 1688 and 1700: 1786 was the latest date to which the world could continue.[17] But later scholars brought the date forward.

The crucial figure for England was the learned Puritan Thomas Brightman, who made the most elaborate study of the last days to date. Brightman died in 1607, and all his books appeared posthumously. They had to be published abroad. He wrote in Latin, but English translations appeared in the Netherlands from 1612, and no doubt circulated clandestinely in England. Brightman's *Revelation of the Revelation* was not published in England until 1644, after the episcopal censorship had broken down. This is evidence that already by the early 17th century attempts to date the end of the world were regarded as seditious. So early had the Elizabethan consensus collapsed, and so important were eschatological studies in polarizing men's attitudes. Brightman's English translator claimed that Brightman "hath so cleared the point of the Jews' vocation as I have not seen any writer the like". Brightman put the calling of the Jews much nearer in the future than his predecessors, dating their full conversion to 1695, though their "first calling shall be about the year 1650". It would be a process occupying several decades. In 1650, Brightman believed, the Euphrates would dry up to facilitate the passage of the first party of Jews from the lost tribes returning to Jerusalem from the East. Their conversion would follow the destruction of Rome and coincide with the overthrow of the Turkish Empire, whose power would begin to reel in 1650, and would be utterly abolished by 1695. The reign of the saints would follow.[18]

Although Brightman's writings were illegal in England before 1640,

---

[15] Willet, *De Judaeorum vocatione* (Cambridge, 1590).
[16] Perkins believed that "it is not possible for any to find out the time of the end of the world" (*Works* 1609–13), III, p. 467.
[17] J. Napier, *A Plaine Discovery of the whole Revelation of St. John* (1593), esp. pp. 12, 16, 179–80.
[18] T. Brightman, *The Revelation of St. John Illustrated* (4th ed., 1644), pp. 518–19, 543–45, 555, 781, 808, 836, 894, 967.

they were clearly well known there.[19] In 1610 the Hebrew scholar Hugh Broughton believed that the conversion of the Jews was imminent, and with it the culmination of human history.[20] After 1640 translations of Brightman's writings, abridgments and summaries began to appear in large numbers. But two other writers must be mentioned before we pass on to the revolutionary decades.

Sir Henry Finch, a lawyer of some standing, wrote *The Worlds Great Restauration or The Calling of the Jews* (1621), the first whole book published on the subject in English. It appeared under the auspices of the eminent Puritan divine William Gouge. Finch accepted Brightman's time-table: in 1650 the Euphrates would dry up and the gathering of the Jews would begin, together with the decline of Turkish power. Gouge was imprisoned for nine weeks until he produced a recantation of his share in this publication.[21]

The earlier date was reinforced by the cautious and scholarly work of Joseph Mede, Fellow of Christ's College, Cambridge, Milton's College. He too had difficulties with the censorship, and refrained from publishing his major works during the sixteen-twenties and thirties. His *Clavis Apocalyptica* (1627) appeared in English translation only posthumously in 1643, published by order of a committee of the House of Commons. A timid man, Mede was clearly (as his correspondence shows) terrified of reprisals from Laud if he spoke out on the subject of his research. In a tract written in 1625 but not published till 1650 Mede suggested a date between 1625 and 1715.

In the sixteen-thirties the Puritans Richard Sibbes and Thomas Adams were convinced that the conversion of the Jews was imminent.[23] George Hakewill in 1627 had thought the future conversion of the Jews so assured that he used it as one of his many arguments that the world was getting better.[24] Even Hakewill's rival, the arch-

---

[19] In 1612 Nicholas Fuller, Puritan lawyer, also expected that the lost tribes would return from the East. He had no doubt been reading Brightman.

[20] H. Broughton, *A Revelation of the Holy Apocalypse* (1610), pp. 50, 264, 269.

[21] Finch, *op. cit.*, esp. pp. 3, 59–60. For Finch see W.R. Prest, "The Art of Law and the Law of God", in *Puritans and Revolutionaries* (ed. D. Pennington and K. Thomas, Oxford University Press, 1978), pp. 94–117.

[22] J. Mede, *Remains, or Some Passages in the Apocalypse*, in *Works* (1672), p. 600.

[23] R. Sibbes, *Works* (Edinburgh, 1862–63), I, p. 99; T. Adams, *A Commentary or Exposition upon the Divine Second Epistle General, written by ... St. Peter* (1633), pp. 1136–38.

[24] G. Hakewill, *An Apologie or Declaration of the Power and Providence of God* (3rd. ed., 1635), p. 549.

conservative Godfrey Goodman, believed in 1653 that Christ would not long be absent.[25]

III

So when the censorship broke down after 1640, when Parliament itself provided for the printing of translations of Brightman and Mede,—as well as of Coke's *Institutes*—a great stimulus was given to thinking about the end of the world. It was shrewd policy to authorize publication of scholarly works discussing the coming millennium, since Parliament's case against a divine right monarchy could be legitimated only by appealing to the higher authority of God. If the last days were at hand, and with them the overthrow of the papal Antichrist, and if Charles's Laudian advisers—and later his military commanders—were no better than papists, then it was right to call on ordinary people to fight for their overthrow. The subversive possibilities of this approach had already been demonstrated in New England, where in 1637 John Wheelwright preached an inflammatory sermon which got him into trouble. In this he declared "We know not how soon the conversion of the Jews may come". It "must come by the downfall of Antichrist, and if we take him away, we must burn him; therefore never fear combustions and burnings".[26] The spread of popular millenarian doctrines in England was like fire along a well-laid trail of powder.

In 1639 Thomas Goodwin foreshortened the dating still further by placing the downfall of Turks and Pope, and the return of the Jews, in 1650 or 1656, at latest 1666.[27] The Jews themselves, he added, have an eye on 1650 for the appearance of the Messiah. Their conversion, Goodwin thought, may fall out even sooner.[28] In an anonymous pamphlet of 1642 the author—an astrologer—said of the mille-

---

[25] G. Goodman, *Trinity and Incarnation* (1653), p. 192.

[26] John Wheelwright, *A Fast-Day Sermon*, in *The Antinomian Controversy, 1636-1638* (ed. D.D. Hall, Wesleyan University Press, 1968), p. 165.

[27] T. Goodwin, *Works*, III, pp. 28-29, 72, 157, 201-02. Goodwin quoted Mede for 1656 (ibid., III, p. 196).

[28] Ibid., III, p. 196, 202-03; cf. *A Glimpse of Syons Glory* (1641), in *Puritanism and Liberty* (ed. A.S.P. Woodhouse, 1938), pp. 233-41. Goodwin may have been reading Sir Henry Blount's *A Voyage into the Levant* (1636)—see p. 26 below. Or he may have talked to Dutch traders.

nium "some do assign one year, some another, yet all agree ... that it is near and even at our door".[29] In the following year a pamphlet entitled *The Rev. Brightmans Judgment* thought that "Rome must be destroyed in 1641 in some of his dominions"[30]—a reference presumably to events in England. Robert Maton in 1642 advocated the return of the Jews to Israel.[31] So did Ephraim Huit's commentary. *The Whole Prophecie of Daniel Explained* (1644).[32]

So preachers and pamphleteers agreed on the years 1650–56 as the crucial period—John Archer in 1642, Raphael Harford in 1643, and many more. In July 1644 Stanley Gower assured the House of Commons that the Jews would be converted in 1650. Next month William Reyner confirmed to them that the overthrow of Antichrist either had already begun or was imminent.[33] Thomas Shepard in 1647–48 expected the Jews to return to Zion within the next few years.[34] Mary Cary, in *The little horns doome and downfall* (1651), looked for the conversion and the return of the Jews in 1655–56, leading up to the millenium in 1701. Her book included introductory material by Henry Jessey, who was not absolutely convinced that 1656 was the year. But he knew the conversion would come before 1658.[35] John Canne thought the Jews would defeat the Turks in 1655 and return home; but they would not be converted until 1700.[36] In 1641 the great Czech reformer Comenius had plans for the conversion of the Jews, since the last days were imminent; but like all the schemes which he devised in England, this one was frustrated by the outbreak of civil war. His disciple Samuel Hartlib accepted the year 1655, and Hartlib's friend John Dury in 1649 felt that "the conversion of the Jews is at hand".[37]

---

[29] [Anon] *The Worlds Proceeding Woes and Succeeding Joyes* (1642), Sig. B 3.
[30] *Op. cit.*, Sig. A3v–A4v.
[31] Robert Maton, *Israels Redemption* (1642), esp. p. 69.
[32] *Op. cit.*, esp. pp. 58–63.
[33] Stanley Gower, *Things Now-a-days, or The Churches Travail Of the Child of Reformation now-a-bearing* (1644), pp. 11–12, 18, 41–42; William Reyner, *Babylons Running-Earthquake and the Restauration of Zion* (1644), pp. 28–33.
[34] J.F. Maclear, "New England the Fifth Monarchy: The Quest for the Millenium", in *Early American Puritanism. Essays on Religion, Society and Culture* (ed. A.P. Vaughan and F.J. Bremer, New York 1977), p. 70.
[35] *Op. cit.*, pp. 207–09; B.R. White, "Henry Jessey: A Pastor in Politics", *Baptist Quarterly*, XXV (1975), p. 101.
[36] B.S. Capp, "Extreme Millenarianism", in Toon, *op. cit.* p. 72.
[37] Ball, *op. cit.*, p. 108; G.H. Turnbull, *Hartlib, Dury and Comenius: Gleanings from the Hartlib Papers* (Liverpool University Press, 1947), pp. 257, 261–62, 267.

So the excitement initially built up by the scholarly chronologists and exploited by Parliamentarian publicists continued and expanded as millenarian radicals became more and more involved in politics. A pamphlet of 1648 indeed referred unsympathetically to "all these Cabbalistical Millenarians and Jew restorers".[38] Among scores of divines and pamphleteers who accepted the mid-fifties as the time for the conversion of the Jews, many were indeed radicals. But they also included such relatively respectable characters as Archbishop Ussher, John Cotton, the Presbyterian Samuel Rutherford and the Directory of the Westminster Assembly.[39] Even so hard-headed a figure as Benjamin Worsley, in or after 1647, noted that most divines conceive that the conversion of the Jews is shortly to be expected. He had no doubts himself.[40] In 1650 the diarist Ralph Josselin was much pre-occupied with the subject: he thought 1654 might be the year in which the conversion would begin, to be completed in 1699.[41] In 1651 Joshua Garment published *The Hebrews Deliverance at Hand*, and Nicholas Culpeper expected their conversion within the next five years.[42] Milton's friend, Moses Wall, also in 1651, looked for the conversion "during this present age in which we live", suggesting 1655 as the date.[43]

Among those who totally rejected a special conversion was the Scot Robert Baillie. Richard Baxter observed sceptically that it would take a long time to convert all the Jews.[44] A radical who believed "the day of the Lord" was "near at hand" but nevertheless rejected any "general visible calling of the Jews in all nations" was John Reeve, founder of the sect later to be called the Muggletonians. "The Lord Jesus," he declared, "will never spiritually gather the seed of those Jews who rated a bloody Barabbas above the Lord of life". But

---

[38] [Anon], *The Great Day at the Dore* (1648), title-page.

[39] Ball, *op. cit.*, pp. 147, 150; Dallison, *op. cit.*, pp. 107, 112–14.

[40] C. Webster, *The Great Instauration* (1975), pp. 381, 565.

[41] Ed. A. Macfarlane, *The Diary of Ralph Josselin* (Cambridge University Press, 1976), pp. 227–28; cf. pp. 257, 266, 268.

[42] B. Capp, *Astrology and the Popular Press: English Almanacos, 1500–1800* (1979), p. 172.

[43] M. Wall, *Considerations upon the Point of the Conversion of the Jewes*, in L. Wolf, *Menasseh ben Israel's Mission to Oliver Cromwell* (1901), p. 53.

[44] R. Baillie, *A Disswasive from the Errours of the Time* (1645), *passim*; W. Lamont, *Richard Baxter and the Millennium* (1979), p. 56; cf. T. Heyne, *Christs Kingdom on Earth* (1645), *passim*.

Reeve also used the word "Jew" to cover those who justify religious persecution.[45]

IV

What we see then is a cumulative process. First the Biblical scholars and the mathematical chronologists evolve techniques for interpreting the prophecies which enable them to arrive at agreed conclusions about dating the events of the last days. These dates are progressively brought back to the first half of the sixteen-fifties. This date is seized upon by the popularizers, the pamphleteers, the Parliamentarian propagandists and preachers in an effort to whip up enthusiasm for the Parliamentary cause and an expectation of the millennium in the foreseeable future. For many radicals the conversion of the Jews was significant primarily as a harbinger of the reign of the saints on earth which was to precede the Second Coming. Soon achieving this reign became an end in itself, by comparison with which the Jews fell into the background.

Gerrard Winstanley for instance equated the English with the Israelites, the chosen people, and declared that "all the prophecies, visions and revelations of Scriptures, of prophets and apostles, concerning the calling of the Jews, the restoration of Israel and making of that people the inheritors of the whole earth," referred to the coming communist society which the Diggers were starting to build in England.[46] Winstanley and Everard told Fairfax that they were "of the race of the Jews".[47]

Echoes of discussions on the conversion of the Jews can be heard in literature. Giles Fletcher the elder was an early English believer in the restoration of the Jews, though his views on the subject were not published until 1677, and I can find no trace of them in the writings of his sons Phineas and Giles the younger.[48] Francis Bacon's Bensa-

---

[45] John Reeve and Lodowick Muggleton, *A Divine Looking-Glass* (3rd ed., 1719), pp. 184-85. This is a reprint of Reeve's original text, before Muggleton tampered with it.

[46] Ed. G.H. Sabine, *The Works of Gerrard Winstanley* (Cornell University Press, 1941), pp. 260-61.

[47] Ibid., p. 15. Winstanley's *The New Law of Righteousness* (1649) was dedicated to "the twelve tribes of Israel that are circumcised in heart."

[48] Vereté, *op. cit.*, pp. 31-32, 49. Fletcher's *The Tartars or Ten Tribes* was published in Samuel Lee's *Israel Redux: Or the Restauration of Israel* (1677).

lem in *New Atlantis* (1627) was inhabited by converted Jews. Twenty years later, in Samuel Gott's *Nova Solyma* (1648), an ideal society was created after the restoration of the Jews. The Turks had been expelled and the Jews converted 50 years before they left for Palestine—by ship from Dover.[49]

In Sir William Alexander's *Dooms-day* (1637) the "signs foreshown" of that event included "some Jews convert".[50] Henry Vaughan in *Silex Scintillans* wrote of the conversion "sure it is not far".[51] The date of publication (1650) suggests that it must be nearly contemporary with Marvell's *Coy mistress*. Abraham Cowley, perhaps in Marvell's more sceptical vein, wrote in the Preface to his *Poems* (1656) "there wants, me thinks, but the conversion of [poetry] and the Jews for the accomplishing of the kingdom of Christ".[52]

V

But other factors contributed to an interest in the conversion, factors perhaps less immediately obvious. To these I now turn.

The conversion of the Jews and "the gathering of the Gentiles" were necessary before the millennium could arrive. This gathering could be furthered by English acquisitions of territory in the New World (Spanish conquests in America of course only extended the kingdom of Antichrist). Take, for instance, Thomas Cooper's *The Blessing of Japheth, Proving The Gathering in of the Gentiles and Finall Conversion of the Jewes,* dedicated in 1615 to the Lord Mayor, Alderman and Sheriffs of London and the Commissioners for Plantations in Ireland and Virginia. "As the Lord hath enlarged himself abundantly unto this honourable City", Cooper said, so "your hearts and purses are enlarged plentifully to the furtherance of this great and glorious work of the gathering in of the Gentiles" by the colonization of Ireland and Virginia. Not for the last time in English history, piety and profit went hand in hand. "Can you do God better service than in promoting his kingdom and demolishing daily the

---

[49] I owe this point to J.C. Davis, *Utopia and the Ideal Society: A Study of English Utopian Writing, 1516–1700* (Cambridge University Press, 1981), pp. 113–15, 146.
[50] Quoted by Ball, *op. cit.*, p. 90.
[51] Henry Vaughan, *Works* (Oxford University Press, 1914), II, p. 499.
[52] A. Cowley, Preface to *Poems* (1656), reprinted in *Poetry and Prose* (ed. L.C. Martin, Oxford University Press, 1949), p. 71.

power of Satan? Can you do better service unto yourselves than not only to ease the land of that rank blood which threatens some great sickness" (a standing concern), "but"—another continuing anxiety among early 17th-century English protestants which historians too easily forget—"especially to provide some retiring place for yourselves if so be the Lord for our unthankfulness should spew us out".[53]

The immediate objective is to strengthen the political and economic power of protestant England. "Hath the Lord begun to enlarge us far and near to Virginia and Ireland, and are not their hopes vain that seek to root God's church out of England? ... Hath not God wonderfully preserved this little island, this angle of the world, that in former ages was not known or accounted to be any part of the world? Have not all the neighbour-nations taken hold of the skirts of an Englishman? Have they not joined themselves to us because the Lord is with us? Are they not happily sheltered under our gracious government?" The reference is to the union of England and Scotland, and perhaps looks forward to the sort of union with the Netherlands which the Commonwealth government was to offer in 1651. Already, presciently, Cooper links Parliamentary government, protestantism, liberty and trade. "So bless thou O Lord the holy meetings of the state that in continuance and increase of the liberty of the gospel we may secure our liberty and advance thy glory, we may provide for the liberty of our posterity, in conveying thy worship unto them, more glorious than we found it".[54]

Those are significant if cautious words: remember that the Parliament of 1614 had just been dissolved without doing anything to secure the liberty of posterity or to advance the glory of protestantism. But Cooper looks forward with confidence to unlimited economic expansion. "Should we not possess all things even when in a sort we have nothing? ... Should we be afraid of men? ... Ought not then the church to strive even for the best with the best? Must she not so run that she may obtain?" (In Cooper's phraseology "the church" means "the commonwealth"). "Oh how may this establish us against the reproaches and contradictions of the world, that we are contentious persons, and strive with the whole earth".[55]

---

[53] *Op. cit.*, Sig. A2–3.
[54] *Op. cit.*, pp. 33–35.
[55] Ibid., pp. 33–34, 42–43.

Despite Cooper's title, the Jews come in almost as an afterthought to this programme for British expansion: but they do come in. "The Jews shall then have a full and glorious conversion, before the Second Coming of the Lord Jesus. . . . Have we not daily experience of the Jews coming in again? . . . This great coming in of the Jew cannot be far off, seeing the fullness of the Gentiles is well-near come in". Meanwhile English merchants must soldier on.[56]

The economic basis of religious belief was not often so makedly exposed. But John Rolfe in 1616 thought the English were "a peculiar people marked and chosen by the finger of God" to possess North America.[57] Conquest of America was linked more closely with the conversion of the Jews by the theory that at least some American Indians were descended from the lost tribes of Israel. This hare seems to have been started in the Netherlands. A Portuguese Jew swore that he had talked Hebrew to some Indians, and the idea spread that the lost tribes were living in America.[58] John Dury among others took the story up.[59] Thomas Thorowgood in *Jewes in America* (1650) linked religion and commercial expansion as crudely as Cooper had done. "Look westward then, ye men of war, thence you may behold a rising sun of glory with riches and much honour, and not only for yourselves but for Christ". The Spaniards are thin on the ground in North America: Indians, Creoles and negroes will turn against them.[60] It reads like a blueprint for Oliver Cromwell's Western Design of 1655.

We are told that those 17th-century Puritans in North America who recorded their opinions believed "almost without exception" that the Indians were descended from the ten tribes.[61] This conviction inspired John Elliott, the "Apostle to the Indians" since their conversion would accelerate the Second Coming. Elliott contributed "Conjectures . . . Touching the Americans" to the 1660 edition of

---

[56] Ibid., pp. 53–55.

[57] Quoted by A. Calder, *Revolutionary Empire: The Rise of the English-Speaking Empires from the Fifteenth Century to the 1780s* (1981), p. 141.

[58] Wolf, *op. cit.*, pp. xxiv, 1–8, and *passim*.

[59] See p. 20 above. Dury published "An Epistolary Discourse"; to Thomas Thorowgood, *Jews in America*, in 1650.

[60] *Op. cit.*, Sig. C3v.

[61] Alden T. Vaughan, *New England Frontier: Puritans and Indians, 1620–1675* (New York, 1979), pp. 19–20.

Thorowgood's pamphlet, seizing the opportunity to distance himself from Thorowgood's commercial approach. "We chose a place where nothing in probability was to be expected but religion, poverty and hard labour, a composition that God doth usually take most pleasure in".[62] Thorowgood, in the less ebullient circumstances of 1660, echoed Cooper's vision of America as a refuge for the godly from "not the violence of enemies so much as our own national and personal sins". The threat now came not from the "encroaching innovations" of (presumably) the Laudians, but from "the falsehood and hypocrisy, the backsliding and apostacy, the avarice and selfishness, the pride and security, uncleanness and adulteries, the bold broaching of errors and heresy", which had accompanied the last years of the Commonwealth and which "do portend no less than a deluge of destruction" unless we repent. Thorowgood seems to have been as unenthusiastic about the restoration as was Milton, whom some of these phrases recall.[63]

In 1649 Parliament established a Society for the Propagation of the Gospel in New England, which among other things subsidized John Elliott. Henry Whitfield in 1652 supported this Society because he hoped that thereby "the calling of the Jews may be hastened".[64] It survived the restoration, and won the continuing support of Robert Boyle, among others.[65] As late as 1707 William Whiston argued that spreading the Gospel to all nations would quicken the conversion of the Jews.[66]

VI

"The chiefest place where the Jews live is the Turkish Empire", Menasseh ben Israel told Oliver Cromwell in 1655.[67] In the early 17th century English trade to the Levant was prospering, outstripping that of France, and Venice, anticipating that of the Netherlands, thanks to expanding production of new draperies, light cloths suit-

---

[62] Thorowgood, *Jewe in America* (2nd ed., 1660), p. 23.
[63] *Ibid.*, p. 51.
[64] Henry Whitfield, *Strength Out of Weakness* (1652), Sig. a, quoted by Ball, *op. cit.*, p. 109.
[65] J.R. Jacob, *Robert Boyle and the English Revolution* (1977), *passim*.
[66] M.C. Jacob, *The Newtonians and the English Revolution* (1976), p. 167.
[67] Wolf, *op. cit.*, p. 85.

able for a Mediterranean climate. As early as 1591 the condemned heretic John Udall was offered commutation of his death sentence if he would go to Syria as minister for the Turkey Company merchants there; but he died in jail whilst negotiating.[68] By 1646 there were at least 22 English merchants in Smyrna alone. They normally conducted their trade through Jewish middlemen: there was little intercourse with Turks. The father of the future Messiah Sabbatai Sevi acted as agent for English merchants in Smyrna. So the merchants, who were held responsible for the behaviour of all their countrymen, and who made a point of entertaining English travellers, would be relatively well-informed about Jewish affairs.[69] With this opening up of English trade, visits to the Levant became feasible. Books like Sir Henry Blount's *Voyage into the Levant* helped to spread knowledge not only of the region but also of the growing anticipations of the Jews for the coming of the Messiah, especially prevalent in the Near East.[70] The Zohar was said to have predicted a return of the Jews to Palestine for 1648.[71]

Among English radical millenarians the idea of leading the Jews back to Jerusalem, or travelling there to assist in the restoration of the Jews, frequently recurs in the two generations before 1640. Ralph Durden in 1586, who thought that the Tudor monarchy was the Beast of Revelation, proposed to lead the Jews and all the saints to rebuild Jerusalem; after which they would defeat all the kings of the earth.[72] Francis Kett, burnt in 1589, grandson of the Norfolk rebel leader of 1549 and friend of Christopher Marlowe, claimed that Jesus was currently in Jerusalem gathering the faithful; all God's people should go and join him there. Whoever will be saved must go to Jerusalem before he dies[73]—an interesting survival in a radical heretic of the mediaeval idea of pilgrimage.

---

[68] *Dictionary of National Biography*.

[69] For all this see A.C. Wood, *A History of the Levant Company* (Oxford University Press, 1935), pp. 43–44, 73, 214, 219–20, 235–36; Gerschom Scholem, *Sabbatai Sevi: the Mystical Messiah, 1626–1676* (1973), p. 107.

[70] Sir H. Blount, *A Voyage into the Levant* (1636), pp. 102–03.

[71] Ed. W. Begley, *Nova Solyma* (1648) (1902 ed.), Excursus F. Begley quotes John Sadler. The book was by Samuel Gott, though Begley attributed it to Milton.

[72] Capp, *The Fifth Monarchy Men*, p. 29.

[73] W. Burton, *Davids evidence, or the Assurance of Gods love* (1592), p. 125, quoted by D.D. Wallace, "From Eschatology to Arian heresy: the Case of Francis Kett (d. 1589)", *Harvard Theological Review*, 67 (1974), pp. 461–62.

Richard Farnham and John Bull, prophets who died in 1642, were believed by their supporters to have sailed away in a boat of bullrushes to convert the lost tribes.[74] Mrs. Attaway, a defender of Milton's doctrine on divorce and a well-known woman preacher, was said to have left London with William Jenny some time before 1646 to await the universal salvation in Jerusalem.[75] The Ranter John Robins was inspired by the Holy Ghost to lead 144,000 men to Palestine, and started training some of them for their arduous expedition on a diet of dry bread, raw vegetables and water.[76] His associate Thomas Tany, who adopted the name Theaureaujohn at divine command, learnt Hebrew with the object of leading the Jews back. In April 1650 he assumed the title of King of the Jews and issued a proclamation announcing the return of his people. Some time later—perhaps as late as 1668—he was said to have disappeared in a small boat which he had built for himself in the hope of getting to Palestine.[77] In the sixteen-fifties Quaker missionaries went to convert the Grand Turk—by whom they were received with more tolerance than in New England.

Intense interest in the return of the Jews led to many stories circulating, most of them without foundation in fact. On All Fools Day 1645 *The London Post* reported that the Jews had sent letters to collect themselves into one body to return to Palestine.[78] Four days later Ralph Josselin in Essex had heard rumours of the Jews' return, no doubt derived from *The London Post*. "Can it be?" he asked doubtfully.[79] In 1647 an anonymous pamphlet, *Doomes-Day: or the great Day of the Lords Judgement proved by Scripture*, announced that the Jews were assembling in Asia Minor, and that the final overthrow of Antichrist was "near, even at the door".[80] There were similar excited expectations in 1648.[81] In 1650 George Foster announced

---

[74] Ed. J. Lindsay, *Loving Mad Tom: Bedlamite Verses of the XVI and XVII centuries* (1969), p. 140; K.V. Thomas, *Religion and the Decline of Magic* (1971), p. 135.
[75] T. Edwards, *Gangraena* (1646), Part III, pp. 26–27.
[76] G.H., *The Declaration of John Robins the false Prophet* (1651), pp. 4, 6.
[77] See my *Puritanism and Revolution* (Panther ed.), p. 143, and references there cited.
[78] J. Frank, *The Beginnings of the English Newspaper* (Harvard University Press, 1961), p. 83.
[79] Josselin, *Diary*, p. 38.
[80] Ball, *op. cit.*, p. 153.
[81] See G. Nuttall, *Visible Saints*, p. 144. At least one Jew was converted to Christianity, and there was one false conversion.

that the Jews were to meet in 1651 in Italy. The Pope would lose his life in 1654, the Head Turk in 1656; after that there would be no Pope, and a classless society would prevail.[82] *A Narrative of the Proceedings of a great Council of Jews assembled in the plain of Ageda in Hungary on 12 October 1650* (published in 1655) had a very circumstantial though largely apocryphal account of the meeting. The author regarded it as "a hopeful sign of the Jews' conversion". The Jews, he added, believe that England has a great love to their nation, because they pray for their conversion. The greatest obstacle to the conversion of the Jews is Rome's idolatry.[83]

VII

Millenarian excitement and commercial interests both contributed to demands for a militant foreign policy which would expedite Antichrist's overthrow, the gathering of the Gentiles and the conversion of the Jews. The radical Puritan Robert Parker, who died in exile in 1614, left a pamphlet called *The Mystery of the Vialls opened*. Unpublishable before 1640, it appeared opportunely in 1651. Parker argued that England would soon take the lead in sacking Rome and converting the Jews—the former a theme of some of Milton's university writings.[84] In 1643 Robert Leslie, commanding the Scottish army in England, was reported as advocating ultimate use of his army to "go to Rome, drive out Antichrist and burn the town".[85] John Eachard in 1645 wrote that "the civil war [now] begun shall last till Rome be burnt and the Jews called". With this magnificent prospect it was absurd for Presbyterians and Independents to squabble among themselves.[86] Peter Bulkeley in *The Gospel Covenant* (1646) similarly anticipated the imminent conversion of the Jews and fall of the Great Turk.[87]

Peter Sterry in 1649 told Parliament that "the outward calling though not the inward conversion of the Jews" was expected near

---

[82] G. Foster, *The Pouring Forth of the Seventh and Last Viall* (1650), pp. 64–66.
[83] In *Harleian Miscellany* (1744–46), I, pp. 369–75. There had in fact been a Jewish Council late in 1650 to deal with the consequences of the Ukranian massacres of 1648.
[84] *Op. cit.*, p. 11.
[85] Ed. J.G. Fotheringham, *The Diplomatic Correspondence of Jean de Montereul* (Scottish History Soc., 1898–99), II, p. 550.
[86] Eachard, *Good Newes for all Christian Souldiers* (1645), Sig. A4v, pp. 1, 3.
[87] The passage was dropped from the 1651 edition of the tract.

this time, adding that "perhaps the affairs of Constantinople, as they now stand, may make way to this desired conclusion".[88] In 1651 the astrologer William Lilly foretold that "we Christians shall recover the Holy Land ... out of the hands of the Turks; then also shall almighty God by miracle withdraw the people of the Jews from their hard heartedness, and from the several parts of the world where they now live concealed, and they shall believe in the true Messias".[89] A year later John Owen, preaching before Parliament, rebuked M.P.s for their inactivity; "the Jews not called, Antichrist not destroyed. ... Will the Lord Christ leave the world in this state and set up his kingdom here on a molehill?"[90] A Fifth Monarchist preacher proclaimed whilst the Barebones Parliament was in session that Blake's fleet would carry the Gospel "up and down to the Gentiles".[91] Morgan Llwyd and the Fifth Monarchists, Christopher Feake, John Rogers and John Tillinghast, all promised that the Army of the saints would overthrow the Turks and the Pope and his helpers.[92] In 1657 George Fox—not yet a pacifist—rebuked Cromwell's Army for its failure to attack Rome.[93]

The Jews' potential usefulness to the development of a forward colonial and commercial foreign policy was an additional reason for English interest in them. As early as 1643 Jews in the Netherlands were said to be financing Parliament. Their command of bullion was enormous; they controlled the Spanish and Portuguese trades; the Levant trade was largely in their hands; they were interested in developing commerce with the East and West Indies. To governments they were useful as contractors and as spies.[94] If the ambitious scheme for Anglo-Dutch union put forward by the Commonwealth in 1651 had come off, then the Jews in the Netherlands would have been taken over together with the Dutch colonial empire and its trade. When the Dutch refused to be incorporated into the British Empire, Dutch merchants were totally excluded from all British possessions by the Navigation Act of 1651. This development made many

---

[88] P. Sterry, *The Comings Forth of Christ* (1650), p. 11.
[89] W. Lilly, *Monarchy or no Monarchy in England* (1651), p. 55.
[90] J. Owen, *A Sermon Preached to The Parliament, October 13, 1652* (1652), p. 126.
[91] My *Puritanism and Revolution*, p. 134; cf. p. 136.
[92] Capp, *The Fifth Monarchy Men*, p. 151.
[93] *Puritanism and Revolution*, p. 146.
[94] Wolf, *op. cit.*, pp. xviii–xix, xxx.

Jews in the Netherlands—especially those trading with the West Indies—anxious to transfer to London; and it redoubled the interest of the English government in attracting them there.[95] The policy paid off: Jewish intelligence helped the preparations for Cromwell's Western Design of 1655.

VIII

So we come to Menasseh ben Israel's attempt to get the Jews formally readmitted to England, from which Edward I had expelled them. In 1648 a pogrom had driven Jews from the Ukraine. It was for them as well as for Jews from the Iberian peninsula that Menasseh hoped to find a refuge in England.[96] There was a contradiction in English attitudes which the Leveller Richard Overton noted in 1645: "our kings and our rulers, our bishops and our priests", would not "suffer a Jew by authority to live amongst them". "What hopes then," he asked, "is there the Jews should be converted?"[97] William Erbery and Selden's friend Christian Ravis also asked why men prayed for the conversion of the Jews if they did nothing about it.[98]

In January 1649 a petition on behalf of the Jews was presented to the leadership of the English Army.[99] The English delegation to the Netherlands in 1651, and especially its secretary John Thurloe, saw a great deal of Menasseh ben Israel. Menasseh's Declaration to Parliament of 1655 stressed that both Jews and Christians "believe that the restoration time for our nation into their native country is very near at hand". To admit them to England might expedite their conversion, it was hinted, and so expedite the last days.[100]

The cause of the Jews had many supporters. Robert Norwood and

---

[95] Ibid., pp. xxx–xxxi, xl–xli.

[96] Ibid., pp. xxxvi–xxxix.

[97] R. Overton, *The Araignement of Mr. Persecution* (1645), in *Tracts on Liberty in the Puritan Revolution* (ed. W. Haller, Columbia University Press, 1933), III, p. 233; cf. p. 225.

[98] F. Cheynell, *An Account Given to the Parliament by the Ministers sent by them to Oxford* (1647), p. 35; Christian Ravis, *A Discourse of the Oriental Tongues* (1648), pp. 61, 70. Margaret Fell, who later married George Fox, was the most active Quaker propagandist for the conversion of the Jews. Between 1656 and 1677 she wrote no less than five pamphlets addressed to the Jews, whilst Fox wrote two (Isabel Ross, *Margaret Fell, Mother of Quakerism* (1949), pp. 89–97).

[99] C.V. Wedgwood, *The Trial of Charles I* (1964), p. 89.

[100] Wolf, *op. cit.*, p. 79; cf. p. 53.

Thomas Collier in 1652 called for permission for the Jews "to live peaceably amongst us, ... whose conversion is promised and we pretend to expect it".[101] Samuel Hering told the Barebones Parliament to call the Jews to England "for their time is near at hand".[102] In 1655 Josselin heard "great rumours of the Jews being admitted into England, in hopes thereby to convert them".[103] Henry Jessey argued for admission, speaking of "hopes of their conversion, which time (it's hoped) is now at hand, even at the door".[104]

By this time the Jews' admission was being officially considered. There was alleged to have been a proposal to this effect in the Barebones Parliament. Pressure for their admittance was said to have given a great fillip to Fifth Monarchists and other sectaries;[105] but the reasons for considering it were not merely religious or political. It was a development of the economic policy contained in the Navigation Act of 1651.[106] "Doubtless, to say no more", observed Major-General Whalley, "they will bring very much wealth into this Commonwealth".[107]

In 1648 Edward Nichols, in *An Apologie for the Honourable Nation of the Jews*, had deplored "the strict and cruel laws now in force" against the Jews.[108] But in fact the judges advised, no doubt under pressure from Cromwell, that there were no legal obstacles to their admission.[109] Jews had long been in England unofficially. In 1652 Elias Ashmole arranged to take lessons in Hebrew from Rabbi Solomon Frank.[110] No official decision to admit the Jews was taken, but Cromwell extended his personal favour to cover *de facto*

---

[101] R. Norwood, *Proposals for the propagation of the Gospel, offered to the Parliament* (1651[-52]), p. 17; T. Collier, *The Pulpit Guard Routed* (1652), p. 41.

[102] Ed. J. Nickolls, *Original Letters and Papers of State Addressed to Oliver Cromwell* (1743), pp. 99-100.

[103] Josselin, *Diary*, p. 358. In 1655 Josselin dreamt that Thurloe was a Jew (ibid., p. 337).

[104] Jessey, *A Narrative of the late proceedings at Whitehall concerning the Jews* (1656), in B.R. White, *op. cit.*, p. 107.

[105] *Thurloe State Papers*, I, p. 387; Wolf, *op. cit.*, pp. xxxvi-xxxvii.

[106] Ibid., p. xli.

[107] *Thurloe State Papers*, IV, p. 108.

[108] Edward Nicholas, *op. cit.*, p. 4. Nicholas expected his book to be attacked by "the Pope and the clergy", especially Jesuits. For Jews, like Puritans, hate idolatry.

[109] See *A Collection of Original Letters and Papers* (ed. T. Carte, 1739), for a curious suggestion that Parliament had "revoked the laws that were made against the Jews", I, p. 233.

[110] Ed. C.H. Josten, *Elias Ashmole (1617-92)* (Oxford University Press, 1966), I, p. 92; II, pp. 560, 606, 609.

admision, despite strong and unpleasantly anti-Semitic opposition from William Prynne and others. Permission was given for building a synagogue in London.[111] Harrington in 1656 saw Ireland as a possible refuge for Jews;[112] many in fact settled in Surinam and the West Indies.[113]

So I see converging trends. (1) The chronological experts fixed on the early sixteen-fifties, and the religious and political propagandists used this in support of Parliament's cause, especially radicals hoping for the rule of the saints. (2) From the time of Richard Hakluyt men had advocated an expansionist policy in North America which would extend God's kingdom and bring profits to Englishmen. Thomas Cooper in 1615 associated this with the conversion of the Jews, an association later reinforced by the idea that the American Indians were the lost tribes. Others, at least from Robert Parker, who died in 1614, called for an aggressive policy in the Mediterranean against the Pope and Grand Turk, as a necessary preliminary to the conversion of the Jews—and this trend too fused commercial with radical religious motives. (3) Finally there was the campaign for the admission of the Jews to England, in which motives were once more mixed.

By 1656 the Jews had been admitted. Cromwell's Western Design had given England a foothold in the Caribbean, and Blake's fleet dominated the Mediterranean. But millenarian expectations of the conversion of the Jews had also stirred up popular excitement and hopes. As the crucial dates passed in the sixteen-fifties with no sign of the millennium, and as the rulers of the Commonwealth grew increasingly conservative, so active millenarianism rapidly declined until the restoration of Charles II in 1660 put "enthusiasm" of any sort out of favour.[114] The Rev. Samuel Lee in 1677 still believed in the restoration of the Jews to Palestine, but by now the date has been moved forward until 1766–1811.[115] It was not until the next great revolutionary age, the seventeen-nineties, that millenarians who fa-

---

[111] W. Prynne, *A short demurer to the Jews long discontinued remitter into England* (1655), pp. 65–66, 89–90; Wolf, *op. cit.*, pp. lvii–lix, lxvii.

[112] Ed. J.G.A. Pocock, *The Political Works of James Harrington* (Cambridge University Press, 1977), p. 159.

[113] J.A. Williamson, *English Colonies in Guiana and on the Amazon, 1604–1688* (Oxford University Press, 1923), pp. 164–65; Wolf, *op. cit.*, pp. xxxvi–xxxvii.

[114] A certain interest attaches to Edward Lane's *Look unto Jesus* (1663), since Lane had been a schoolfellow of Milton's. *Look unto Jesus* contained an appendix showing the certainty of the calling of the Jews.

[115] Samuel Lee, *Israel Redux*, pp. 120–222. Lee's book was reprinted several times.

voured the French Revolution hoped that it would give occasion for the conversion and calling of the Jews.[116] Napoleon in Egypt at least got nearer to Palestine than Cromwell did. When in the present century a Jewish national state was established in Israel it did not coincide with "the conversion of the Jews."

IX

The conversion of the Jews had been hoped for until about 1656—a date after which it is unlikely that *To his coy mistress* was written. So we come back to Marvell. He might, I hope you will agree, have heard of the conversion of the Jews. His contemporaries, accustomed to thinking in analogies, would naturally expect the Flood to lead to the conversion of the Jews. It is not, *pace* Ransom, "the logic of a child", but of a sophisticated 17th-century wit.

It would be pretty safe, I think, to date "To his coy mistress" between 1646 and 1656. "Ten years before the Flood" would be *anno mundi* 1646. If the end of the world is coming in 1656, the lady may not have so long as we thought for her refusal. I am not of course suggesting that Marvell himself expected the conversion of the Jews in 1656. We do not know, but my guess would be that he did not. An interesting paper by Hugh Ornsby-Lennon recently suggested that in *Upon Appleton House* Marvell plays with modish alchemical ideas in a way that seems serious but is almost certainly ironical:[117] that is exactly what I am suggesting he does with fashionable millenarian ideas in "To his coy mistress."

By 1656 the millennium had not come, nor were there conversions in any significant number of either Jews or American Indians. On the other hand, the new English foreign policy had been triumphantly achieved by the Navigation Act and Cromwell's conquest of Jamaica. The conversion of the Jews seemed less urgently relevant. What survived was a secularized millenarianism in which the conversion of the Jews plays little part, and English commercial enterprise is central.

The Horatian Ode's lines,

> As Caesar he ere long to Gaul,
> To Italy an Hannibal,

---

[116] Véreté, *op. cit.*, pp. 26–27.
[117] H. Ornsby-Lennon, *Futurist Poets of the English Civil War* (xerox, 1981). I am grateful to the author for allowing me to read this article in advance of publication.

perhaps catch something of the earlier revolutionary internationalism. But in *The First Anniversary of the Government under O.C.* Marvell recognized that millenarian hopes were now doubtful.

> If in some happy hour
> High grace should meet in one with highest power ...
> Fore-shortened time its useless course would stay
> And soon precipitate the latest day.

Cromwell was the obvious focus for such hopes:—

> If these the times, then this must be the man.

But too many

> Unhappy princes, ignorantly led,
> By malice some, by error more misled,
> Indians whom they should convert, subdue;
> Nor teach, but traffic with, or burn, the Jew.
> Hence that blest day still counter-poised wastes,
> The ill delaying what th'elected hastes.

It is the only mention of Jews in the poem: note their association with Indians.

What matters now is England's national power and national trade. In this respect Charles II could easily succeed to Oliver Cromwell. In 1652 the Welshman Arise Evans had proclaimed Charles II "to be the great deliverer of the Jews". This remarkable suggestion was repeated in 1658 by Walter Gostelow and by a royalist pamphleteer in 1660.[118] Menasseh ben Israel quoted a Frenchman to the effect that the King of France would be leader of the Jews "when they returned to their country".[119] Traditional nationalism is taking over from the religious internationalism of the interregnum radicals.

Dryden, like Marvell a former Cromwellian civil servant, resumed the theme of national commercial greatness in *Annus Mirabilis*, whilst ignoring any idea of an anti-catholic crusade or the conversion of the Jews. After Dryden pseudo-millenarian predictions of a glorious imperial and trading future for London and England became

---

[118] See my *Change and Continuity in Seventeenth-Century England* (1974), pp. 55, 58, 77, 158, 310.

[119] Menasseh ben Israel, *Vindiciae Judaeorum* (1656), in Wolf, *op. cit.*, p. 124.

common form.[120] We are back where we started with Thomas Cooper. But as the defeat of "the Puritan Revolution" allowed the Church of England to take over Sabbatarianism and "the protestant ethic", so the secular content of millenarian foreign policy could be taken over once millenarianism was no longer dangerous.[121]

A few die-hard survivors refused to give up the dream. George Wither wrote of the Jews in 1666:

> "More than most nations we are thought
> Their restoration to have sought."

He was advocating complete toleration for Jews in England. But then Wither still believed the end of the world was "at hand".[122] Milton was much less committal on the conversion of the Jews than he was on most theological subjects. In his *De Doctrina Christiana* he merely cited the relevant texts and said "some authors think" that the calling of the Jews will be a further portent of the Second Coming.[123] In *Paradise Regained* the Son of God leaves the question open—

> Yet he himself, time to himself best known
> May bring them back repentant and sincere.[124]

Milton's eager millenarian expectations had been disappointed so many times that his caution is understandable. Yet Northrop Frye argued that "the prophecy of Michael in *Paradise Lost* presents the whole Bible as a miniature contrast-epic, with one pole at the apocalypse and the other at the Flood".[125] The pattern does not depend on the dating 1656 a.m./1656 A.D.; but it is a suggestive thought for our theme. If the whole Bible proceeds from the Flood to the conversion of the Jews, Marvell hardly needed his rhyming dictionary.

To his coy mistress is a running joke about time. Marvell starts by jumping from 1656 a.m. to 1656 A.D. His "vegetable love shall grow / Vaster than empires and more slow;" he ends "If we cannot make

---

[120] M. McKeon, *Politics and Religion in Restoration England* (Harvard University Press, 1975), pp. 63, 153, 174–75, 249, 268–81.

[121] See my *Society and Puritanism in Pre-Revolutionary England*, pp. 490–94.

[122] Wither, *Vaticania Poetica, or, rather A Fragment of some Presages long since written* (1666) in *Miscellaneous Works* (Fourth Series, Spenser Society, 1875), pp. 15–19.

[123] Milton, *Complete Prose Works*, VI, pp. 617–18.

[124] Milton, *Paradise Regained*, Book III, lines 433–34.

[125] Northrop Frye, *Anatomy of Criticism: Four Essays* (Princeton University Press, 1957), p. 324.

our sun / Stand still at least we'll make him run". It is not a facile conclusion, I think intentionally so. For in between had come the terrifying lines, the axis on which the poem turns:—

> At my back I always hear
> Time's winged chariot hurrying near.

The chariot carries not the Messiah but death, and a death which appears to offer no immortality:—

> And yonder all before us lie
> Deserts of vast eternity.

The lines remind me of Pascal's cry, as he contemplated the consequences of the new astronomy: "the eternal silence of those infinite spaces terrifies me". That was written in the sixteen-fifties too.

C.S. Lewis called Milton our first poet of space.[126] On the strength of the lines just quoted, Marvell has some claim to be our first poet of an eternity associated neither with the bliss of heaven nor with the torments of hell. Its blank and empty silence corresponds to the blank infinity of the Copernican universe. It does not seem very Christian. Lovers may take the counter-offensive against Time and so avoid languishing in his slow-chapped power. But Time wins in the end. We are dead for a very long while. To this extent the conclusion is factitious.

Marvell avoided the other standard ending to this type of *carpe diem* poem: that the poet will win eternity if the lovers do not. Marvell's echoing song will not resound in the marble vault of the lady, but is still resounds in the Clark Library and in countless other lecture halls in the English-speaking world. Marvell of course might have preferred silence.

---

[126] C.S. Lewis, *Words* (Cambridge University Press, 1960), p. 251.

STEVEN N. ZWICKER

ENGLAND, ISRAEL, AND THE TRIUMPH OF ROMAN
VIRTUE

My subject is the way in which people imagine themselves and their own time. The issue is complex and broad, but its scope should not entirely defeat attempts to describe the cultural and political imagination of a particular moment or to understand changes in that imagination. And it is these changes, or rather a specific change, that I want to talk about here. To put the case as simply as possible, in 1650 the central book of English culture was Scripture; by 1700 the texts men chose to talk about themselves were those of Roman history and Roman politics. By 1700 it was Juvenal, not Jeremiah, whom satirists invoked; the Roman senator, not the Mosaic lawgiver, embraced as parliamentary ideal; commercial empire, not the end of time, for which ministries toiled; Roman virtue, not Hebraic righteousness, that defined civic morality.

That Rome had become a central fixture in the English imagination by 1700 is of course a convention of our literary history. Nor did we invent or impose the idea of English augustanism. The English themselves were busy assembling such an identity at the close of the century, and its character, especially in literary expression, has been carefully studied.[1] Why the English stopped imagining Elect Nation and chose Rome in its stead are problems less frequently addressed.[2] The displacement was gradual and its character involved not only a new exploration of Roman politics and Roman history, but as well the decline of righteousness as a moral code and prophecy as a political agenda.

Roman virtues came into cultural predominance toward the end of the seventeenth century, but they did not suddenly then emerge. Roman history became a crucial analogue for English politics in the

---

[1] The bibliography on this topic is vast; two primary studies are Paul Fussell, *The Rhetorical World of Augustan Humanism* (Oxford, 1965), and J.W. Johnson, *The Formation of English Neo-classical Thought* (Princeton, 1967).

[2] A notable exception is J.G.A. Pocock, *The Machiavellian Moment* (Princeton, 1975), ch. 11, especially pp. 401–05.

1690s, but such discovery was not revelation. In fact, the strand of Roman history as cultural and political analogue is continuous in this century.[3] Shakespeare's Roman plays, Jonson's tragedies and lyrics, the Tacitism of Bacon's *History*, the writings of the English republicans before and after the civil wars all argue the continuity of the analogue. But to cite a history is not to explain its force or character at a particular moment. The continuity of the trope is evident, but the reasons for its sudden predominance at the close of the century are not. And the problems in assessing seventeenth-century scripturalism are similar. The predominance of Elect Nation at midcentury is not at issue, nor is the presence of scriptural language in political texts after the fall of the Puritan theocracy. What is not so clear, however, is the force as praise and prophecy that Scripture retained after midcentury, the capacity for public belief and self-imaging that such language continued to sustain. I suspect that with both languages what we are dealing with is not the sudden emergence or disappearance of cultural and political institutions, but rather widening and narrowing bands of propriety and use, congruent and at points interconnected histories of dislocation and renewal.

The English have had a long romance with the Jews, the mingling of their histories not least significant in our own time. But the conjoining in modern history can be dated rather precisely with the emergence of Elect Nation in the sixteenth century.[4] At first, the analogue was part of an effort to establish a reformed church; sixteenth-century Protestants sought the authority of Scripture, the language of covenant and election, to challenge Rome. But the language did not remain ecclesiastical. The Protestant agenda broadened to a national program. By the 1640s it is right to speak of something like national election.[5] Cromwell's armies marched to battle singing Psalms, members of parliament argued sharply and cogently from Scripture, the highest decisions of state were charted on a calender that provided dates for the defeat of Roman antichrist and the inauguration of Christ's thousand year rule. Nor was it fanatics

---

[3] See, for example, B.N. de Luna, *Jonson's Romish Plot* (Oxford, 1967), especially ch. 1, "Notes of the Precedent Times"; Fred J. Levy, *Tudor Historical Thought* (San Marino, 1967); and Paul Cantor, *Shakespeare's Rome* (Ithaca, 1976).

[4] William Haller, *The Elect Nation; The Meaning and Relevance of Foxe's Book of Martyrs* (New York, 1963).

[5] William M. Lamont, *Godly Rule; Politics and Religion, 1603–1660* (London, 1969); Christopher Hill, *Antichrist in Seventeenth-Century England* (London, 1971).

alone who spoke Scripture as politics. So cool and scrupulous an intellect as Andrew Marvell adopted the high apocalyptic mode in thinking on English history in the early 1650s.[6] And Royalists were not to be denied the use of Scripture in creating political theory or political rhetoric. It was in the 1640s that Filmer constructed his defence of Royal absolutism by a careful reading of the patriarchal character of the Old Testament,[7] and the martyrology of Charles I turned on a rather special scripturalism of its own.[8] In 1650 Scripture was not a party text; its dominion was such that both those who had mounted the attack on the crown and the crown itself were forced to speak the same language. Men denounced one another for betraying Scripture, for falsely crumbling and wrongly applying the holy writ, but neither the authority of that writ nor the propriety of conceiving national politics in its terms were questioned. And yet, despite the wide application of Scripture, the Old Testament was the book of the Puritan elect. The triumph of the Hebrew spirit was the triumph of parliament and the rule of Oliver Cromwell. And in such ligature between righteousness and revolution, the demise of that righteousness as a political language was written. It was not, after all, Anglican Royalists who studied Hebrew and printed Hebrew grammars and dictionaries in the 1650s in order to achieve immediate communion with God, "in his words, even to the very ravishing of the soul and spirit in such communion."[9]

A few, like Venner, attempted holy war after the Restoration,[10] but when serious revolution was an aim, it was not advocated in the Hebrew tongue. The marching orders in the Exclusion Crisis and in 1688 were not issued out of the Bible, and the political reasons for avoiding Scripture in these crises are not far to seek. The long and

---

[6] See Zwicker, "Models of Governance in Marvell's 'The First Anniversary'," *Criticism*, vol. 16 (1974), 1–12.

[7] See Peter Laslett, "Sir Robert Filmer," *William and Mary Quarterly*, V, no. 4 (1948); and Laslett, *Patriarcha and Other Political Works of Sir Robert Filmer* (Oxford, 1949).

[8] See, for example, Thomas Pierce, *A Sermon preached ... the 29th day of May* (London, 1661); John White, *The Parallel Between David, Christ, and K. Charls* (London, 1661); the verse in *Domiduca Oxoniensis* (Oxford, 1662); J.W.'s *King Charles I. his imitation of Christ. Or the parallel lines of our Saviours and our kings sufferings; drawn through forty six texts of Scripture* (London, 1660).

[9] Robertson, *A Key to the Hebrew Bible* (London, 1656), "The Preface to the Readers," Bl^r.

[10] On Venner's uprising see Cobbett, *Parliamentary History of England* (London, 1803), vol. 4, 186, n.

deep association of prophecy with the rule of the saints made the language a dangerous one for men to apply to affairs of state when they were attempting to force change. Prophecy excited associations of enthusiasm and fanaticism, of uncontrolled passions that would lead men to civil war, and none but the most fanatic could suffer to imagine that fate. The most powerful imperative after the collapse of the Protectorate was to avoid disorder and fracture of state. The efforts at healing and settling in 1660 were widespread and significant.[11] Vengeance was a motive after the return of the king, but neither that return nor the Exclusion Crisis nor the expulsion of James II resulted in purge or widespread bloodshed, and these are significant testimonials to the fear of civil war. Men avoided Scripture as a political language because it was tainted by association.

But it was not only association that determined the fate of this language. The moral and political schemes of the Old Testament allow no room for compromise. The moral agenda of the Old Testament is clear and unforgiving; embracing such schemes and principles had exacted a cost. Men eschewed sacred history as a national program because they had no wish to be driven again by its imperatives to civil war. God's chosen people are opposed only by the damned, the rule of Christ impeded only by the body and agents of antichrist. The political lessons of Scripture are not diplomacy, concealment and halfmeasure; and the pressing need after 1660 was for something like political negligence, for a language of public exchange that defused rather than heightened the meaning of religious differences. Moreover, what had made Scripture useful for political revolution and social reform—for Adamites at one end of the social scale and for zealous, self-seeking Presbyterian merchants at the other—rendered it unsuitable for returning Cavaliers. If Scripture celebrated the priesthood of all believers and the aristocracy of the spirit, it did not celebrate the aristocracy of land, and the restoration of the king was a restoration of an aristocratic court and its clients. The social utility of the Old Testament must have been marginal for these men.

Given such imperatives and implications, the continued political use of Scripture after 1660 may at first be surprising. But the afterlife is not inexplicable. For one thing, dominant languages do not just disappear. Scripture was now the wrong book with which to challenge

---

[11] See J.P. Kenyon, *The Stuart Constitution* (Cambridge, 1966), pp. 357–58, 365–70.

the court and administration of a Stuart king, but it was not necessarily the wrong book with which to celebrate that court. Indeed, it must have been a pleasure for the crown to rescue prophecy from the Puritans. Nothing could have been more obvious in 1660 than the failure of what enemies of the crown had once billed as national election. Now David the suffering servant could return from hapless exile, and that figure is invoked more than once for Charles Stuart in the years following his restoration. There is some justice in saying that Royalists could turn to Scripture with a vengeance, and often that is what they did. Royalist vindication reclaimed materials that Puritans had once used to celebrate their triumphs; but Royalists also looked harshly and derisively at Puritan scripturalism: prophecy now revealed as self-interest, as political frenzy, as fanaticism for gain. The combination of Puritan demise and Royalist vindication complicated the potential for Scripture as a social and political language, but eventually such complication also undermined its authority, its capacity to sustain praise and the burden of a national life imagined in its terms.

Scripture had been a language of public humiliation and correction in the years before the Restoration, and so it remained, but the satiric and corrective voice was heard more frequently in Roman than Hebraic accents toward the end of the century. The biblical language of correction and humiliation is an essential facet of Protestant spiritualism, and as a language of personal discipline, Scripture endured. But as a language of public correction, Scripture was undercut both by the failure of spiritual politics and by changes in those public institutions that needed correction. The sexual manners of the Restoration court were different from those of the Caroline court; the corruption of parliament through systematic bribery was sharply different from earlier efforts to force parliament into conformity with the court. Indeed with the growth of the electorate in the later seventeenth century, bribery became a convention of electoral politics, and with a significant increase in government bureaucracy, we witness a commensurate growth in the practice of corruption by place.[12] The mismanagement and diverting of public funds for personal gain, not itself a new fact of political life, was certainly remark-

---

[12] Clayton Roberts, "Party and Patronage in Later Stuart England," unpublished paper; J.H. Plumb, *The Growth of Political Stability in England* (London, 1967), esp. ch. 3, "The Growth of Oligarchy."

ed with a new and relentless ferocity in these years;[13] and the deception practised by politicians and publicists came to characterize public discourse as never before.[14] What moralists discovered in the face of such behavior was the pertinence of Roman satire to the sins of the nation; Juvenal, Persius, and Martial provided more exact counters and models for the censure of public morals than did the Hebrew prophets.

And finally, the demise of Elect Nation as a public language must in some way be linked to the perception of the Jews themselves. The English developed an identity as Elect Nation in virtual ignorance of the Jews; the fantasy of election came from a book. The metaphor took shape in a world without Jews; perhaps such are the conditions for metaphors of national identity: Israel, Arcadia, Arthurian Britain, all were safely remote. And while it remained unlikely for Englishmen to meet Arthurian Britons, they did in fact begin to meet Jews in the 1650s.[15] No longer were the Jews simply history, and though the history remained, the remnant was not so easily romanticized as the history. And the perception of that history and its application to national life began to change at a time when the Jews became a subject of contested inquiry. The sudden attention came with the agitation in favor of and unofficial re-entry of the Jews into England in the early 1650s. The nexus of Jewish and Christian millenarian motives for the readmission is a separate chapter in this story;[16] what concerns me here is the attention to the Jews as remnant. Some of this attention was philosemitic, but much of it was not. A book entitled *The Wonderful, and Most Deplorable History of the Jews* went through seven editions in the second half of the century, and it is but one of such histories.[17] Josephus was re-edited, re-

---

[13] See, for example, the satiric advice-to-painter poems and Marvell's attack on Hyde, "Clarendon's Housewarming," *Poems on Affairs of State*, vol. I., ed. George de F. Lord (New Haven, 1963).

[14] Zwicker, "Language as Disguise: Politics and Poetry in the Later Seventeenth Century," *Annals of Scholarship*, I, 3 (fall 1980), 47–67.

[15] On the re-entry of the Jews see Lucien Wolf, "Cromwell's Jewish Intelligence," *Essays in Jewish History* (London, 1934), 115–44; Salo W. Baron, *A Social and Religious History of the Jews*, 2nd ed. (New York, 1952), vol. 15, pp. 74–160; Gershom Scholem, *Sabbatai Sevi* (Princeton, 1973), 339 ff.

[16] See Richard H. Popkin, "Jewish Messianism and Christian Millenarianism" in *Culture and Politics from Puritanism to the Enlightenment*, ed. Perez Zagorin (Berkeley, 1980), pp. 67–90.

[17] Josephus Ben Gorion, *The Wonderful, and Most Deplorable History of the Later Times of the Jews* (London, 1652). Later editions include, 1653, 1662, 1669, 1673, 1684, 1699.

translated, and re-introduced, and there is an extensive contemporary travel literature in which the country and peoples of Palestine are examined.[18] Much of this writing has a detachment and a sharpness of tone that is quite different from the literature of prophetic calling that we identify with Puritan scripturalism.

When Josephus was dedicated to Charles, Lord Howard, in 1602, book and patron were linked in commendation, "I have chosen your Honour out for a most noble Patron of this most famous and accomplished History of the Jews: which (for dignity and antiquity of subject, the elegance and puritie of the Style, the choices propriety of copious words, the gravitie and variety of Sentences, the alterations and memorable events, and lastly for the birth and dignity of the author) requireth a spirit of no less wisdom, courage, and nobility than yourself."[19] But in 1675, in *The Present State of the Jews*, we hear of the "fatal impediments respecting the Jews Conversion ... their own ingrafted perverseness, and obstinate adherence to the Doctrine of their Fore-Fathers. As to the former, the Jews are notorious therein above all other people."[20] And here are the Jews in a 1684 edition of *The Wonderful, and Most Deplorable History*, "The City of London was guilty at that time, of all these Ugly and Enormous Crimes, and maybe said to be led all along by a true Jewish Spirit; and concerning the last, viz., the Crucifixion of our Savior, though no Comparison made without a high propheness, yet the manner of Murdering Charles the First may be said to bear a kind of Analogy, and resemblance with it. Nay the Jews whereof there are Swarms now in this City will not stick to say, that it was a murther beyond theirs."[21] And, finally, a new perception of Jewish history itself, this from the 1708 translation of Basnage's *History of the Jews, From Jesus Christ to the Present Time*.[22] Here are the topics for an analysis of Moses, "He kills an Egyptian for making an Israelite a Cuckold. His reign in Ethiopia. How he went over the Red Sea. A ridiculous Story. His Tiranny. Crimes he committed. His miracles

---

[18] For bibliographical guidance to this literature see, *A Reference Guide to the Literature of Travel* (Seattle, 1935), 2 vols.; and *Early Travels in Palestine*, ed. T. Wright (London, 1848).
[19] *The Famous and Memorable Works of Josephus* (London, 1602), p. 2.
[20] L. Addison, *The Present State of the Jews* (London, 1675), p. 1.
[21] *The Wonderful, and Most Deplorable History*, p. A7^v.
[22] *The History of the Jews, From Jesus Christ to the Present Time ... Written in French by Mr. Basnage ...* translated into English by Thomas Taylor (London, 1708).

and his hardness," and here, the conclusion of this study, "The design and end of Moses in getting his People out of Egypt was to settle the Empire in his own House ... he was ambitious, a Tyrant, and an Enemy of the People subjected to his laws."[23]

Part of what we are listening to is an attack on the authority of Scripture which belongs to a phase in the history of natural religion;[24] but I think there is something like a sociology of these ideas too, and part of the social dimension of this language impinges on the metaphor of Elect Nation in the very years when that metaphor was in decline. What was an Englishman to think when told that a curse had fallen on the Jews, "witness those uncouth looks and odd casts of eye, whereby they are distinguished from other people. As likewise that rankish kind of scent, no better than a stink, which is observed to be inherent and inseparable from most of them above all other nations."[25] Under such assault, the romance with Israel must have been difficult to sustain.

There are perhaps other dimensions to the history of this demise, but the issues that I have touched on stress the connections between political circumstance and the languages men use to understand and to give authority to their needs and institutions. What we witness in the later seventeenth century is not the natural or inexplicable rise and decline of speech idioms, but the expression of social and political imperatives that made it desirable and in some cases necessary to distance and devalue one language while exploring or re-inventing another. I have earlier suggested the continuous presence of the Roman analogy; students of the republican tradition in seventeenth-century England have charted this Roman theme over the whole of the century and beyond, arguing its classical sources, its continuity, its force in political crises.[26] Imperial Rome is also a continuous strain in the literature of courtly and civic praise. And it hardly needs stressing that Latin literary models were not a discovery of the 1690s.

---

[23] *The History of the Jews*, pp. 228–30.
[24] Hans W. Frei, *The Eclipse of Biblical Narrative* (New Haven, 1974), 51–105; Margaret Jacob, *The Radical Enlightenment* (London, 1981), chapts. 1 and 2.
[25] *The Wonderful, and Most Deplorable History*, p. A7^v.
[26] See Z.S. Fink, *The Classical Republicans: An Essay in the Recovery of a Pattern of Thought in Seventeenth-Century England* (Evanston, 1945); Caroline Robbins, *The Eighteenth-Century Commonwealthsman* (Cambridge, Mass., 1959); J.G.A. Pocock, *The Machiavellian Moment* (Princeton, 1975); and Blair Worden, "Classical Republicanism and the Puritan Revolution," *History and Imagination* ed. Hugh Lloyd-Jones, Valerie Pearl, and Blair Worden (London, 1981), 182–200.

Who more than Ben Jonson had created an English idiom from the forms and voices of Latin poetry? And yet availability is not dominance, nor is the presence of literary models social or political urgency. Rome may be a steady presence in the seventeenth century, but it does not become dominant until the last decades of that century, until Scripture as a public idiom had suffered irreparable decline.

It is too simple to say that men had had enough of enthusiasm and godliness, but it is interesting to see how soon after the Restoration such words as "zealous" and "enthusiastic" became abusive epithets.[27] The cooler temperatures of the Roman past were part of the invitation after 1660, but there is a more complex structure that lies below the temperate surface. In 1650 reason of state had been argued as revelation; at midcentury arcana imperii suggested more than statecraft; something like a penetration of divine wisdom. But the Roman mode in politics was a demystifying mode; its application to English public life is part of an effort to demystify those politics. The Roman past was construed not as the record of men waiting on signs from God, not the story of ceaseless intervention, scourging, and salvation, but as the history of a city that had raised itself to universal empire solely by human endeavor. Rome had achieved greatness because its people were:

> wise, frugal, justly and passionately studious of Glory, a people whose Prudence in their Counsels, whose Maturity in Deliberation, whose Diligence in Execution, whose profound Secrecy in the most important affairs, and whose noble resolution in unavoidable dangers and the greatest extremities ought to be remembered to all Ages. It is a history of a state that grew so mighty from small beginnings, all by its patient daring, by its perseverence, by its exact observation of the Laws, by the inviolable severity of its discipline, by training up a well-regulated and courageous soldiery. It was a nation that was virtuous and courageous through a pure Principle of Honour, whose valour was more the product of the head than the Heart.[28]

How different from election. Valor and prudence are virtues that can be cultivated without revelation or grace. There is inherent in this

---

[27] See Ronald A. Knox, *Enthusiasm* (Oxford, 1950); Susie I. Tucker, *Enthusiasm* (Cambridge, 1972); Michael Heyd, "The Reaction to Enthusiasm in the Seventeenth Century: Toward an Integrative Approach," *Journal of Modern History*, vol. 53 (June 1981), 258–80.

[28] Laurence Echard, *The Roman History* (London, 1695), "The Preface," sig. *a–*a^v.

historical model not only a new set of principles for the conduct of public life but also a rejection of the imperatives of Jewish history. Such rejection might well have a polemical edge—the spurning of prophecy as political opportunism—but the denial of sacred history cut across political allegiance and party lines.[29] Here at the height of the Exclusion Crisis is an exclusionist arguing against the application of Jewish history to English politics, indeed to any politics at all:

> There is one Opinion which prevails much in the World, Which as it is false, so it does a great deal of hurt, and that is this: that every Government in the World was constituted by God himself; but that cannot be so; for it would follow, that God is unjust which he cannot be. There neither is nor was any Government of that Sort but only that of the Jews; the rest of the World left to themselves, to frame such a government as suited best their Inclination; and to make such Rules and Laws as they could best obey and be governed by.[30]

Of course, those who advocated exclusion did not court association with the men who had raised arms against Charles I; but more significantly, if government might wholly be dissociated from a sacred model, indeed if the divine will could simply be ignored in the constitution of human government, then the whole structure of divine right monarchy with its apparatus of passive obedience and the sanctity of lineal descent might conveniently be put aside. This is part of what Royalists feared of the implications of that famous book of royalist apologetics, *The Leviathan*;[31] and perhaps such reasoning also explains the odd contiguity of the two treatises of Locke's *Two Treatises of Government*, the first of which argues so closely from Scripture and the second of which argues from Scripture almost not at all. The careful dismantling of Filmer in the first treatise is executed in the idiom of Filmer's patriarchal argument (itself cast in scriptural terms in order to participate in and refute the political implications of Puritan scripturalism in the 1640s).[32] But where Locke accounts for the

---

[29] See the debates over the "Bill for abrogating oaths of supremacy and allegiance," Anchitell Grey, *Debates in the House of Commons*, 10 vols. (London, 1763), II, p. 301; pp. 445–47.

[30] *The History and Proceedings of the House of Commons* (London, 1742), II, p. 138 f.

[31] For the contemporary response to Hobbes see S.I. Mintz, *The Hunting of Leviathan; Seventeenth-Century Reactions to the Materialism and Moral Philosophy of Thomas Hobbes* (Cambridge, 1962).

[32] On the troubled issue of the dating of *Patriarcha* see, John Wallace, "The Date of Sir Robert Filmer's *Patriarcha*," *The Historical Journal*, XXIII, 1 (1980), pp. 155–65.

nature and rise of human government, he argues without historical models. If the sanctity of human government is denied, then the antiexclusionist argument based on that model can be dismissed. If government is convenience rather than fiat, and if the Catholic James Duke of York is thought to be inconvenient, then he might properly be set aside for a more convenient ruler. As Professor Pocock has shown, what is radical about Locke's second treatise in the context of political argument in the late seventeenth century is not contract or convenience but the ahistorical character of its argument.[33] Locke's contemporaries did not argue in this way, and he was ignored by them because he was arguing outside the mainstream of political discourse, outside the authorizing models of history, models that his contemporaries felt they could not do without.[34]

And Rome was one such model. Rome could authorize republic and empire, monarchy and aristocracy. It could provide the history of valor and the history of luxury; it could authorize the rule of the strong sovereign and the inviolability of the senate. It offered an unlimited array of politicians and political conduct characterized by corruption, treachery, and deceit. It could as well provide the most august and revered examples of men whose laws and literary acts were unmatched for correctness and sublimity. It could provide authority for the conduct, the celebration, and the censure of public life in a nation bent on or being bent toward bloodless revolution, commercial empire, and the rage of party politics.

And it is the congruence of this last term with the Roman analogy that I would like to explore for a moment. English politics from the civil wars through the end of the century are dominated by conflicting interests; yet the idea of party was abhorrent to most men. Party was wholly outside the canon of political conduct until very late in the seventeenth century. When men had gone to war against the king, they did so to protect him from evil ministers, and in the end to protect him from himself. Perhaps this was convenient hypocrisy, yet the necessity of the convenience is a revealing one. In the face of civil war, it was difficult if not impossible to admit to party, and this remains

---

[33] See Pocock on Locke in *The Ancient Constitution and the Feudal Law* (Cambridge, 1957).
[34] Richard Ashcroft has recently challenged this view, "Revolutionary Politics and Locke's *Two Treatises of Government*," *Political Theory*, VIII, 4 (Nov., 1980), 429–86.

true until very late in the century. The failure to acknowledge party does not argue an inability to see the partisan character of political conflict; it suggests, rather, the power of certain concepts of political conduct. The court was the country, its fullest and most brilliant expression; the king in parliament was the most complete realization of the nation's will. Court and monarch acted against such a will only through the influence of evil counsellors. And on that altar a number of men were sacrificed. But the resistance to party over the course of the century must also be linked to the pressure of sacred politics, a model of governance that excluded the possibility of party, of loyal opposition, of competing and equally legitimate political interests. It seems more than coincidence that with the gradual repudiation of sacred politics we watch the emergence of party. And it was an essential characteristic of Roman political history not simply to allow the expression of party, but to give party an authority and vocabulary of its own. Roman politics made it imaginatively and rhetorically possible for England to become a state in which men might oppose one another with equally legitimate political interests and traditions.

The Roman analogy had cooled the temperature of political discourse to a point where the kingdom of the spirit might finally be severed from the kingdom of the sword, a point at which Locke's *Two Treatises* might assume the status of a classic of political philosophy. But the Roman analogy provided for more than severance; it provided a complex and powerful alternative to Elect Nation. It allowed men to replace zeal and chiliastic fervor with valor and prudence; it allowed them to contemplate English history as progressive empire without the trap of eschatology. It offered an expansive model and at the same time provided a literature that brilliantly analyzed the failures of the Roman enactment of its own ideal. And both the expansive model and the corrective analysis were adopted in England, at times pitched against one another, but neither the model nor the corrective implied holy war or the end of time.

It is beyond the scope of this paper to trace the entry of Latin authors into later seventeenth-century public texts, a route to begin with of a very large number of editions, translations, prefaces, paraphrases, adaptations, allusions, commentary, and discourse, but the numbers alone suggest the magnitude of this entry, the romanization of English literary and political culture at the end of the century.[35] The political implications of the Roman past were many and

---

[35] Peter Burke, "A Survey of the Popularity of Ancient Historians, 1450–1700." *History and Theory*, V (1966), 135–52.

complex; my immediate point however is not that diversity but the fact that Roman history had begun to assume the status of a central cultural text, one that allowed and indeed by its authority compelled men to find self-explanation and self-assertion in its terms. Such is the position that Scripture had occupied at midcentury, and such is the position that the Roman analogy had come to occupy at the close of the century. Whatever its inherent disposition—and that disposition would have had to be sufficiently broad to allow such dominance—all men might draw comfort from its various strands. Roman history was cited to reveal the true meaning of the primary culture, to express its political, social, ethical, and cultural ideals. It was at once self-assertion and satiric trope. Such dominance did not preclude other analogies and other strands of historical and polemical self-explanation—Roman piety subsumed under Christian charity—but the central analogy not only allowed for contrary positions but by its history and rhetoric proved the legitimacy of both those interests. Not only did Rome provide a various political history but it showed that piety and prudence were the underpinnings of both empire and republic, that the defense of liberty was a trope to be used from without and within,[36] by country against court, by Whigs against Tories, by defenders of the Revolution, and by Jacobite critics of that daring breach of legality and legitimacy. It may not be surprising to hear the "prudence of the ancients" cited against Stuart tyranny.[37] But here, in defense of that very tyranny, is the Roman analogy. The date is 1686, the occasion is James's act of indulgence, and the text is an *Address of Thanks to a Good Prince, Presented in the Panegyrick of Pliny upon Trajan, the Best of Roman Emperors.*[38] Pliny's panegyric is applied to James because "nothing pen'd at so wide a distance comes so nearly up for an application to our own time. For sure a gratitude for the comforts of an easie Government, and a recognisance of the merits of a gratious Prince were never more requisite, never more opportune."[39] But even more than the panegyric modeled on Pliny, it is the dedication of the *Address* to Sir William

---

[36] On opposition rhetoric see, Isaac Kramnick, *Bolingbroke and His Circle* (Cambridge, Mass., 1968), and Quentin Skinner, "The Principles and Practice of Opposition," *Historical Perspectives*, ed. Neil McKendrick (London, 1974).
[37] John Ayloffe, "Brittania and Raleigh," *POAS*, I, ed. George de F. Lord (New Haven, 1963), p. 236.
[38] *An Address of Thanks* (London, 1686).
[39] *An Address*, sig. A3r.

Glynne, one of James's trusted servants, that interests me here:

> My adorning these Papers with your worthy Name, is not a meer design of getting them the more plausibly recommended to the world .... For this Laudatory Address being rendered from that authentick Language wherein you are so accurately skilled, I may not only sollicite you for a Friend, but refer to you as a Judge of the performance, and if You, Sir, would approve, it would be too bold a Criticism in any else to condemn. For you are an unquestion'd Master in the proprieties of either Speech, and can so pierce into the genuine and unpresumed sense of the primitive Author, that you could have obliged us with a much politer Version, if your admirable faculty at Translating the Roman virtues, had not lifted you above the drudgery of so dealing with the Roman Tongue.[40]

I cite this text not with any claim to its cultural or political importance, but for its mode of praise, because, quite independent of political position, what a gentleman might aspire to late in this century and what a writer might best find to praise a patron for is that "admirable faculty at Translating the Roman virtues."

It is the happy coincidence of my subject, though I think it more than coincidence, that the great and representative examples of satire and epic in the late seventeenth century should turn, respectively, on Elect Nation and Augustan England. The satire is *Absalom and Achitophel*, and the epic that poet's translation of Virgil's *Aeneid*. It is no discovery to suggest that these poems are historical texts; it is still something of a novelty to insist that they are highly polemical texts;[41] but what I want to add here is that the central metaphors of these poems, their very premise and identity, also have social and political histories. These poems engage Elect Nation and Augustan England from a particular angle, at a certain moment in flight; and we must know not only text and history, but also the point and conditions of their coincidence, how and to what ends the historical languages entered the literary text.

If my account of Elect Nation is accurate, then we ought to find *Absalom and Achitophel* balanced somewhat precariously near the edge of a demise, and indeed Dryden's efforts at achieving the semblance of balance—of sustaining the meaning and implications of prophetic history while simultaneously exploring those implications

---

[40] *An Address*, third to fourth preliminary leaf.
[41] See Steven Zwicker and Derek Hirst, "Rhetoric and Disguise: Political Language and Political Argument in Absalom and Architophel," *Journal of British Studies*, XXI, 2 (Fall, 1981), 39–54.

in harsh and derisive ways—seem to me the defining characteristics of this poem. The strength of the performance comes from its daring, from the freedom that Dryden felt in exploiting the satiric potential of sacred history while insisting that its emotional and intellectual powers remained politically cogent, that it retained sanctity and authority, its complex patterning in figural application and prophecy. Taking up this language rather late in its life as a serious political idiom allowed Dryden to extend its potential as derision in quite powerful ways, and yet he must have understood that if this poem were to be more than derision, satire could not utterly overwhelm prophecy. Indeed, it is the residual meaning of the metaphor that makes the satire, practised in its terms, so telling as an instrument in 1681, and it is the wit and daring of the application that allow us to take seriously the prophetic schemes as they might seem to be born out in the reviving fortunes of Stuart monarchy in 1681. If men were tiring of Elect Nation in 1681, then Dryden thrusts against that weariness a brilliant portrait of the English as murmuring Jews, the French as gourmandizing Egyptians, the wicked lunacy of Titus Oates as debased prophecy. And if they resented sacral kingship in the person of Charles II, then Dryden offered them the resistance of laughter and benignity, the fortunate, amusing and quite undeniable coincidence of Charles and David in their paternity and in their kingship. The genius of the poem is to make us see that the satire takes force from sacred history and that such history is deepened and renewed through satire.

> The *Jews*, a Headstrong, Moody, Murmuring race,
> As ever try'd th' extent and stretch of grace;
> God's pamper'd people whom, debauch'd with ease,
> No King could govern, nor no God could please;
> (Gods they had tri'd of every shape and size
> That God-smiths could produce, or Priests devise:)
> Those *Adam*-wits, too fortunately free,
> Began to dream they wanted libertie;
> And when no rule, no president was found
> Of men, by Laws less circumscrib'd and bound,
> They led their wild desires to Woods and Caves,
> And thought that all but Savages were Slaves.[42]

What did it mean so to portray Englishmen in 1681? At the height

---

[42] Citations are to the Kinsley edition, *The Poems of John Dryden*, ed. James Kinsley (Oxford, 1962), 4 vol., I, ll. 45–57.

of the Exclusion Crisis those ranged against the King and his Catholic brother included the political heirs and beneficiaries of men who had raised arms against Charles I. They composed an audience for and an important subject of the poem. Dryden wrote for them a history of Exclusion in a tongue which they had once claimed passionately as their own. Of course in 1681 they did not embrace the language of this history with its associations of civil war, of political experimentation, and regicide. But the function of Dryden's poem is to act as memory.[43] Unlike the King in 1660, Dryden will deny these men oblivion; this poem will fix the enemies of the court in a history which they may wish to distance, but whose sanctity they would be hard pressed utterly to deny or disclaim. Dryden knew what this history meant and so did his audience, Whig and Tory alike. And it is because of this knowledge and because at the height of Exclusion the parallels to '41 were so relentlessly worked in the pamphlet literature that he could run his own parallel history.

But Elect Nation is a different identity in 1681 than it was in 1641; it is not only the English past but also the history of the remnant; and the thrust and particularity of Dryden's portrait of the Jews seems to fix them more exactly in their "deplorable" present than in their polygamous and heroic past. Part of the wilful and clever sleight of hand in this poem is the arrangement of incongruous histories into a progressive narrative that allows us to conflate past and present and to have both take meaning from such juxtaposition. David acts the vigorous patriarch at some moment of Jewish urhistory, but the Jews draw their identity from the political history of Elect Nation, and from the perception of the remnant late in the seventeenth century, from their "ingrafted perverseness, their inveterate obstinacy against truth. They are a nation justly rendered the object of divine displeasure." The portrait could not have been turned in this complex manner in 1640 or in 1720. But in 1681—rather far along the road from Israel to Rome, removed from theocracy but quite alive to the memories and implications of holy war—Elect Nation deals with civil disorder as Jewish history and Jewish character. In 1640 the metaphor could not have sustained so wide and so genial a satiric margin. There were of course royalists who after the execution of the king denounced the Puritan savagery as Jewish deicide, but such denunciation was not

---

[43] Kinsley, *The Poems*, I, ll. 575, 633.

accompanied by laughter. In 1720 the metaphor would have been Augustan England, the overtones Virgilian or Horatian; Elect Nation was by then a past, distant and without authority.

But to suggest Elect Nation only as derision in 1681 is to ignore both the structure of this poem, the ascent to law and prophecy, and the steady and quite powerful tradition of scriptural figuralism that had once drawn Scripture into continuous alignment with the politics of a puritan theocracy. The meaning of Elect Nation in this poem is civil disorder; it conjures as well the remnant—that wonderful and deplorable history of the Jews—but the metaphor also argues renewal; the restoration prophesied at the end of the poem turns on both the triumph of the law and the renewal of the people. Exactly how far the metaphor might now sustain public belief and assent is a measure that we cannot take with precision.[44] But we ought not too quickly to dismiss the political meaning of scriptural promise even so late as 1681. Without the idea of that promise, without the possibility of a godly nation knowing their lawful lord, such restoration would have a compromised and cynical meaning in this poem; and I think neither history nor tone conveys cynicism. Dryden knew the complexities, indeed the unlikelihood, of prophecy; he understood how difficult a task he faced in attempting to turn the energies of this poem fully toward biblical restoration. But he was careful to insist that his composition was neither history nor satire. It is a poem; it has the structure of a fiction, the capacity to imagine the meaning of prophecy among a people though miserably fallen, yet still within reach of salvation. If the gestures of prophecy seem strained at the poem's close, there can be little wonder; it was late in the complicated and now harried life of this language; it was a point at which the Virgilian overtones of the poem's close must have seemed an agreeable, indeed compelling, harmony.[45]

The great Roman and romanizing work of this age came sixteen years later, in Dryden's translation of Virgil. But Dryden's *Virgil* did not altogether celebrate empire. That Virgil's great epic was a signal Roman text needs no elaboration; but the ways in which it was a romanizing work need to be explored. To claim Virgilian identity in

---

[44] The force of apocalyptic in the later seventeenth century is the subject of William Lamont's recent *Richard Baxter and the Millennium* (London, 1979).
[45] See R.G. Peterson, "Larger Manners and Events: Sallust and Virgil in *Absalom and Achitophel*," *PMLA*, LXXXII (1967), 236–44.

the 1690s was to invoke sublimity and authority, but it was not to invoke a fixed political identity or a specific interpretation of English politics. Neither Roman history as a whole nor Virgil's poem had become party property, though attempts to fix Roman history into a Whig or Tory interpretation of English politics would come in the following decades.[46] Of course, individual strands of Roman history and particular authors had inescapable political meaning for seventeenth-century Englishmen, and the republican tradition exemplifies such a treatment of antiquity.[47] But republicanism was not a narrow political program, nor did Roman history assume its cultural dominance as republicanism. Dryden undertook his last great political meditation on a text that was not, in the early 1690s, a political code. Indeed, it was the political ambiguity of the metaphor that allowed Dryden to conduct this translation as commentary and meditation. In 1681 Elect Nation was a set of complex but sharply fixed integers; but Augustan England in the early 1690s was an emerging identity, its protean shape certainly not fixed in the confusions and rapid shifts of party politics of that decade. When Dryden took up this translation in 1693, he engaged a metaphor and a text of enormous and longstanding cultural prestige; but to translate Virgil in the aftermath of the Glorious Revolution was a wholly different enterprise than to apply II Samuel at the height of Exclusion. All might claim and aspire to Roman virtue in 1697; and while men understood that Roman history was both republican and imperial order, the high authority of that history would serve more than one political end.

It is an interesting and revealing fact that Dryden's Whiggish publisher, Jacob Tonson, thought that he might have Dryden's *Virgil* honor William III by altering the figure of Aeneas in the plates interleaved through the book to resemble the hook-nosed king.[48] Although Tonson was unable to force from Dryden an explicit dedication of the *Aeneis* to the king—that honor went to the Earl of Mulgrave—I suspect that the crude alteration in the plates might have been sufficient to convince the king that such an honor was intended, that this translation of Virgil's great poem of empire was indeed a

---

[46] Addison Ward, "The Tory View of Roman History," *SEL* IV (1964), 413–56.

[47] Blair Worden, "Classical Republicanism in the Puritan Revolution," *History and Imagination*, ed. Hugh Lloyd-Jones, Valerie Pearl and Blair Worden (London, 1981), 182–200.

[48] Charles E. Ward. *Letters of John Dryden*, (Durham, NC, 1962), p. 93.

celebration of the new order, an England turned more sharply toward European interests than ever before, a panegyric to a foreign prince and to a king bound by marriage to the throne. Indeed, the fit between mythic and historical figures is rather neat, and such analogy was not lost on Dryden. Not only did he conceive his translation in political terms, but he saw or claimed to see Virgil's poem as political commentary: a warning to Augustus Caesar on the dangers of tyranny and elective kingship.[49] This is hardly the analogy that Tonson intended, but it was crucial to Dryden's reading of Virgil, an understanding of the Latin poet that can be traced through the dedicatory essay and that animates the whole of the translation, quite overtly at moments, less sharply and in a more sustained manner over the brooding and melancholy whole. What Tonson intended as honor, Dryden conceived very differently; for he understood Virgil's celebration of empire more subtly, in more compromised and less heroic ways, than Tonson could have imagined. I suspect that in its oblique and difficult relationship to the idea of heroic conquest and the fate of empire, Dryden's *Virgil* is more our poem than Tonson's, more contemporary than its indefatigable couplets will at first allow.

Listen for a moment as Dryden's Juno addresses Venus at the opening of Book 10, harshly and ironically rehearsing the causes and the character of the war that is about to unfold between Trojans and Rutulians:

> You think it hard, the *Latians* shou'd destroy
> With Swords your *Trojans*, and with Fires your *Troy*:
> Hard and unjust indeed, for Men to draw
> Their Native Air, nor take a foreign Law:
> That *Turnus* is permitted still to live,
> To whom his Birth a God and Goddess give:
> But yet 'tis just and lawful for your Line,
> To drive their Fields, and Force with Fraud to join.
> Realms, not your own, among your Clans divide,
> And from the Bridegroom tear the promis'd Bride:
> Petition, while you publick Arms prepare;
> Pretend a Peace, and yet provoke a War.[50]

Here and throughout the translation, Trojan entry is made to conjure invasion and conquest. In part the translation of this passage is exact;

---

[49] Kinsley, III, 1014, *Dedication of the Aeneas*, ll. 433–53.
[50] Kinsley, III, 1323, ll. 112–23.

but Dryden also invents, at points shades the political idiom to accommodate his own concerns with the injustice of the Glorious Revolution, "Hard and unjust indeed, for Men to draw/Their Native Air, nor take a foreign Law." The tone is resentful and xenophobic, and the language has no original in Virgil. Nor does the following line, "Realms, not your own, among your Clans divide." Dryden is translating "avertere praedas," to carry off plunder, with the phrase above.[51] And the closing lines of the passage draw the *Aeneis* close to the charges laid against the expanding European war which Dryden and others claimed was draining the English treasure in an endless European escapade, and moreover resulting in the awards of lavish grants and English estates to foreigners.[52] The topics derive from Virgil, but the particular thrust of the language is Dryden's own.

I don't want to suggest that Dryden conceived the translation of the *Aeneis* as an allegory, but rather that he saw a relationship between the conduct of Roman politics in the century of the Caesars and English history in his own time. He read Roman history in terms of English politics; he conceived this poem to have been Virgil's meditation on Roman politics, and he used Virgil for his own political ends. Dryden's subjects in his *Aeneis* were conquest and usurpation; oaths and bonds; the role of providence in the disposition of governments; the complaint of justice against fate. But because of the peculiar character of the 1690s and the fluid state of the metaphor, neither Tonson nor Dryden need have missed in their perception and application of the Roman analogy. Virgil's poem might have been and indeed was applied in both directions. In Thomas Fletcher's 1692 translation of Book I of the *Aeneis*, Jove's prophecy of Aeneas's bloody triumph was intended as an allusion to and celebration of William's victory at Boyne:

> A long and bloody, but successful, War
> Waits his Arrival on th'*Italian* Shore.
> Till Victories his fatal Title show,

---

[51] Virgil, *Aeneid*, Loeb Edition (London, 1950), p. 174, l. 78.

[52] On the question of William's grants to his Dutch compatriots see Frank H. Ellis, *A Discourse of the Contests and Dissentions Between the Nobles and the Commons . . . by Jonathan Swift* (Oxford, 1967), pp. 14–27; and the debates in the 1695 parliament, *A Collection of the Parliamentary Debates* (London, 1739), III, 52–57.

And barb'rous Nations to his Scepter bow;
Barb'rous, till he within just Bounds restrain
The savage Race, and break them into men.[53]

But the *Aeneis* might also be turned against the Revolutionary settlement, against the European wars and foreign interests, against the legitimation of invasion and conquest. This was a daring political application, and I suspect that if the integers of Roman history had been more clearly fixed in the political languages of the 1690s, Dryden could not have undertaken this translation in the manner that he did. Irony and insinuation were the mode of the commentary, and Dryden must have thought the screen sufficient to conduct his reading in this way.

Such an understanding of Virgil is evident throughout the translation, but it is most explicit in the dedicatory essay where historical digression suggests exactly how Dryden saw and used the Roman past:

> I must now come closer to my present business: and not think of making more invasive Wars abroad, when like *Hannibal*, I am call'd back to the defense of my own Country. *Virgil* is attack'd by many Enemies: He has a whole Confederacy against him, and I must endeavour to defend him as well as I am able .... But we are to consider him writing his Poem in a time when the Old Form of Government was subverted, and a new one just Established by *Octavius Caesar*: In effect by force of Arms, but seemingly by the Consent of the *Roman* People. The Commonwealth had receiv'd a deadly Wound in the former Civil Wars betwixt *Marius* and *Sylla*. The Commons, while the first prevail'd, had almost shaken off the Yoke of the Nobility; and *Marius* and *Cinna*, like the Captains of the Mobb, under the specious Pretence of the Publick Good, and of doing Justice on the Oppressours of their Liberty, reveng'd themselves, without Form of Law, on their private Enemies. *Sylla*, in his turn, proscrib'd the Heads of the adverse Party: He too had nothing but Liberty and Reformation in his Mouth; (for the Cause of Religion is but a Modern Motive to Rebellion, invented by the Christian Priesthood, refining on the Heathen:) .... Such was the Reformation of the Government by both Parties. The Senate and the Commons were the two Bases on which it stood; and the two Champions of either Faction, each destroy'd the Foundations of the other side: So the Fabrique of consequence must fall betwixt them: And Tyranny must be built upon their Ruines. This comes of altering Fundamental Laws and Constitu-

---

[53] Thomas Fletcher, *Poems on Several Occasions, And Translations* (London, 1692), p. 83.

tions .... Thus the *Roman* People were grosly gull'd; twice or thrice over: and as often enslav'd in one Century, and under the same pretence of Reformation.[54]

The passage begins with a defense of Virgil, but Virgil was a poet who hardly needed Dryden's defense; he was the most esteemed of ancient poets, and this epic revered as the culmination of a form that expressed for Renaissance poets and theorists the highest attainment of the literary intellect. The defensive posture follows not from Dryden's understanding of Virgil's condition but from the translator's sense of his own embattled circumstances as he began his romanizing work. By defending Virgil, Dryden in fact undertook a reading of the Roman poet that justifies his own circumstance and his own enterprise. The coincidence of poet and translator emerges from the large analogy that Dryden pursues through his description of politics in Augustan Rome, "... we are to consider [Virgil] as writing his Poem in a time when the Old Form of Government was subverted, and a new one just Established ... In effect by force of Arms, but seemingly by the Consent of the *Roman* People." Dryden is describing Roman politics in the century of the Caesars, but the language suggests as exactly the Jacobite reading of the Glorious Revolution. Stuart loyalists maintained that the revolution was effected by force of arms, that it was an invasion conducted under the pretense of a protection of property and liberty, a subversion of the government that had in fact altered fundamental laws and constitutions. Dryden's summary of Roman political history is in fact an outline of the course of politics in England from the civil wars through the end of the century, and this application would have been difficult for his audience wholly to ignore. Not only do key words and phrases argue those connections, but the whole scheme of political history as disguise fits the conduct and perception of politics in the later seventeenth century.

The subversion of government under the pretense of reform, the use of arms under the guise of public consent, the tyranny consequent on altering fundamental laws and constitutions: none who spoke politics could have mistaken the English meaning of this Roman history. Some among Dryden's audience would have resented or scorned his implications, but all would have recognized the contemporary

---

[54] Kinsley, III, 1011–13, *Dedication*, ll. 318–419.

meaning of those words and phrases, the special fit of Roman history to English politics. And that fit was pursued not only in sweeping analogies but also in daring particulars. On the administration of tyrants, Dryden wrote in the *Dedication*:

> The last *Tarquin* was Expell'd justly, for Overt-Acts of Tyranny, and Male-Administration; for such are the Conditions of an Elective Kingdom: And I meddle not with others: being, for my own Opinion, of *Montaigns* Principles, that an Honest Man ought to be contented with that Form of Government, and with those Fundamental Constitutions of it, which he receiv'd from his Ancestors, and under which himself was Born.[55]

The initial application of the passage is obvious; the conflation of tyranny and elective kingship was an insult directed to William III and his supporters; the satiric literature of the 1690s had made current the identification of William and Mary with Tarquin and Tullia,[56] those models of despotism and filial impiety; but the slur of elective kingship aims at constitutional as well as personal issues. The parliamentary convention of 1689 had scrupled so minutely over the language with which to describe James's departure from England in order to avoid two implications: that William's descent into England was an invasion and that his title was founded on election or conquest.[57] The parliamentary bill for the Exclusion of James, Duke of York, from succession had been defeated in 1681 on the strength of the argument that such exclusion would turn the kingship into elective monarchy; none who supported William's kingship would have had his title hinged on so precarious a term: "*Tarquin* was Expell'd justly, for Overt-Acts of Tyranny, and Male-Administration; for such are the Conditions of an Elective Kingdom." But this argument by slur and implication does not close with the reference to Tarquin. The citation from Montaigne raises the same issue, though in more oblique fashion. The contentment of Montaigne's "Honest Man" is not simple piety, it is a form of civic virtue that recognizes the binding force of personal and national inheritance. Dryden insists on the same

---

[55] Kinsley, III, 1014, ll. 444–49.
[56] Cf. Arthur Mainwaring, "Tarquin and Tullia," *POAS*, V, ed. William J. Cameron (New Haven, 1971), pp. 46–54; "The Female Parricide," *POAS*, V, 157; and Cameron's commentary.
[57] For the debates of Convention Parliament see W. Cobbett's *The Parliamentary History of England*, V (London, 1809), pp. 31–136; and Chapter 1 of J.P. Kenyon, *Revolution Principles* (Cambridge, 1977).

principles in *Absalom and Achitophel*:

> If those who gave the Scepter, coud not tye
> By their own deed their own Posterity,
> How then coud *Adam* bind his future Race?
> How coud his forfeit on mankind take place?
> Or how coud heavenly Justice damn us all,
> Who nere consented to our Fathers fall?[58]

The issues are buttressed by a fuller moral, legal, and theological argument in *Absalom and Achitophel*, but the position in the *Dedication*, though suggested with greater tact, is the same.

Nor is Tarquin the only analogue for the English king. There are comparisons with Aeneas and Augustus, and a rather pointed contrast with Latinus, that paradigm of kingly legitimacy. The ways in which Aeneas and Augustus are used to think about William is one of the most complex issues in the *Dedication* and in the translation; Dryden's strategy in the dedicatory essay is not to analogize either Aeneas or Augustus directly with William but to present the Roman figures in a language that would argue the circumstances of William's kingship. Hence the peculiar passage on succession and title as they bear on Aeneas's claims to the Trojan office:

> *Aeneas* cou'd not pretend to be *Priam*'s Heir in a Lineal Succession: For *Anchises* the Heroe's Father, was only of the second Branch of the Royal Family: And *Helenus*, a Son of *Priam*, was yet surviving, and might lawfully claim before him. It may be *Virgil* mentions him on that Account. Neither has he forgotten *Priamus*, in the Fifth of his *Aeneis*, the Son of *Polites*, youngest Son to *Priam*; who was slain by *Pyrrhus*, in the Second Book. *Aeneas* had only Married *Creusa, Priam*'s Daughter, and by her could have no Title, while any of the Male Issue were remaining. In this case, the Poet gave him the next Title, which is, that of an Elective King.[59]

For Dryden, Virgil is instructing and warning Augustus on the nature of the Roman emperor's title: elective kings rule at the pleasure of the people. Dryden has Virgil raise this subject so that he, Dryden, can scorn the legitimacy of William's rule and warn those who claimed for the Dutchman the sanctity and rights of lineal descent that they had in fact sanctioned revolution and usurpation. The debate over the nature of William's title had not been settled in 1689; it was raised

---

[58] Kinsley, I , 236–37, ll. 769–74.
[59] Kinsley, III, 1016–17, *Dedication*, ll. 541–51.

throughout his kingship, and with special force the year before the *Virgil* publication. The assassination plot of 1696 had caused parliament to vote an Association proclaiming loyalty to William as rightful and lawful king. But in the debate over the Association, even so late as 1696 and even in the face of the Plot, members of parliament still scrupled over the title.[60] Dryden's *Virgil* depicts Aeneas's Trojan office as elective kingship so that Augustus Caesar might be instructed in the character and dangers of such a title. The analogy is two-fold: first, between the Virgilian models of elective kingship—Aeneas, Mezentius, and Tarquin—and William III; second, between the Roman emperor and the English king. The Virgilian models, pious and restrained in the person of Aeneas, but brutal and corrupt in the persons of Mezentius and Tarquin, demonstrate the extremes. Augustus Caesar, conqueror and despot, needs the instruction of Virgil's poem so that he might become the best of the bad lot to which he belongs. By arguing that Virgil draws Aeneas to the measure of Augustus Caesar, Dryden is free to raise the problems of Caesar's kingship as they are illustrated in Virgil's epic. The distortion is curious but with William in mind we can see its point. "Our Poet, who all this while had *Augustus* in his Eye, had no desire he should seem to succeed by any right of Inheritance, deriv'd from *Julius Caesar*; such a Title being but one degree remov'd from Conqest. For what was introduc'd by force, by force may be remov'd." In this complex arrangement of poetic models and historical figures, William falls somewhere between Aeneas and the worst examples, Mezentius and Tarquin. One assumes that Dryden found a greater affinity between Tarquin and William than between Aeneas and the English king, but perhaps the closest analogue is Caesar. The language in which Dryden casts Virgil's deliberation over the character of Aeneas's sovereignty and the nature of Caesar's rule is strikingly appropriate to the debate over the revolutionary settlement: under what conditions had William entered the country and by what rights did he now wield power? The whole of this problem is of course reflected in the translation, especially Book 7, Aeneas's entry into Latium, where the steady shading of the language, the consistent impulse to render entry as conquest, can only be the translator brooding over the injustice and perhaps the inevitability of such conquest, of Latium by Aeneas and of England by William III.

---

[60] Cobbett, V, pp. 987–93.

The contemporary application of the whole discussion of legitimacy and sovereignty is sharpened by the introduction of Latinus:

> Our Author shews us another sort of Kingship in the Person of *Latinus*. He was descended from *Saturn*, and as I remember, in the Third Degree. He is describ'd a just and a gracious Prince; solicitious for the Welfare of his People; always Consulting with his Senate to promote the common Good. We find him at the head of them, when he enters into the Council-Hall. Speaking first, but still demanding their Advice, and steering by it as far as the Iniquity of the Times wou'd suffer him. And this is the proper Character of a King by Inheritance, who is born a Father of his Country. *Aeneas*, tho' he Married the Heiress of the Crown, yet claim'd no Title to it during the Life of his Father-in-Law.[61]

Perhaps the idea of Latinus as James II—gracious father to his people and sage parliamentarian—would have roused the scorn of much of Dryden's audience, but who could have missed the analogy between Aeneas and William, the thrust of the end of this passage?

Not all contemporary issues are argued so openly as this. Some topics are raised only by allusion and not pursued through extended analogy. But we can hear the contemporary harmonies in Dryden's handling of such themes as ingratitude and constancy. Gratitude as a political virtue had been constantly extolled by those Stuart apologists who saw in the system of patronage and in the generosity of Charles II an ideal of governance and kingship. Dryden was hardly alone in the Exclusion Crisis when he scored the ingratitude of those who had battened on the King's largesse and then turned against their benefactor. Gratitude was in fact a linch-pin of Stuart politics, and the language of Dryden's *Dedication* in 1697 conjures a powerful political argument that takes meaning not only from the disloyalty of those who raised arms against James II but from the whole history of disloyalty to Stuart kings, from that highest crime of regicide which gave particular force to this theme: "... want of Constancy, and Ingratitude after the last Favour, is a Crime that never will be forgiven."[62]

Nor is gratitude the only theme thus handled. There are glancing references to "dispensing powers," a subject that Dryden treats in purely literary terms, but none who heard the phrase could ignore its political meaning, the long history of a struggle between two Stuart

---

[61] Kinsley, III, 1017, *Dedication*, ll. 561–71.
[62] Kinsley, III, 1027, ll. 953–55.

kings and truculent parliaments that were unwilling to allow their laws to be suspended at will by kings bent on what they thought was the destruction of the Protestant religion and the imposition of Catholic slavery. "Any thing might be allow'd to his Son *Virgil* on the account of his other Merits; That being a Monarch he had a dispensing Power, and pardon'd him. . . . To Moralize this Story, *Virgil* is the *Apollo*, who has this Dispensing Power. His great Judgement made the Laws of Poetry, but he never made himself a Slave to them."[63] Virgil like Apollo could supersede mechanical rules for the same reason that a "Monarch may dispense with, or suspend his own Laws, when he finds it necessary so to do; especially if those Laws are not altogether fundamental."[64] If this seems a slightly off-hand way of conducting a political argument, the mode is explained by its history. The battle had been long and bitterly fought, and Dryden's use of Virgil's looseness with chronology and fables to demonstrate the inevitable rights of monarchy is not so much an argument as it is a memory of a political contest.

Dryden's discussion of the coinage crisis makes a similar use of poetics, not exactly to conceal a political argument, but to allow suggestion and metaphor to enlarge the range of meaning that links politics with poetry, "Words are not so easily Coyn'd as Money: And yet we see that the Credit not only of Banks, but of Exchequers cracks, when little comes in, and much goes out."[65] The enormous expenditures that supported William's European wars are clearly alluded to here and in the following passage on the coining of words, "I carry not out the Treasure of the Nation, which is never to return: but what I bring from *Italy*, I spend in *England*: Here it remains, and here it circulates; for if the Coyn be good, it will pass from one hand to another."[66] The passage begins with the contrast between the debased currency of the 1690s and Dryden's coining which, I suspect, he knew would be valued and endure; but the real contrast that Dryden is after is not wholly contained by the metaphor; what he wants to juxtapose is king and poet, warfare and translation. This poem reverses the history of luxury and decline; Dryden's trade with the ancients and moderns enriches England, King William's wars end in waste and destruction.

---

[63] Kinsley, III, 1030, ll. 1046–54.
[64] Kinsley, III, 1031, ll. 1080–82.
[65] Kinsley, III, 1058, *Dedication*, ll. 2105–07.
[66] Kinsley, III, 1059, *Dedication*, ll. 2167–70.

There is something touching if incongruous about the circumstances and the daring of the whole project. When Dryden began to translate the works of Virgil, he had been ejected from the laureateship, he had converted to Roman Catholicism, and he maintained what can only seem to us a preposterous loyalty to James II; for these principles he had lost favor and patronage. He was a man precarious in his safety, his health, and his finances, depending on the leavings of a few minor gentry and loyal patrons who bore him no grudge in what he himself perceived as rather shabby circumstances. And yet he now chose to make an English *Virgil*, to translate a poem of empire and sublimity, not perhaps the most likely enterprise for this old age. Dryden took up this translation because he needed money; but he also knew that an English *Virgil* would both honor the Roman poet and enshrine the translator who thought himself Virgil's likeness and heir. By maneuvering the poem into an opposition stance, such a work gave this Jacobite a way of asserting his literary and civic identity, and that assertion is itself a commentary on the range of meaning that Rome offered at the close of the seventeenth century. The analogy with Rome allowed Dryden to see himself as patriot; it allowed him to celebrate those families that still obliged him as the Roman nobility, and to scorn the revolution that had displaced the legitimate king and poet laureate with tyranny and the mob. The analogy with Rome provided a language and a history for such assertion. How clearly the political assertion was perceived is difficult to know; but Dryden's *Virgil* also suggested eternity, and in that invocation the poet was not wrong.

HARRY M. BRACKEN

BISHOP BERKELEY'S MESSIANISM*

In this lecture I ask a question which I cannot properly answer. My question is: why did Berkeley set out upon his American Project? I can only offer a suggestion as to what fired up Berkeley's imagination and led him to devote almost a decade of his life to a most extraordinary scheme.

First, a word about Berkeley: he is well-known to Americans because Berkeley, California is named after him. Indeed, his portrait adorns the city seal. Moreover, Yale University contains a Berkeley College. His American philosophical disciple, Samuel Johnson, became the first president of King's College (later Columbia University). George Berkeley was born near Thomastown, Ireland, probably in 1685. He graduated from Trinity College, Dublin, entered the Anglican priesthood, and was elected a college fellow. The philosophical work for which he is now best known appeared between 1709 and 1713. In 1709 his *Essay towards a New Thory of Vision* was published. It is primarily a study of both the optics and the psychology of human visual perception. His *Principles of Human Knowledge* appeared in 1710. It is in this text that he advances his famous—or infamous—thesis that the being of things consists in their being perceived, i.e. *esse* is *percipi*. Berkeley argues that philosophers are wrong to think that there are such things as material substances; that is, things which are said to exist independently of their being perceived. Philosophers who have postulated material substances are driven into a hopeless scepticism because there is no way of telling if

---

* Some of the research for this paper was supported by grants from the Social Science and Humanities Research Council of Canada and from McGill University. For their thoughtful, and often extensive assistance, I wish to thank David Berman, James Force, Elly van Gelderen, Patrick H. Kelly, F.R.J. Knetsch, and Jean-Paul Pittion. I particularly wish to thank Richard H. Popkin both for inviting me to participate in this series of lectures and for the scholarly help and encouragement which he has always given me. I am also profoundly indebted to Mary P. Pollard, Deputy Keeper of Older Printed Books and Special Collections, and to Charles Benson, both of the Trinity College Dublin Library, for the wide range of assistance—bibliographical, historical, and philosophical—which they have given me. Finally, my thanks to Norman Thrower, Director, and Thomas Wright, Librarian, of the William Andrews Clark Memorial Library, for their generous cooperation.

what *appears* to us corresponds to anything in the philosophers' world of 'real' material substance. In other words, Berkeley analyses material substance as being an unknowable absurdity. He concludes that what appears to us in perception *is* what is real. Berkeley's revolutionary move is thus to identify two things (*to be* and *to be perceived*) which, when separated, he takes to constitute the very root of scepticism. With this brilliantly simple dissolution of the conceptual structure of the philosophers' account of material substance, Berkeley claims that he also provides a sound basis for science, as well as proofs for the existence of God and of an immaterial and substantial perceiving self. The world, however, was not convinced. The London wits greeted the new philosophy with laughter.[1] And so in 1713 Berkeley cast the same arguments in dialogue form and sought to anticipate all possible objections. His *Three Dialogues between Hylas and Philonous* is now both a literary and philosophic classic. During the remainder of his life, Berkeley published on a wide range of topics including philosophy, economics, mathematics, and medicine.[2]

In the years immediately after his graduation and election to Fellowship, Berkeley travelled in England, France, and Italy and in 1717 was named a Senior Fellow of the College, i.e., a member of the governing body. He taught divinity, Hebrew, Greek, and served as librarian. In May 1724 he resigned from Trinity to become Dean of Derry. By 1724, however, something quite remarkable had happened in his life. He writes his friend Percival, 4 March 1723: "It is about ten months since I have determined with myself to spend the residue of my days in the Island of Bermuda, where I trust in Providence I may be the mean instrument of doing good to mankind."[3] He refers to the Bermuda "scheme" again in a letter to Percival of 4 June 1723. "[It] is now stronger on my mind than ever, this providential event having made many things easy in my private affairs which were otherwise before."[4] He produced a *Proposal for the better Supplying of*

---

[1] See my *Early Reception of Berkeley's Immaterialism: 1710–33*. 2nd ed., rev. (Den Haag: Martinus Nijhoff, 1965), and David Berman, "Berkeley's Reception after America," *Archiv für Geschichte der Philosophie*, LXII (1980), 311–20.

[2] See A.A. Luce, *The Life of George Berkeley*, (Edinburgh: Thomas Nelson, 1949).

[3] *The Works of George Berkeley*, ed. A.A. Luce and T.E. Jessop, 9 vols., (Edinburgh: Thomas Nelson, 1948–57) VIII, 127.

[4] *Works*, VIII, 130. Luce takes this 'providential event' to be the legacy unexpectedly left Berkeley (by Swift's Vanessa) and referred to in the previous paragraph. I incline to the view that it refers to the Bermuda project, partly for grammatical reasons

Churches in our Foreign Plantations, and for Converting the Savage Americans, to Christianity, by a College to be erected in the Summer Islands, otherwise called The Isles of Bermuda,[5] and by 1725 had a royal charter for St. Paul's College. He spent several years politicking both for private funds and governmental grants to underwrite the project. In September 1728 he set sail for Newport,[6] R.I. and arrived 23 January 1729, in the company of his wife of a year as well as John Smibert, "the pioneer of portrait painting in America."[7] Four fellows of Trinity College 'signed on' to become fellows of St. Paul's but did not accompany Berkeley on the trip.[8] A.A. Luce, Berkeley's most recent biographer and co-editor of the standard edition of the *Works of Berkeley* sees Berkeley motivated by missionary concern, as well as educational and imperial interests. He makes two points about Berkeley's decision to go to Rhode Island. (1) The Project required both Crown and private support. He needed to show private contributors that he was serious—a matter about which questions had been raised. However, no sooner was he out of town than the politicians who had promised Crown appropriations reneged on their undertakings. (2) The royal charter for St. Paul's College specified that the Deanship of Derry would fall vacant eighteen months after his arrival in Bermuda.

As even the title of the *Proposal* makes clear, Berkeley has two goals: a college that would prepare the sons of colonists for the Church, and would also educate Indian boys so as to convert the Indian populations. He chose Bermuda because it seemed to be roughly equidistant from the several colonies, because not being important to trade it would not have corrupting influences, and because it had a mild climate. In fact he never got to Bermuda. He remained in Rhode Island for almost three years. When it was clear that the Bermuda plan had failed, he set sail from Boston 21 September 1731 and reached London 30 October. While in America he wrote *Alciphron*, he acquired some disciples, and he left a collection of books plus the

---

and partly because I do not think a Christian of Berkeley's sort would consider an award of cash useful in 'private affairs' as 'providential'. That is, I take the Project to have given meaning and direction to Berkeley's 'private affairs'.

[5] *Works*, VII, 345 f.
[6] Cf. Edwin S. Gaustad, *George Berkeley in America*, (New Haven: Yale U.P., 1979).
[7] Luce, *Life*, 113.
[8] *Ibid.*, 103.

deed to his house and land to Yale. In 1734 he became Bishop of Cloyne, a small rural diocese adjoining Cork.

His friend Jonathan Swift seems to have found the American scheme "romantic" but he supported it.[9] Others found the entire enterprise absurd. As Edwin Gaustad has shown, those with first-hand knowledge of the American Church or educational scenes were profoundly distressed with Berkeley's ignorance. It is clear that for many years, Berkeley was seen as something of a nut. His friends were obliged to negotiate with care in order to arrange meetings between Berkeley and Queen Caroline lest talk about Bermuda ruin his chances for preferment. "Give me leave to be," writes Baron Wainwright, interceding with Mrs. Clayton [later Viscountess Sundon, Mistress of the Robes to Queen Caroline], "as I have often been, an advocate for the Dean with your Ladyship ... Forget Bermuda, and he will shine among the clergy and do honour to the Church by his virtue and learning." He then goes on to discount the rumor that Berkeley is mad.[10] Hertz writes that "it was thought a waggish thing, after [Berkeley] had been consecrated to the see of Cloyne in 1734, to use the phrase, 'when the Bishop of Cloyne sets out a second time for Bermuda' as a synonym for never."[11]

When Berkeley threw himself totally into the American project, he must have realized that it would damage his reputation. But he plunged ahead. Even the prospect of three months confined on a small vessel of 250 tons must have induced consternation in a man whom both J.O. Wisdom[12] and David Berman[13] have suggested, for quite different reasons, was much concerned with symbols of purification. And yet the Project totally consumed his energies for almost a decade. Why?

In his *Berkeley's American Sojourn*[14] Benjamin Rand suggests

---

[9] *Ibid.*, 101.

[10] *Memoirs of Viscountess Sundon* ... ed. Mrs. Thomson, 2 vols. (London: Henry Colburn, 1847), II, 165 f.

[11] Gerald Berkeley Hertz, *British Imperialism in the Eighteenth Century*, (London: Archibald Constable, 1908), 225–26. Hertz cites *Orrey Papers* (ed. 1903), I, 224, for his reference.

[12] J.O. Wisdom, *The Unconscious Origin of Berkeley's Philosophy*, (London: Hogarth Press, 1953).

[13] David Berman, "Bishop Berkeley and the fountains of living waters," *Hermathena*, CXXVIII (1980), 21–31.

[14] Benjamin Rand, *Berkeley's American Sojourn*, (Cambridge: Harvard U.P., 1932), 9–10.

that Berkeley's "ardent spirit was evidently now controlled by the desire for philanthropic endeavors. Hence it was that romance and philanthrophy became united as the essential factors that animated his subsequent scheme of founding a college in America." As will become evident, Berkeley had an explicit motivation which can hardly be described as 'philanthropic'.

Or was he consumed with missionary zeal? I think we can dismiss that reason. If Berkeley were motivated by a desire to convert natives, he could have started in Ireland. Catholics outnumbered Protestants in, e.g., Cloyne, by eight to one. The Anglican Church in Ireland expended considerable effort to bring the Protestant religion and English language education to the "native Irish" during this period.

Or was it because he was tired of the Old World and saw hope only in the New? George Davie[15], has argued, I think persuasively, that in *Alciphron* (the book written in Rhode Island) Berkeley is analysing the threat to the social and moral order posed both by the rising commercialism and by one of its most brilliant apologists, Bernard Mandeville, author of *The Fable of the Bees: or, Private Vices, Publick Benefits* (1714). Berkeley is seeking a new foundation on which to base the social order in the light of the profound changes he sees Western civilization undergoing. There is no doubt that Berkeley was distressed by the implications of that financial collapse known as the South Sea Bubble (in the 1720s). Davie also suggests that with his fellow Irishman, Francis Hutcheson, Berkeley sets the stage for that explosion of ideas we now call the Scottish Enlightenment—including the work of David Hume, Adam Smith, and Thomas Reid. In any case, Berkeley can be seen as a social commentator who was pessimistic about the situation in Great Britain and Europe.

But neither ordinary missionary activity nor disillusionment with Europe adequately explains Berkeley's motivation. Bear in mind also that Berkeley has a reputation for holding reasonable views on matters of social policy. He often expresses concern for the welfare of his Irish Catholic neighbors and he seems to have been well-regarded by them. In the American context, he suggests that colonial Protestant planters "might learn from those of the Church of *Rome*, how it is in their Interest and Duty to behave. Both *French* and *Spaniards* have

---

[15] George Davie, "Berkeley, Hume, and the Central Problem of Scottish Philosophy," in *McGill Hume Studies*, eds. David Fate Norton, Nicholas Capaldi, Wade L. Robison, (San Diego: Austin Hill Press, 1976), 43–62.

intermarried with *Indians*, to the great Strength, Security and Increase of their Colonies."[16] English planters, however, reveal "an irrational Contempt of the Blacks, as Creatures of another Species." On the other hand, Berkeley does not oppose slavery. Instead, he sees the conversion of blacks as being beneficial to the slaves and in the interest of slave owners. Owners would then "have Slaves who should *obey in all Things their Masters according to the Flesh, not with Eye-service as Men-pleasers, but in Singleness of Heart as fearing God* [and who would understand] that Gospel Liberty consists with temporal Servitude; [owners should realize] that their Slaves would only become better Slaves by being Christians."[17] Some planters feared that if their slaves became Christians they would be entitled to freedom—or at least entitled to Sunday as a day of rest. Berkeley answers the first worry by obtaining a ruling from the Solicitor-General to the effect that converted slaves need not be freed. Perhaps Berkeley hoped that Christianity would bring freedom in its train; he reportedly baptised his own (Rhode Island) house slaves. Berkeley is, however, sensitive to coercion in religious matters.[18] He suggests, e.g., that Catholics should be given an economic stake in Ireland, the opportunity to attend the University of Dublin, and generally that consciences should not be forced.

When we turn to Berkeley's American Project Proposal, we find him advocating a policy which is surely as oppressive and coercive as any which falls under the bloody history of the traditional Christian doctrine: "Compel them to enter." [*Luke* 14: 23] Where were the Indians, whose conversion is one of the two purposes of the proposed Bermuda college to come from? It must have been a very providential event indeed which prompted him to write: "The young *Americans* necessary for this Purpose, may in the Beginning be procured, either by peaceable Methods from those savage Nations, which border on our Colonies, and are in Friendship with us, or by taking captive the Children of our Enemies."[19] So Berkeley would have us take captive the children of our enemies—being careful to select only those who "are under ten years of Age, before evil Habits have taken a deep root; and yet not so early as to prevent

---

[16] SPG Sermon, 1732. *Works* VII, 122.
[17] *Works* VII, 346. See also Gaustad, *op. cit.*, 91–94.
[18] E.g., *Works* VI, 160.
[19] *Works* VII, 347.

retaining their Mother Tongue, which should be preserved by Intercourse among themselves." Now we have two related questions: why did Berkeley get involved with America? How did he get himself into the position of proposing to found a college in the New World with a student-body obtained by such means?

Does it really make sense that a man who in later life can spend twenty years in Cloyne with hardly so much as a visit even to Dublin[20] should suddenly be prepared to sacrifice a promising career in the Church to kidnap and then to convert Indian children on an island he has never seen off the coast of a continent he knows virtually nothing about?

The only clue I have found is in Berkeley's *Verses on America*. They were, according to reliable evidence adduced by Luce[21] written on or before 10 February 1726. The last stanza has often been read as messianic. Antonello Gerbi[22] reports that the opening line, amended to read "Westward the Star of Empire takes its way," stands at the head of the west stairway of the US Capitol in Washington. The poem is entitled: "America or the Muse's Refuge: A Prophecy." In the 1726 form in which it was sent to Percival, the last stanza reads:

> Westward the Course of Empire takes its Way;
>   The four first Acts already past,
> A fifth shall close the Drama with the Day;
>   Time's noblest Offspring is the last.

When published in Berkeley's *Miscellany* (1752) the last line is amended to read: "The world's great Effort is the last."[23]

I take the symbolism of the final stanza, the four plus one Acts, to be from *Daniel*, chapter 2, where the four kingdoms, usually taken to be Babylon, Persia, Greece and Rome, shall be succeeded by a fifth: "And in the days of these kings shall the God of heaven set up a kingdom, which shall never be destroyed ..." (2:44) Traditionally, the Saints are not said to come marching in until the four empires have disappeared. Christian (especially Protestant) interpretations of *Daniel* as presaging the Second Coming abounded in the English Civil War period—a matter Christopher Hill[24] has examined. A number of

---

[20] Cf. Luce, *Life*, 173, also (Dublin 1738) letter 190, *Works* VIII, 246–47.
[21] *Works* VII, 369.
[22] Antonello Gerbi, *The Dispute of the New World*, transl. Jeremy Moyle, (Pittsburgh: U.P., 1973?), 138.
[23] *Works* VII, 370, 373.
[24] *The World Turned Upside Down*, (Harmondsworth: Penguin, 1975) and many

groups expected 1666 to be *the* year. That was also the year in which Sabbatians expected the Messianic age to begin. The Sabbatian movement had an impact across Europe and even in America as Gershon Scholem[25] shows. Berkeley makes a negative reference to some of these sects at *Querist* I, 303: "Whether every plea of conscience is to be regarded? Whether, for instance, the German Anabaptists, Levellers, or Fifth Monarchy men would be tolerated on that pretence?"[26]

Not everyone finds Berkeley's poem a piece of prophetic literature. E.L. Tuveson, in *Redeemer Nation: The Idea of America's Millennial Role*[27] strongly rejects the notion that Berkeley's poem is really prophetic because it fails either to provide an account of an apocalyptic struggle or to envisage what Tuveson takes Berkeley to deny, i.e., an universal millennium. So far as Tuveson is concerned, Berkeley's ideal is only that America should become a better Europe.[28] In response one should note three factors: (1) Millennialists usually see some particular historical events as marking the beginning of the millennium even if the millennium is said to be universal. (2) There is no indication that Berkeley is excluding the possibility that America will effect changes worldwide. (3) Berkeley subtitles his poem, *Prophecy*.

David Berman[29] has argued that Tuveson misreads Berkeley. Berman thinks the prophetic text is not Daniel but Isaiah xliv, 6, partly on the basis of an SPG Sermon (1730) by Zachary Pearce, who was involved in fund-raising for the American Project. Pearce argues, says Berman, that the *Isaiah* prophecy is to be fulfilled in America, i.e. "salvation unto the end of the earth."

> It is observable that this so lately discovered World lies in the very Route and Road, which Christianity seems to have all along taken: in the East, we know, it first appeared; and, as it spread itself, it shaped its Course with that of the Sun, the Emblem of its Light and Glory: to the Westward it travelled, and in length of time took possession of the *European* Countries, which are now called *Christendom* ... (p. 26) [London 1730]

---

other works. See also Peter Toon, ed., *Puritans, the Millennium and the Future of Israel*. (Cambridge: James Clarke, 1970).
[25] Gershom Scholem, *Sabbatai Sevi*, (Princeton: U.P., 1973).
[26] *Works* VI, 161.
[27] (Chicago: U.P., 1968).
[28] *Ibid.*, p. 94.
[29] David Berman, "Berkeley's Prophecy," *Scriblerian*, XIII (1980), 38–39.

Berman proposes that we use Pearce's *Sermon* as a gloss upon Berkeley's poem and thus that the Acts mentioned in the poem "are the different phases in the spread of Christianity ... The fifth Act, clearly, and the close of the religious Drama, was to be the general conversion of America." But as I have already said, my view is that Daniel is the text alluded to in Berkeley's *Prophecy*, a view which Donald Greene[30] shares.

I think we are now in a better position to deal with the questions I posed: if it is granted that Berkeley hoped to use the traditional symbolism of Daniel so that he might characterize America in messianic terms then we have a partial answer to the point of the American Project. To repeat: Berkeley does not tell us what struck him in 1722. But he does tell us, and he tells us in print, that he proposes to convert the Indians by kidnapping Indian children who are to be educated to become missionaries.

I suggest that the key to this extraordinary proposal is that Berkeley accepts the popular view that the American Indians are the Lost Tribes of Israel. As Jews, their conversion is especially dear to God and each conversion promises, as Paul tells us in *Romans xi*, to bring closer the Second Coming. Unfortunately for my suggestion, Berkeley does not mention the widely-held Jewish-Indian thesis. But I submit that an explanation of this sort is required to make sense of the incredible and totally out-of-character savagery recommended in his American prophetic dream. American millennial thinking is driven both by the Jewish-Indian notion and by the belief that America is the hope of Protestant Europe. Berkeley, however, is not merely interested in Protestantizing the New World—he wants to convert the Indians.

In his history of the Indies, published in both Spanish and English editions at the outset of the seventeenth century, Joseph Acosta[31] makes it clear that the Jewish-Indian thesis is widely held as an explanation, compatible with the Bible, for the origin of the people in the New World. So much so that he feels obliged to devote a chapter to refuting it, entitled: "*That the opinion of many which holde, that the first race of the Indians comes from the* Iewes, *is not* true."[32] Hardly a philo-semite, he writes:

---

[30] Donald Greene, "More on Berkeley's Prophecy," *Scriblerian*, XIV (1981), 58. See also Berman's Reply, w.c., 58–59.

[31] Joseph Acosta, *The Naturall and Morall Historie of the East and West Indies*, transl. by E.G., (London: Val: Sims for Edward Blount and William Aspley, 1604).

[32] *Ibid.*, Lib. I, ch. 23.

> There are great signes and arguments amongst the common sort of the *Indians*, to breed a beleefe, that they are descended from the *Iewes*: for commonly you shall see them fearefull, submisse, ceremonious and subtill in lying. And moreover they say, their habites are like vnto those the *Iewes* vsed; for they weare a short coat or waste-coat, and a cloake imbroidered all about; they goe bare-footed, or with soles tied with latchets over the foot ...[33]

Notwithstanding this, Acosta rules out the Jewish-Indian thesis because Jews, unlike Indians, use a written language, are circumcised, and avoid idolatry.

On the other hand, Thomas Thorowgood, in his *Jewes in America, or, Probabilities That the Americans are of that Race*,[34] takes up Menasseh ben Israel's Lost Tribe thesis; included is a Dedicatory Epistle by John Dury supporting this view and citing Comenius as well. Dury sees "the dissolution of the States and Empires of the world, [tending] towards some great works, and extraordinary revolution which may shortly come to pass." Thorowgood gives a number of Biblical citations when he writes: "The Jewes before the end of the world shall be converted to Christianity; this truth is to be found in the Old and New Testament."[35] He cites a letter from "Master R. Williams" of New England, who learned an Indian language and sought to convert Indians. Williams finds evidence of Jewish practices among the New England Indians, e.g., the separating of menstruating women and belief in a God overhead. Thorowgood also writes that de Groot asserts confidently that "we have so many witnesses that the Americans be circumcised, as it becomes not a modest man to deny it ..."[36]

According to Dury's biographer,[37] Dury co-operated with a group of "Puritans in securing the passage of an act of Parliament in 1649 providing for the incorporation of 'The Society for the Propagation of the Gospel in New England,' which was to have as its object the diffusion of Christianity and education among the American Indians. Dury persuaded his friend, Thomas Thorowgood, to publish his pamphlet, *The Jewes in America* ..."[38] Dury seems to have been in-

---

[33] *Ibid.*, 75–76.
[34] (London: Printed by W.H. for Tho. Slater ..., 1650). Popkin has discovered that the 1660 edition is significantly different, e.g., the essay by Dury is omitted.
[35] *Ibid.*, p. 22.
[36] *Ibid.*, p. 9. Thorowgood cites *In Laet*. p. 2, p. 59.
[37] J. Minton Batten, *John Dury: Advocate of Christian Reunion* (Chicago: U.P., 1944).
[38] *Ibid.*, 139.

volved with a wide range of political, religious, and philosophical people. He married a relative of Sir Robert Boyle, the Irish scientist. In 1662, Boyle became governor of the Society which Dury had helped incorporate.[39] Dury was closely associated with Samuel Hartlib and Comenius.[40] Dury's 'circle' also includes William Penn, Hugo de Groot, Irish Archbishop James Ussher, Menasseh ben Israel, Descartes, and John Milton. His daughter marries Henry Oldenburg, first secretary of the Royal Society. Jacob writes that it was "To promote [the work of conversions] in New England" that brought Comenius to London in 1641. "The Comenians saw their work in the conversion of non-Christian people to the true religion as being a sign that the millennium might be dawning. Boyle shared such sentiments ..."[41] Batten writes that Dury's correspondence with Menasseh ben Israel set in motion a series of developments that culminated in a major effort to secure the readmission of the Jews to England [under Cromwell]."[42]

Thorowgood's little book, which Dury encouraged, also contains a poem by George Herbert. The lines are well-known:

> Religion stands on tip-toe in our land,
> Ready to pass to the *American* strand,
> When height of malice, and prodigious lusts,
> Impudent sinning, witchcrafts, and distrusts,
> (The marks of future bane) shall fill in our cup
> Unto the brimme, and make our measure up;
> When *Sein* shall swallow *Tiber*, and the *Thames*
> By letting in them both pollutes her streams:
> When *Italie* of us shall have her will,
> And all her calender of sinnes fulfill
> Whereby one may foretell, what sinnes next yeare
> Shall both in *France* and *England* domineer:
> Then shall religion to *America* flee:
> They have their times of Gospel, ev'n as we.[43]

In a seventeenth century anthology entitled *Prophecys concerning the*

---

[39] J.R. Jacob, *Robert Boyle and the English Revolution*. (New York: Burt Franklin, 1977), p. 148.
[40] Cf. Vivian Salmon, *The Works of Francis Lodwick*, (London: Longmans, 1972).
[41] Jacob, *Robert Boyle* ... pp. 148–49.
[42] Batten, *Dury*, p. 140.
[43] From "The Church Militant," in *Works of George Herbert*, ed. F.E. Hutchinson. (Oxford: Clarendon, 1941), 196–97.

return of Popery into England, Scotland and Ireland,[44] Herbert's lines also appear.

Thorowgood cites a 1648 pamphlet by Thomas Shepard, *The Clear Sun-shine of the Gospel breaking forth upon the Indians in New England*.[45] Shepard writes: "I beleeve the calling in of a few *Indians* to Christ is the gathering home of many hundreds in one, considering what a vast distance there hath been between God and them so long, even days without number; considering also how precious the first fruits of *America* will be to Jesus Christ, and what seeds they may be of great harvests in after times ..."[46]

Another of Dury's friends, William Penn, holds the Jewish-Indian thesis. He is delighted[47] to encounter live members of the Lost Tribes, whereas Berkeley is thoroughly shaken by meeting his first Narragansett Indians.[48] In a letter about the Indians, Penn writes:

> For their original, I am ready to believe them of the Jewish race; I mean, of the stock of the ten tribes, and that for the following reasons: first, they were to go to a 'land not planted or known,' which, to be sure, Asia and Africa were, if not Europe; and He that intended that extraordinary judgement upon them, might make the passage not uneasy to them, as it is not impossible in itself, from the easternmost parts of Asia, to the westernmost of America. In the next place, I find them of like countenance, and their children of so lively a resemblance, that a man would think himself in Duke's-place or Bury-street in London, when he seeth them. But this is not all; they agree in rites, they reckon by moons; they offer their first-fruits, they have a kind of feast of tabernacles; they are said to lay their altar upon twelve stones; their mourning a year, customs of women, ...[49]

I think it is clear that many people in the seventeenth century took the view that the Indians were the Lost Tribes. Indeed, it may have been the majority view among Protestants.[50] There were others whose

---

[44] By Archbishop *Usher*, Mr. *Herbert*, Dr. *D. Pareus*, Mr. *Burroughs*, Mr. *Selden*, Mr. *Baxter*, Dr. *M. Luther*, Arch-bishop *Grindal*, Bishop *Jewel*, Bishop *Gauden*, Mr. *Hooker*, Dr. *Sutcliffe*. (London: A. Bancks, 1682).

[45] (London: R. Cotes for John Bellamy, 1648).

[46] *Ibid.*, pp. 37–38.

[47] Batten, *Dury*, p. 196.

[48] Cf. Maureen T. Lapan, "George Berkeley: Friends and Experiences in the Narragansett Country in Rhode Island," paper delivered at the 1981 annual meeting, American Society for Eighteenth Century Studies. See also Berkeley's SPG Sermon (1732), *Works* VII, 121 f.

[49] *The Select Works of William Penn*, 3 vols. 4th ed. (London: William Phillips, 1825), III, 232–33 (§ xxvi).

[50] Daniel Neal says that it is "pretty certain" that the American natives "are not

prophetic vision about America seems to have been less tied to the Indian conversion question. Popkin has brought to my attention a passage from *A Brief Description of the Future History of Europe* (1650): the Fifth Monarchy spoken of in *Daniel* will not only begin in 1710, it will begin in America, "for God hath now transplanted his Gospel from *Europe* unto a more grateful and pregnant soyl, which will bring forth the fruits thereof in due season."[51]

Jonathan Edwards could hardly have influenced Berkeley but he does make much of the fact that America was discovered around the time of the Reformation and that the old continent, although the "source and original of mankind," crucified Christ. "God has therefore probably reserved the honour of building the glorious temple to the daughter that has not shed so much blood."[52] He also expected the New Jerusalem to descend upon New England—presumably around the time of the Great Awakening in the 1740s, a period Edwin Gaustad has chronicled.[53] Cotton Mather,[54] writing at the end of the

---

the Posterity of *Jews, Christians,* or *Mahometans,* because there were none of the Footsteps of those Religions found among them ..." *The History of New-England ... to the Year ... 1700,* 2 vols. (London: J. Clark, et al., 1720), I, 1. Edward Stillingfleet, Bishop of Worcester, whose work was presumably known to Berkeley and whose library constituted the core of Archbishop Marsh's Library, (Dublin) reserves judgment on the question and merely provides references to the controversies between Hugo de Groot and Johannes de Laet as well as to Menasseh ben Israel and his critic Theophili Spizeli; cf. *Origines Sacrae,* (London: Henry Mortlock, 1663), Bk. III, ch. iv, pp. 575 f.). In his *Elevatio Relationis Montezinianae de Repertis in America Tribubus Israeliticis* ... (Basileae: Joannem König, 1661) Spizelii relies heavily on Acosta's reasons for rejecting the Jewish-Indian thesis. William Whiston, in his *Supplement to the Literal Accomplishment of Scripture Prophecies,* (London: J. Senex, et al., 1725) holds that Adam and Eve, Abel and Seth, etc., "were proper whites." Because of Cain's wicked life, "God chang'd him to the remotest Species and Colour of a perfect Black ..." (p. 109). While Whiston considers all mankind one species in the sense of being derived from Adam, he also believes that Africans and Indians are the posterity of Cain and Lamech. He takes himself to be following Stillingfleet in saying that the peopling of America remains an unsolved question and cites (p. 130) *Origines Sacrae,* Bk. III, ch. iv.

[51] *A brief description of the future history of Europe, from Anno 1650, to An. 1710. Of those grand and famous Mutations yet expected in the World, as, The ruine of the Popish Hierarchy, the final annihilation of the Turkish Empire, the Conversion of the Eastern and Western Jews, and their Restauration to their ancient Inheritances in the holy land, and the Fifth Monarchy of the Universal Reign of the Gospel of Christ upon Earth. With principal Passages upon every of these, out of that famous Manuscript of Paul Grebner, extent in Trinity-College Library in Cambridge ...* (1650 s.l.) p. 18.

[52] Edwards, *Works,* 8 vols. (London: James Black, 1817), VI, 56.

[53] *The Great Awakening in New England,* (New York: Harper, 1957).

[54] *Magnalia Christi Americana: or, the Ecclesiastical History of New England ...* (London: Thomas Parkhurst, 1702), I, 2.

seventeenth century, suggests that the devil sought to place the Americans on a distant continent so that they could not hear the Gospel. That theme is echoed in Edwards[55] as well as in John Eliot, *The Day-Breaking, if not the Sun-Rising of the Gospel with the Indians in New-England.*[56] Mather also expects the New Jerusalem in America. Joseph Mede, of Cambridge University, is perhaps the most distinguished scholar of prophetic literature in the seventeenth century. Although his prophecies often seem to have a cautious air, Mede thinks America has only been inhabited "since our Saviour and his Apostles times, and not before."[57] He thinks it most unlikely that the New Jerusalem will descend on America.

I have not placed before you the great mass of prophetic material published in the seventeenth and early eighteenth centuries. As I suspect you have come to realize in the course of this series of lectures, there is hardly a single great mind of the period which is not involved in millennial thinking. Henry More,[58] Sir Isaac Newton, and Sir Robert Boyle may be the names best known to academic philosophers. I would add Berkeley to the list. I appreciate that we find huge tomes in which the analyses of the 'real' meaning of, say, *Revelations*, are difficult to understand. But both the English Revolution and the Revocation of the Edict of Nantes (1685) produced massive out-pourings of this sort of analysis of historical events.[59]

---

[55] Edwards, *Works* V, 221–22.

[56] (London: R. Cotes for F. Clifton, 1647).

[57] Mede, *Works*, (London: Roger Norton for Richard Royston 1677), IV, 798–800. Epistle xlii.

[58] Berkeley's gift of books to Yale includes Henry More's *Opera Theologica*,[(London: J. Macock, 1675)]. Unlike the English version of 1708, this edition includes his tract on the Apocalypse (with illustrations) and indeed, it is presented at the outset, pp. 15–47. Berkeley's gift also includes several of the Boyle Lectures, e.g. William Whiston, *Accomplishment of Scripture Prophecies . . . [Being Eight Sermons . . .]* An edition was published in 1708. See Andrew Keogh, "Bishop Berkeley's Gift of Books in 1733," *Yale University Library Gazette*, VIII (1934), 1–28. For a discussion of the range and philosophical complexity of More's thought, see Alan Gabbey, "Philosophia Cartesiana Triumphata: Henry More (1646–71)," in *Problems of Cartesianism*, eds. Thomas M. Lennon, John M. Nicholas, and John W. Davis, (Montreal: McGill-Queen's University Press, 1982).

[59] Pierre Jurieu, Huguenot refugee scholar, political activist, and commentator on prophecy whose work was widely disseminated, discerned (1687) in the apocalyptic texts that 1785 promised to bring a new day to France and Europe. See his *Accomplishment of the scripture prophecies, or the approaching deliverance of the Church . . . Faithfully Englished from the New French Edition, Corrected and Enlarged by almost a third part, with the explication of the visions of Daniel, and the Revelation.* (London: 1687). I have found no references to America in that text, but F.R.J. Knetsch nas noted

However, if Berkeley's millennialist or messianic views help to explain the motivation for his American sojourn, it should be emphasized that such views were also common in his Irish environment. For example, in the seventeenth-century, Armagh Archbishop James Usher—from whom Luce says Berkeley may have been descended[60]—was much involved not only in calculating the age of the world but also in matters of prophecy. Second, within Berkeley's circle of friends is Robert Clayton. Clayton was a Fellow of Trinity College and Berkeley's 'associate' in the Bermuda Project. Also, Clayton's wife was the sister of Anne Donnellan. Popkin points to evidence suggesting that Berkeley was romantically involved with Anne prior to setting off for Rhode Island with his new bride, Anne Forster.[61] In brief, Berkeley's connections with Clayton are extensive. Bishop Clayton's *A Dissertation on Prophecy* (London: 1749) presents a detailed account of the Biblical case for the Second Coming and the conversion of the Jews. He argues that many Christian doctrines, especially those of Rome, inhibit Jews from acknowledging Jesus as the Messiah. Their conversion will occur shortly before the (next) arrival of the Messiah.[62] Clayton's anti-Trinitarian views are frequently articulated in this period.

Millennialist and messianic forces continue to be present in Irish thought through the balance of the century. As is well known, the American and French revolutions had considerable impact on Ireland. But one of the more interesting instances of this sort of think-

---

two other passages in which references are made. (1) *L'esprit de M. Arnaud ... Premiere Partie ...* where he comments on the religious excellence of the work of Protestant missionaries among the New England Indians. Indeed, he suggests these Indian groups seem to have the quality of genuine apostolic communities. (2) In his *Lettres Pastorales ...* Jurieu quotes a letter by Crescent Mather to Johannes Leusden which refers to the work of the John Eliot mentioned above. Cf. *Lettres Pastorales ... Seconde Anne'e ...* (Rotterdam: Abraham Acher, 1687). Lettre xvii, p. 135. *L'Esprit de Mr. Arnaud ...* (Deventer: Chez les Heritiers de Jean Colombius, 1684), Pt. I, 225–26, cf. also Pt. II, 186 f. See F.R.J. Knetsch, *Pierre Jurieu: Theoloog en Politikus der Refuge*, (Kampen: J.H. Kok, 1967).

[60] A.A. Luce, *Life* ... p. 111. For another connection with Berkeley see David Berman, "Berkeley, Clayton, and *An Essay on Spirit*," *Journal of the History of Ideas*, XXXII (1971), 367–78.

[61] Richard H. Popkin, "Bishop Berkeley and Anne Donnellan," in his *The High Road to Pyrrhonism*, eds. Richard A. Watson and James E. Force. (San Diego: Austin Hill, 1980).

[62] Robert Clayton, *A Dissertation on Prophecy*, (London: rev. ed. 1749). See esp. pp. 141 ff.

ing is in the efforts of Francis Dobbs, an MP[63] in the last Irish Parliament, to block the British Act of Union in 1800. On the basis of an examination of Hebrew and Gaelic place names Dobbs argues that the Second Coming must occur on a hill in Armagh. But if Ireland ceases to be, then the place at which Jesus is to appear also ceases to be. Hence, as a profound impediment to the Second Coming, the Act of Union must be rejected. Although Dobb's argument at the very least startled his fellow legislators, the British had bought enough votes to guarantee the passage of the Act and thus the cancellation of the Second Coming. Mystical elements are always a feature of nationalist movements and these forces continue to play a role in Irish thought in the twentieth-century, for example, in the Easter Rising (1916).

To conclude: I have tried to show both from Berkeley's prophetic poetry and from his plan for his American Project, that Berkeley has millennialist ideas.[64] I have suggested that the suppressed premise in his argument is that the Indians are the Lost Tribes of Israel, and in accordance with the New Testament, their conversion is absolutely essential to the millennial era. I have briefly indicated that the Jewish-Indian thesis was well-known and often discussed and also that America was seen as having a glorious role in the post-reformation world. Given what we know about Berkeley, we must find a reason not only for his committing himself so completely to his American dream, but especially for the savagery he was prepared to inflict on Indian children. I submit that the Jewish-Indian thesis provides the required explanation.

---

[63] Cf. W.E.H. Lecky, *A History of Ireland in the Eighteenth Century*. Abridged by L.P. Curtis, Jr. (Chicago: Univ. Press, 1972), p. 466.

[64] Berkeley seldom tells us much on these matters. He does, however, seem to attribute some divine significance to earthquakes. He concludes his *Observations on Earthquakes*, (1750) with these sentences: "I see nothing in the natural constitution of London, or the parts adjacent, that should render an earthquake impossible or improbable. Whether there be any thing in the moral stage thereof that should exempt it from that fear, I leave others to judge." *Works* IV, 256. The short essay appeared in *Gentleman's Magazine*, April 1750, Vol. 20, p. 166.

G.S. ROUSSEAU

MYSTICISM AND MILLENARIANISM: "IMMORTAL DR. CHEYNE"

> ... if there might not, I say, be higher, more noble, and more enlightening *Principles* revealed to Mankind *somewhere* ...
> (George Cheyne, "The Case of the Author," 1733, 331)
>
> ... this material *Metaphysicks* of a *Regimen*.
> (George Cheyne, *ibid.*, 367)

I. *"Immortal Dr. Cheyne": The Literary Response*

If contemporary anthropologists and sociologists are correct in believing that cult figures in every age are trusted by their devotees while viewed suspiciously by the rest of the world, then George Cheyne deserves to be categorized as a cult figure. For almost everyone who knew him well trusted him and liked him, whereas those who did not either disliked or despised him. And most educated people knew who he was and were aware of his reputation as a celebrated physician and author. But here the agreement ended. The only other consensus was his weight. Cheyne swelled to 448 pounds—"32 stone"[1]—and whereas no handy eighteenth-century *Guinness Book of Records* is

---

[1] George Cheyne, "The Case of the Author," *The English Malady* (London, 1733), 342, henceforth cited merely as *CA*. It is best to state—here at the start—that I consider this a reliable source for the shape of Cheyne's life. Given the romantic excesses and mystical turns of Cheyne's temperament, it is possible that he exaggerated the pain he suffered during the various crises he endured. It is also possible that during the composition of these memoirs in the early 1730s, his memory distorted or confused events that had occurred three decades ago. But no reason exists to believe that Cheyne intentionally distorted the facts of his past life in order to endow posterity with a better image of himself, or that the agony and anguish of repeated breakdowns and collapses had put him out of touch with a minimal reality. The failure of scholars who have not relied on these memoirs must be attributed to their lack of interest in Cheyne's life, or to their sheer neglect and ignorance of the work. In the notes below, all names of publishers have been omitted, and unless noted otherwise the place of publication of all works cited is London. I am grateful to Professors Richard Popkin, M.E. Novak, James Force, and Donald Greene who commented on several versions of this essay, although my acknowledgement should not imply that they agree with my conclusions about Cheyne.

extant to report whether he was the fattest man of the Enlightenment, he certainly must rank among the heaviest.[2]

Literary evidence demonstrates the attitude of his contemporaries better than any other source. For example, Pope knew Cheyne well and relished his eccentric blend of reason and madness: "... so very a child in true Simplicity of Heart, that I love him; as He loves Don Quixote, for the Most Moral and Reasoning Madman in the world."[3] This reference caresses Cheyne and is one of many vignettes of the doctor that abounds in Pope's correspondence. "He is," Pope later affirmed, echoing the book of St. John, "a kind of living Parson Adams, in the Scripture language, an *Israelite in whom there is no Guile*, or in Shakespeare's, *as foolish a good kind of Christian Creature as one shall meet with*." All Pope's estimates of the childlike Cheyne portray the doctor as a fundamentally good man; deluded, eccentric, confusing windmills and giants, but nevertheless a man who was as good as the salt of the earth. Fielding's patron Lyttelton agreed with Pope: "... Immortal Doctor Cheyne. ... The Doctor is the greatest Singularity, and the most Delightful I ever met with."[4] Every Scriblerian, even Swift, adored Cheyne, the only famous physician in England who escaped their venomous collective pen.[5] John

---

[2] There is no twentieth-century biography in any language, although several short articles exist. The fullest of these is H.R. Viets, "George Cheyne," *Bulletin of the History of Medicine*, XXIII (1949), 435–54. The only lengthy account is W.A. Greenhill's *Life of George Cheyne, M.D.* (Oxford, 1846), but it is anecdotal, based on secondary sources, and often unreliable. An estimate of Cheyne as an "eccentric genius" is found in J.H. Burton, *History of the Reign of Queen Anne*, 3 vols. (Edinburgh, 1880), vol. 3 , 429. Though it is limited in its explanations about Cheyne, W.G. Hiscock's (ed.) *David Gregory, Isaac Newton and their Circle: Extracts from David Gregory's Memoranda 1677–1708* (Oxford, 1937) is far more useful. Valuable information is also found in G.D. Henderson, *Mystics of the North-East* (Aberdeen, 1934), still the best source on Cheyne's relation to the circle of George Garden, M.D. Altschule, *Origins of Concepts in Human Behaviour* (Washington, 1977), 53–74, and in L.S. King, "George Cheyne: Mirror of Eighteenth-Century Medicine," *Bulletin of the History of Medicine*, XLVIII (1974), 517–39. Need exists for a detailed modern scholarly biography.

[3] George Sherburn (ed.), *The Correspondence of Alexander Pope*, 5 vols. (Oxford, 1956), IV, 208.

[4] Ibid., IV, 46.

[5] Cheyne is nowhere mentioned in *The Memoirs of Martinus Scriblerus* (1714), a natural locus in view of the satires of science and the lampoons of doctors and their hypotheses found in this collaborative work, but he is discussed as a "mathematical authority" in William Wotton's *Defence of the Reflections upon Ancient and Modern Learning* (1705), 10. The reference in Wotton makes it clear that by 1705 Cheyne was well-known to Bentley and others whom Swift attacked in *A Tale of a Tub* (1704).

Gay continued to be overwhelmed by "Cheyne huge of size" whom he greets in *Mr. Pope's Welcome from Greece*;[6] and Edward Young nostalgically immortalized Cheyne in a central passage in the *Epistle II. to Mr. Pope* when imprecating for "three ells round huge Cheyne."[7] Fielding was far too robust for Cheyne's lettuce and milk diet, but even he nodded at "the learned Dr. Cheyne" in *Tom Jones*.[8] Richardson was much more devoted. He and Cheyne were in constant correspondence for many years—certainly throughout the composition of *Pamela*—indeed for such a long time that Richardson may not have enjoyed the necessary perspective to determine precisely who Cheyne was. And Richardson relied monolithically on Cheyne for professional medical advice, as well as for literary guidance in the composition of *Pamela*. He told Stephen Duck, the "thresher poet," that Cheyne "was so good as to give me a Plan [in *Pamela*] to break Legs and Arms and to fire Mansion Houses to create Distresses."[9] Few patients who were also novelists ever trusted their doctor to this degree of compliance.

The catalogue of comments is endless. In January 1742 Thomas Gray concocted an "Imaginary Conversation" between ancient and modern geniuses, including Aristotle, Virgil, Locke, Swift, and Cheyne, wherein Cheyne is made to recite his own aphorism: "Every Man after forty is either a fool or a Physician."[10] The young Hume turned to Cheyne for medical advice about his mysterious illness in 1734, entreating Cheyne as if he were Galen or Hippocrates.[11] Lord

---

[6] John Gay, *Mr. Pope's Welcome from Greece* (1725), 1. 133.

[7] Edward Young, *Epistle to Pope* (1757), I, 199. Young read at least one of Cheyne's books. In February 1746 he visited Richardson, and "inadvertently stole one of [his] books." A few days later he wrote to Richardson: "On turning over my cargo, I find Dr. Cheyne among my other books." See H. Pettit (ed.), *The Correspondence of Edward Young 1683–1765* (Oxford, 1971), 231. It is impossible to know which book of Cheyne's this is, but Young apparently knew of Cheyne's *Philosophical Principles* (1705 edition) in *The Force of Religion* (1714).

[8] M. Battestin (ed.), *Henry Fielding: The History of Tom Jones, A Foundling*, 2 vols. (Oxford, 1975), II, 605, and n. 73 below.

[9] See J. Carroll (ed.), *Selected Letters of Samuel Richardson* (Oxford, 1964), 52 and C.F. Mullett (ed.), *The Letters of Doctor George Cheyne to Samuel Richardson (1733–1743)* (Columbia, Missouri, 1943), cited henceforth as *Letters to Richardson*.

[10] See P. Toynbee (ed.), *The Correspondence of Gray, Walpole, et al*, 2 vols. (Oxford, 1915), II, 19.

[11] J.Y.T. Greig (ed.), *The Correspondence of David Hume*, 2 vols. (Oxford, 1932), I, 12. Ernest Mossner attributes this letter to Dr. Arbuthnot rather than to Cheyne but his reasons as given in *The Life of David Hume* (Oxford, 1980), 84, are unconvincing. Hume's self-diagnosis was "melancholic mania," the eighteenth-century term for

Chesterfield intensely disliked metaphysics but valiantly wrote to Cheyne to say that, if ever he were compelled to choose "a system," he would select Cheyne's as the most probable.[12] Lord Hervey, Pope's rival in politics and love, considered Cheyne the most eminent physician in England and was not abashed to say so.[13] The wealthy and lovely Countess of Huntingdon became the patron of Cheyne, the only man in the Realm—except for the Methodist preacher George Whitefield—fortunate enough to have captured her attention.[14] Even Wesley, the great reformer, converted to Cheyne's diet and advocated it in his popular handbook of medicine, *Primitive Physick*.[15] William Somerville the poet versified Cheyne's best-selling book *The English Malady* in his poem *The Hip*. John Hill, a notorious if eccentric *enfant terrible*, extolled Cheyne in *The Construction of the Nerves* (1768) and praised his theories of nervous physiology. The medical writings of the too-little known William Porterfield are permeated with approving glances at Cheyne.[16] Porterfield was the first Secretary of the Edinburgh Literary and Philosophical Society; from him many who were later to become lights in the Scottish Enlightenment first heard about "immortal Doctor Cheyne." The "Great Cham" told the lecherous Boswell that he ought to read Dr. Cheyne's books on temperance and health, advice Boswell probably never heeded but which abundantly adumbrates Johnson's very high esteem.[17] Thomas Tyers, who was apparently one of Johnson's favorite people, wrote the first biographical sketch of Johnson a day after he died on 13 December 1784 and while Tyers mourned he composed a "Set of

---

manic depression, and he wrote to Cheyne as the leading authority on melancholy.

[12] Cheyne dedicated his last book—*The Natural Method of Cureing [sic] the Diseases of the Body* (1742)—to Chesterfield.

[13] Hervey, MSS, 31 January 1738.

[14] See C.F. Mullet (ed.), *The Letters of Dr. George Cheyne to the Countess of Huntingdon* (San Marino, 1940). On p. 17 of *Letters to Richardson*, Mullett notes: "There is no reason to suppose that the letters printed by me constituted the entire correspondence of Cheyne with her ladyship." A limited search has failed, however, to produce further letters.

[15] *The Works of John Wesley*, 2 vols. (1865), XI, 493, entry for 12 March 1742.

[16] See the many references, for example, in W. Porterfield's *A Treatise on the Eye, the Manner ... of Vision*, 2 vols., (Edinburgh, 1759).

[17] G.B. Hill (ed.), *Boswell's Life of Johnson*, rev. L.F. Powell, 6 vols. (Oxford, 1934–50), III, 26–27; see also H.R. Viets, "Johnson and Cheyne," *TLS*, Feb. 5, 1954, 89. Johnson admired Cheyne's *The English Malady, or a Treatise of Nervous Diseases of All Kinds* (1733) as the best account of modern melancholia, frequently cited it, and owned a copy. See D.J. Greene, *Samuel Johnson's Library: An Annotated Guide* (Victoria, B.C., 1975), 48.

Resolutions" founded on Cheyne's principles: "especially to make exercise a part of one's Religion," and "to be religiously observed."[18] This material represents just the tip of the iceberg that constitutes the literary evidence:

> Not all the Gemmy Treasures of the East,
> Nor yet the Spicy Odours of the West;
> Not all the Glorious Trophies of the Great,
> Would please so much, or form one joy compleat,
> Like that I feel, great wond'rous Genius, when
> I scan th' amazing Beauties of thy Pen.

Thus an anonymous poet rhapsodized Cheyne in 1733 on reading his works.[19] Lyrical though the mode is, the praise is specific:

> Long did the Sacred Art in Bondage mourn,
> Become the Jest of Fools, or else their Scorn;
> 'Till Heav'n, to set the fetter' Science free,
> And pit'ing abject Man, created Thee.
> Made Thee to act of Gods the healing Part
> And live a Pillar to the Noble Art,
> To be the only shining acting Sage,
> Not giv'n, but lent from them to heal this Age.
> Great Wonder from above, thou Boast of Men,
> Accept these Offerings from a Namesake's Pen.

The fact that this catalogue of response can be extended considerably is only the first of my points today, as is the repeated strain about Cheyne's corpulence and medical eminence, although it is intriguing to notice in history how often physical size is equated with heroic greatness. Cheyne's contemporaries were no doubt amazed by his weight reduction from 448 pounds to 130.[20] The further fact that he practiced what he preached about the relation of weight and diet also lent him credibility lacked by many eighteenth-century physicians. But the public's image of Cheyne in the eighteenth century was nevertheless jaded and distorted—was not at all the sense of himself he had. Obesity vanquished; a long life of 72 years in an epoch when so many died in youth or early adulthood; national fame as a writer; a close friend of so many famous and influential Britons: these unas-

---

[18] John Nichols, *Literary Anecdotes of the Eighteenth Century*, 8 vols. (1812), VIII, 82.

[19] "To Dr. Cheyne of Bath. On Reading his Works," *Gentleman's Magazine*, III (1733), 205. For other similar poems, see *Letters to Richardson*, 126–37.

[20] Cheyne himself is probably the best source for this figure; see *CA*, 342.

sailable facts were important to Cheyne, but they were distant from the center of his intellectual and private emotional life. Cheyne's idea of selfhood and the niche he had carved depended to a certain extent on these incontrovertible facts, but rested equally, if not more so, on other private beliefs which can only be understood in the light of his chronological biography. Without this crucial background, the flow of his ideas over five decades remains a muddle and a mystery.

II. *Chronological Biography and Intellectual Development*

Cheyne was born in Aberdeen in 1671 in a Scottish Episcopalian family that intended him, like his father and both grandfathers, for the Church. His early education was classical, as were his university studies in Edinburgh where he read mathematics. One teacher alone, Archibald Pitcairne, the illustrious mathematician and physician, enjoyed remarkable sway over him. Both had an Episcopalian religion in common, and Pitcairne urged Cheyne to follow in his iatromathematical footsteps: to apply mathematics in the service of medicine.[21] Cheyne ardently followed the advice, obtained a medical degree (at Aberdeen), and even became Pitcairne's staunchest defender in fierce paper wars about iatromathematics. Yet Pitcairne's impact on Cheyne extended beyond this sphere. As Boerhaave's most important teacher at Leyden, Pitcairne had attracted the best minds there and was known throughout Europe as a towering intellect, as the most distinguished iatromathematician of the seventeenth-century *fin de siècle*.[22] His protèges rapidly became fervid Newtonians— especially Freind, Mead, and James Keill—and built a kind of "school of iatromathematics" around him in which Newtonian calculus, or fluxions, was applied to medical theory. But Pitcairne was also

---

[21] Cheyne describes this influence in *CA*, and in *The English Malady* (1733), and there is mention of Cheyne in Pitcairne's correspondence; see W.T. Johnston (ed.), *The Best of Our Owne: Letters of Archibald Pitcairne* (Edinburgh, 1979). See also W.G. Hiscock (n. 2), 23–26.

[22] For example, when someone calling himself "Sir Edward Ezat," attacked Pitcairne as "Apollo Mathematicus" in *The Art of Curing Diseases by the Mathematicks, According to the Principles of Archibald Pitcairne* (1695), Cheyne counter-attacked brilliantly in several pamphlets and showed how effectively he could demolish the enemy. Cheyne's first book, *A New Theory of Fevers* (1701), which originally appeared as a Latin dissertation, was an attempt to combine Newtonian mathematics with Pitcairnean mechanics, but the Newtonian disapproved of it and their dispraise in the years 1702–1706 eliminated Cheyne from consideration as a future Boyle lecturer.

an enthusiast in religion, and generated his medical theory with the zeal of an apostle, a characteristic of personality Cheyne discovered to be temperamentally compatible with to his own personality.[23] Calculus, geometry and medicine filled only part of Cheyne's imagination during his twenties[24]—intellectually his most formative period—the rest of his energy occupied by a deep-seated religious mysticism. He joined a group of Scottish mystics in the 1690s centered around George Garden, the Quietist. Through them he obtained a post as tutor to the young Earl of Roxburgh; but more importantly, he made friends who remained loyal to him for the rest of his life and who joined him later on in his endeavor to become one of Britain's main distributors of Quietist literature.

Why did the young Cheyne have such conflicting aspirations: iatromedicine on the one hand, and mystical religion on the other? The 1690s was understandably the great decade of chiliasm and millenarianism in Western Europe,[25] and although Cheyne was too young personally to have witnessed the events of the 1650s, he was attentive to those of the 1690s. He heard much millenarian talk at Roxburgh House, the great country estate where he lived in comfortable circumstances during those years. He had also heard millenarian talk at home and in Aberdeen.[26] He knew about Jane Lead and the English Philadelphians, and about her prediction of an imminent millennium commencing in 1700. At Roxburgh he had read

---

[23] In precisely which year in the period 1695–1706 Cheyne absorbed, rather than paid lip service to, Pitcairne's influence, it is difficult to say.

[24] According to Cheyne (*Essay on Health and Long Life*, 1724, 47) during the 1690s he had read the works of: Sir William Temple, Willis, Glisson, and Borelli. In *The English Malady* (1733), 78–80, he claims also to have read Glisson, Bernoulli, Molieres, Sydenham, and, of course, Newton and Pitcairne.

[25] See D.P. Walker, *The Decline of Hell* (1964); E. Tuveson, *Millenium and Utopia* (Berkeley, 1949); K. Thomas, *Religion and the Decline of Magic* (1971); R.T. Vann, *The Social Development of English Quakerism 1655–1755* (Cambridge, Mass., 1969); M.C. Jacob, *The Newtonians and the English Revolution 1689–1720* (Ithaca, 1976), chap. iii; P. Toon (ed.), *Puritans, the Millennium and the Future of Israel* (Cambridge and London, 1970); Desiree Hirst, *Hidden Riches: Traditional Symbolism from the Renaissance to Blake* (1964); and still a standard work for the radical millenarian sects of the 1690s, Nils Thune, *The Behmenists and the Philadelphians* (Uppsala, 1948). Craig believed that the millennium would commence when faith left the earth; and by applying the law of the inverse square he calculated the rate at which faith was disappearing.

[26] Religious talk abounded in his house, especially on his paternal side; yet there were clergymen on both sides of the family, and Cheyne's mother was Thomas Burnet's second cousin.

about the chiliastic interpretations of the year 1697: that the Treaty of Ryswick which finally brought peace to Europe was evidence—"public testimony"—of the Deity's intention to commence the millennium. And he certainly read John Craig's *Theologiae Christianae Principia Mathematica* (1699), which applied Newton's inverse square law to derive the precise year of the Second Coming, for Cheyne continued to refer to it and quote from it.[27] Cheyne was also related to Thomas Burnet, the author of the *Sacred Theory of the Earth*, and knew Burnet's descriptions of millennial life. Although Burnet had not dated his predictions, he implied they were soon to occur. Furthermore, through Pitcairne Cheyne had been introduced to the most devoted young Newtonians—especially to David Gregory and the Keill brothers—and discovered, if he had not already realized it, that iatromathematics could be compatible with mystical religion. This discovery cannot be precisely dated, but it must have occurred sometime around 1699 or 1700, a crucial millenarian moment. Finally, there was the example of Pitcairne himself. Pitcairne was not a hardened mystic, but he showed mystical tendencies. He was anything but a solid member of the Scottish Church ("the Kirk"), a fact that hindered his academic career after he returned to Scotland from Leyden,[28] and which caused him to be attacked by the medical profession.

Cheyne's career drastically changed after he migrated to London in the winter of 1701/2.[29] Now, daily, he saw before his own eyes the millenarian fervor about which he had heard and read so much in Scotland. If there were relatively few Philadelphians or Quietists in Roxburgh, or even in Edinburgh, there were many in London. Here was millenarianism of another magnitude. Medical degree in arm, and letters of introduction too, Cheyne arrived in a city riven by diverse opinion about the politico-religious development at the turn of the century. This was especially true among the Fellows of the Royal Society, with whom Cheyne was closely associated when he

---

[27] See the prefaces of both versions of Cheyne's *Philosophical Principles* (1705; rev. 1715). Hiscock (n. 2) briefly discusses the reception of work by the Newtonians, and shows how they laughed it straight out of court.

[28] See W.T. Johnston (ed.), *Our Owne: Letters of Archibald Pitcairne* (1979), 42.

[29] Edinburgh University MSS 38,305 (anonymous) describes reasons for his departure from Scotland, as well as the basis for his medical degree: "He's not only our owne countryman, and at present not rich, but is recommended by the ablest and most learned Physicians in Edinburgh as one of the best mathematicians in Europe; and for

arrived. He had been resident in London only a few weeks when the War of the Spanish Succession broke out. To some mystics this gruesome event signified that the Deity had interrupted his millenarian intentions, and demonstrated his dissatisfaction with English national behavior. Cheyne had not yet arrived in London when the Philadelphians read in public their famous Proclamation on Easter Sunday 1699,[30] but he certainly heard accounts of their radical prophecies. During his first spring and autumn in London—1702—he focused his energy, as he recounts in his autobiography, on establishing a successful medical practice. He pursued this goal by appearing in the "right" coffeehouses, and by cultivating the wealthy and the great in their private saloons and drawing rooms.[31] Years later, Cheyne described this period of his life as one of immense "luxury, gluttony, and upper-class vice without exercise," and typified it in his memoirs by the act of forever "taking snuff out of a ponderous gold box."[32] (An essay is not the place to discuss the sociology of medicine in the eighteenth century; but it should be noted that while Cheyne's method of gaining patients was common, his degree of application was not.) During these years he also sat in Batson's and Child's, and in the townhouses of dukes and duchesses; and he wrecked his health through drink and gluttony. The talk Cheyne heard in these places must concern us as preponderantly as his dissipation. Here he was apprised of the aspiring physician's need for written credentials and word-of-mouth recommendation. But he also heard about the mounting war on the Continent, and the radical prophecies interpreting it. On street-

---

his skill in medicine he hath given a sufficient indication of that by his learned Tractat *De Febribus* [see n. 22 above], which hath made him famous abroad as well as at home; and he being just now goeing [sic] to England upon invitation of some of the members of the Royal Society." The invitation may have come from Arbuthnot, who Cheyne met upon arrival and with whom he quickly became closely associated. The two Scots remained associates for three decades.

[30] *A Declaration of the Philadelphian Society of England* (1699), which is discussed by Cheyne's friend Richard Roach in *The Great Crisis* (1725–1727), a mystical work containing a description of millenial life. Roach's description on p. 181ff. also bears similarities with Thomas Burnet's position in *De Statu Mortuorum & Resurgentium [Of the State of the Dead and of Those that are to Rise]*. But few copies of Burnet's book were printed before 1727, as Frances Wilkinson, Burnet's literary executor, explains. It would be interesting to know whether Cheyne had seen a copy before 1727. For Roach, see his six volumes of diaries in The Bodleian Library, Oxford.

[31] Dr. Richard Mead's medical career had rocketed to fame in just this way, and may have been held up as a paragon to Cheyne by his friends in the Royal Society. In any case Cheyne and Mead were friends by 1703.

[32] *Letters to Richardson*, 73.

corners he saw freethinkers and mystics chanting about the millennium come or interrupted, and heard tales about the hysterical uprising of the Camisards in the Cevennes.[33] Cheyne's urban hedonism was extravagant, but apparently not so extreme as to prevent him from writing a mathematical treatise in 1703,[34] which so annoyed Newton that he dropped Cheyne from the circle of young disciples to whom his bounty was given. Cheyne suffered the Newtonian fall miserably. He repressed it, and never again commented on it in any of his autobiographical memoirs.

Newton's dispraise however, did not prevent Cheyne from setting to work shortly thereafter—probably in 1703—on another book that proved far more theological than the previous two. Two years earlier, late in 1701, Cheyne proclaimed the need for a *Principia Medicinae Theologia Mathematica* based on Newton's *Principia*—one that would integrate medicine and mathematics. Cheyne's idea derived, in part, from John Craig's 1699 *Theologia ... Mathematica* which Cheyne read and acknowledged in the preface of the new book. But Cheyne's desideratum is not what he wrote. Hoping to reingratiate himself with the Newtonians—by 1703–1705 the most powerful scientific coterie in the Royal Society—Cheyne abandoned mathematical medicine, and composed a type of "Boyle-lecture" which he called *Philosophical Principles of Natural Religion* (1705), modelling the title, as well as the book, on Newton's *Mathematical Principles*. Not surprisingly, *Philosophical Principles* was greeted by the Newtonians with more hostility than Cheyne's previous book.[35] Dislike was based on two grotesque and unpardonable errors: first, that Cheyne had misunderstood the essence of Newtonian gravity, and, then, that his analogical method of reasoning was altogether unscientific. Cheyne replied to the first charge that Newton had "stolen" certain points in the *Queries* appended to the Latin *Opticks* from him "in

---

[33] A picture of religious street-life at the time is found in D.P. Walker, *The Decline of Hell*, 245ff. and in Hillel Schwartz, *The French Prophets: The History of a Millenarian Group in Eighteenth-Century England* (Berkeley, 1980), 37ff.

[34] *Fluxionum methodus inversa* (1703). For the response of the Newtonians, see Hiscock (n. 2), 15 and R. Schofield, *Mechanism and Materialism: British Natural Philosophy in an Age of Reason* (Princeton, 1970), 59, who comments: "Scorned by Gregory and attacked by deMoivre, it provoked Newton into publishing his *Tractatus de Quadratura Curvarum* as an appendix to the 1704 *Opticks*. This was its only virtue and it was quickly forgotten ..."

[35] For the reception, see Hiscock (n. 2), 24–25.

private conversation,"[36] an argument no one then seems to have construed seriously. At least it did not persuade the Newtonians, old or young, that Cheyne understood anything about gravity, or that he ought to be readmitted to the clique. The second charge—unscientific analogy—appeared less critical in 1705, but this is the aspect of Cheyne's writing that renders him such a unique figure in the physico-theological world of the early eighteenth century. It is also the strand of his thinking that leads directly to his curious doctrines of early eighteenth-century millenarianism.

Cheyne's analogies derive from a "Universal Law of Attraction, whereby all the parts of Matter endeavour to embrace one another."[37] From this given "Law" he reasons that a "Divine Providence permeates" both the natural and supra-terrestrial universe. Yet almost every conclusion he draws from this point forward is at odds with the basic assumptions of Newtonian thinking. Moreover, Cheyne's inability to grasp the inconsistencies and obliquities of his own principles in relation to those of Newton constitutes the best comment on his scientific abilities. Such defect of talent certainly did not go unnoticed by the English Newtonians, who now began to wonder if Cheyne was a scientist at all; and the mere fact of an earned medical degree counted for nothing—especially inasmuch as it was granted in Aberdeen—in an epoch when medicine was commonly anything *but* scientific. Geoffrey Bowles has argued that Cheyne's discussion of short-range attraction is the most interesting feature of *Philosophical Principles*, observing as well that Newton had not pronounced publicly on this matter until 1706.[38] Bowles' contention is that Cheyne's

---

[36] *Ibid.*, 35. In fairness to Cheyne, it must be noted that the extant evidence comes primarily from Gregory, who was no friend of Cheyne's. Gregory also persuaded Arbuthnot that Cheyne was a poor scientist, and attempted to intercept their association.

[37] *Philosophical Principles* (1705), 104.

[38] See G. Bowles, "Physical, Human and Divine Attraction in the Life and Thought of George Cheyne," *Annals of Science*, XXXI (1974), 473–88, especially the discussion on 481. Other commentators have been less sympathetic to Cheyne. H. Metzger discovered little of scientific value in *Philosophical Principles* and categorized the book, disparagingly, as "Neo-Platonist" in *Attraction Universelle et Religion Naturelle chez quelques Commentateurs Anglais de Newton* (Paris, 1938), 139–53. D. Kubrin is more sympathetic, but has discovered little that is original in Cheyne's 1705 *Principles*; see "Newton and the Cyclical Cosmos: Providence and the Mechanical Philosophy," *Journal of the History of Ideas*, XXVIII (1967), 325–46. Cheyne's skepticism about "the mechanical philosophy" is as pervasive in these 1705 *Principles* as is his hermetic notion of analogy. See, for example, *Philosophical Principles* (1705),

method of analogical reasoning permitted him to make an intuitive leap: reasoning from long-range to short-range attraction. This may be true, but the English Newtonians hardly saw the matter in this light. They grasped on to Cheyne's mathematical errors, and were troubled by the Stoic undertones of his concept of Providence. Only Jean LeClerc, head of the Remonstrant-Arminian Seminary in Amsterdam and himself an ardent theologian, reviewed Cheyne's book.[39] Otherwise, the book went unnoticed and bitterly disappointed Cheyne. In this capacity, it did not matter whether or not his medical practice was a success, or whether his urban hedonism had wrecked his physical health.[40] He had lost the support of the Newtonians and other fellows of the Royal Society whose approval he direly sought. A second attempt to re-enlist himself proved futile. Now he had elicited their fury twice.

III. *Collapse and Crisis*

The result was breakdown and collapse in 1706. It may never be known whether this condition was primarily physical or mental. But Cheyne's account of the collapse is so detailed, that he must be believed when commenting that at this time (1706) he "went about like a *Malefactor* condemn'd, or one who expected every Moment to be crushed by a *ponderous* Instrument of Death."[41] However, Cheyne's attribution of the collapse to his London hedonism, and to the defects of his physiological constitution, is probably incomplete, although not inaccurate. 440 pounds of human flesh will afford even the soberest human being with a perfect rationalization for anything that ever happens, or happened, to him! What counts for more is the curious way that Cheyne permitted his breakdown to determine the course of his whole future career.

12: "But if any one can tell by what Laws of Mechanism, any one Animal or Vegetable ws produc'd, or from what Mechanick Principles the Planets describe Elliptick Orbits, I shall for the sake of these allow their [i.e. the mechanists'] whole Scheme to be true."

[39] J. LeClerc, *Bibliotheque ancienne et moderne. Pour servir de suite aux bibliotheques universelle et choisi* (Amsterdam, 1715), III, 41–157. Although LeClerc waited ten years to publish the review, he reviewed the 1705 first edition of *Philosophical Principles*.

[40] Years later, Cheyne confided to Richardson a progression throughout his life of composition and publication, followed by illness. See *Letters to Richardson*, 69: "I never wrote a Book in my Life but I had a Fit of Illness after." There are many other versions of this self-confession in the Cheyne-Richardson correspondence.

[41] *CA*, 327.

He swiftly departed from London—from the hub of luxury and glut—and fled to the country, hoping to die in pastoral simplicity. He was uncertain about many things; but he was sure, at thirty-five, that death could not be far away. He also "fix'd on one, a worthy and learned *Clergyman* of the *Church of England*, sufficiently known and distinguished in the *Philosophical* and *Theological* World (whom I dare not name, because he is still living, tho' now extreamly old)."[42] This may have been Whiston whose Arianism and disavowal of the coeternity of the Father and Son were notorious by late 1706. Ill and despondent, Cheyne, following Whiston's example, "resolved to purchase, study, and examine carefully such *Spiritual and Dogmatic Authors*, as I knew this *venerable Man did* most approve and delight in."[43] These were works of primitive Christianity, "a *Set of religious Books* and *Writers*, of most of the *first Ages* since *Christianity*." They confirmed Cheyne's developing sense that the material world was proximate to dissolution and the New Jerusalem imminent. They encompassed the writers of the first four centuries who had not been contaminated by the Council of Nicea and the Apostolic Succession. Cheyne and Whiston probably did not meet: Cheyne was in Bath, Whiston in Cambridge. But there is a good deal of circumstantial evidence to suggest that Whiston is the "now extreamly old"—now as Cheyne writes in 1733, not 1706—scientist and philosopher whose "primitive Christianity" subdued his misery in illness.

But Cheyne did not remain in "the country" (wherever that may have been) throughout 1706, the year of collapse. He very often returned to London, and may have been there when the first French

---

[42] Ibid., 332. George Garden (1649–1733), the religious centerpiece of the Aberdeen mystical group with which Cheyne had been involved in the 1690s, was also "now extream'ly old," but had not been scientifically distinguished. Besides, Cheyne would not have described the mystical Garden in this way. Other possibilities—Samuel Clarke, John Craig, Newton himself—were either dead or incapable of this description in 1733. Andrew Michael Ramsay (1686–1743), the direct link between Madame Guyon and George Garden's mystical group in Scotland, was hardly old in 1733; see D.P. Walker, *The Ancient Theology* (1972), 232. Five or six others may be possible candidates, but no one fits the whole description and context of the allusion as well as Whiston.

[43] Ibid., 332. By this time—1706–1707—Cheyne probably read much that Whiston had written, and may have heard about or read Whiston's theory of attraction. But Whiston's Boyle Lectures, *The Accomplishment of Scripture Prophecies*, were not delivered until the following year—1707—and were not published until 1708. Useful information on Whiston's Boyle Lectures is found in M. Farrell, *The Life and Work of William Whiston* (New York, 1981), 262–66.

prophets arrived that autumn.[44] Fatio, Newton's disciple, quickly enlisted himself in the service of Elie Marion, their leader, and introduced David Gregory, and possibly Cheyne, to the prophets. But whereas Gregory was resistant, Cheyne was sympathetic. By Christmas 1706, the prophets predicted that the millennium had arrived and that the "hidden keys of Divine Wisdom" were daily being revealed to women, children and common folk. During these months at the end of 1706, Cheyne—ill, despairing, believing he was near to death— began to connect the apocalypse with medicine, and started to realize that his life could serve a higher purpose than he ever dreamed.

Strangely, he soon began to improve, this after six or seven months. His near-fatal illness, he concluded, was clear revelation: not only that he should instantly mend his ways—his whole style of life then— but also that he should serve his Maker by delivering "a message" to mankind. When Cheyne reflected (in 1733, thinking about the curve of his whole life) on the validity of the cosmological picture he had painted in *Philosophical Principles*, he was altogether dissatisfied. "I found," he writes, "that *these [Philosophical Principles]* alone were not sufficient to quiet my Mind at that Juncture."[45] Then he describes the new vision acquired since his illness:

> ... especially when I began to reflect and consider seriously, whether I might not (through Carelessness and Self-Sufficiency, Voluptuousness and Love of Sensuality, which might have impaired my Spiritual Nature) have neglected to examine with sufficient Care: If there might not be more required of those, who had had proper *Opportunities* and *Leisure*; if there might not, I say, be higher, more noble, and more enlightening *Principles*[46] revealed to Mankind *somewhere* ... and lastly, if there were not likewise some clearer Accounts discoverable of that State I was then (I thought) apparently going into, than could be obtained from the mere Light of *Nature* and *Philosophy*.

This "mere Light of *Nature* and *Philosophy*"—especially Cheyne's new perception of the limits of science—constitutes the source of his mental frame during the next decade. Now, more than before, he

---

[44] The most authoritative study to date is the work by Hillel Schwartz (n. 33) from which I have learned much. See also M.C. Jacob, "Newton and the French Prophets," *History of Science*, VI (1978), 134–42, who concludes on the basis of manuscript evidence that Newton was not altogether hostile to the prophets during the first few years of their residence in Britain.

[45] *CA*, 331, i.e., narrating the events of the summer and autumn of 1706.

[46] I.e., than those "principles" Cheyne had studied in his last book, *Philosophical Principles*, 1705.

believed that religion was revelation; and that the body of man had been the most sorely neglected source within the Book of Nature.

IV. *Healing and Rebirth*

Still believing himself close to death in 1707, Cheyne heard the voices of another type of natural revelation than those he had heard on London street-corners or read about in books. Medicine, like mathematics, had been part of the Deity's grand plan from the start;[47] but now Cheyne understood how the Deity would reveal his wisdom and might through suffering and healing. The body of man, like the Book of Nature, was a major seat of revelation; and anatomy and physiology its correlatives within "natural philosophy." Cheyne's illness—his "crisis of 1706"—was then a part of a larger providential plan. Had there not been evidence of revelation through the body of man in recent social events as well? Sudden healing of the sick poor; the unprecedented establishment of alms houses; other medical services that rescued men and women who would have been given over for dead only a few years ago?[48] It seemed to Dr. Cheyne that the millennium had commenced or soon would, and that he had been chosen to be instrumental in the establishment of the New Jerusalem in England. This was a far more important calling, he reasoned, than the previous Newtonian one.

---

[47] Suffering and healing had, of course, entered everywhere into millenarian discussion, especially in sermons, but medico-theologies had not been delivered in the Boyle Lecture series. There are many reasons for this absence, not least the fact that iatromathematics was unpopular with the Newtonians. It may be, then, that Cheyne now (1706–1709) returned to an old project, one whose idea had germinated ca. 1699–1700, at the turn of the century, when talk of the millennium peaked and shortly after Cheyne read and discussed John Craig's *Theologiae Christianae Principia Mathematica* with the author. The profuse acknowledgements to Craig in the preface of *Philosophical Principles* suggest this chronology and development. It is also possible that John Freind of Christ-Church, Oxford, with whom Cheyne had been in correspondence before 1704, played some role in the genesis of *Philosophical Principles*. Whatever the case actually was, Cheyne's statement in the preface that he composed the work "to record his dialogues in the 1690s, with his former pupil, the Earl of Roxburgh," is inadequate as explanation. The likelier reason is that Cheyne wrote the book to win back the support of the Newtonians.

[48] H. Schwartz (n. 33) is right to remind historians of science on p. 250 that many scientists in the apocalypse "sought a tincture that would cure every disease because it was in essence a microcosm of the soul's union to the body and of God's relationship to Christians. The panacea was the apex of medicine just as the perpetual motion machine was the apex of physics. Universal perfect health, like universal perfect

Now persuaded that the body could not be overlooked, Cheyne turned elsewhere in the apocalypse than to mathematics or iatromathematics. His primary task, as he recounts in his "case history," was to recover. He persuaded himself that by practicing the most vigilant temperance he could avert further collapse. He increasingly renounced London, returned there less frequently, and abjured its indolence and luxury. Precisely why he did not join Fatio and the other prophets remains a mystery,[49] unless his decision owed something to the personal or public intervention of his mentor Whiston. By the autumn of 1706 Whiston's *Essay on the Revelation of Saint John* had appeared, announcing that certain of his earlier prophecies had been fulfilled and that others were yet to come. Cheyne may not have read this work, but he probably heard or read Whiston's Boyle lectures delivered in the next winter (1707–1708) and printed the following summer. Here Whiston argued that scriptural prophecy is capable of one and only one interpretation; he also fixed the precise date of the millennium as 1736, which he later updated to 1766. More urgently for Cheyne, Whiston warned against the placing of trust in the French prophets,[50] a position that may have weighed somewhat in Cheyne's decision not to join them. One further consequence of possible Whistonian influence was Cheyne's apparent realization that he (Cheyne) had been wrong about the source of the "Universal Attraction" discussed in *Philosophical Principles*. At least, this line of argument—that Cheyne revised his theory as a consequence of Whistonian influence—is more likely than the arcane explanation that for a third time he tried to regain the bounty of the Newtonians.

Alone then in the country, ailing but improved, and no longer near death, Cheyne set about to revise his "philosophical principles" in a

---

motion, was as close as the apocalypse." See also such works as, anon., *Universal Health ... made possible for the Poor* (1697), a rare treatise in the Wellcome Institute Library for the History of Medicine.

[49] While Fatio was swiftly converted, Gregory was hostile and skeptical of the new prophets; Cheyne's role in the early days (1706–1709) is unclear, as is that of Dr. James Keith and several other members of the Aberdeen-Garden mystical group who had by now migrated to London. By 1709, however, Cheyne had befriended a number of the prophets' leaders, especially Cuninghame (a friend of the Garden group) and Roach, and was engrossed in reading mystical literature. See n. 52 below.

[50] In his *Boyle Lectures*, 2 vols. (1739), II, 329, Whiston warned his countrymen to beware of the "dangerous and false" prophets: "If any person in this age, who pretend to a prophetic spirit do foretell events, whether of mercy or of judgment, which do not come to pass according, we have the warrant of God himself for their rejection."

manner that would take account of his "great crisis" of 1706. "If my life was to be sav'd," he comments in his memoirs looking back at these years between 1706 and 1709, "it was only by this [temperate] Regimen." Cheyne's solace in his illness was that he had learned to understand Grace in a new light: "if my Time of *Dissolution* was come, I knew I should die under Misery . . . [rather] than by an other Means."[51] By 1709 he settled in Bath, close to the mineral waters in case further crises of health should arise. Here he could practice medicine if he recovered, but the main attraction was the pure quality of the air and the proximity of the spa. He arose early and retired early; his diet consisted exclusively of vegetables, milk, and seeds; he sought out no patients and lived frugally. In the terms of modern psychoanalysis, his ego underwent radical redefinition. If a patient visited him, he would treat him, but he no longer craved to be a fashionable London physician. James Cuninghame (1665-?), one of the four main French prophets, sought him out while recuperating from his own illness in Bath early in the spring of 1709, and filled Cheyne's ears with talk about the prophets' activities and the imminence of apocalypse.[52] Cuninghame read Augustine Baker's *Sancta Sophia* during recuperation, while Cheyne still scanned the works of the early Christian fathers, and possibly of Boehme.[53] It must have occurred to them how remarkably parallel their lives were. Both men were Scots who craved worldly recognition in England; both had been introduced to mystical religion by the Aberdeen-Garden group; both had recently been afflicted with a near-fatal illness; the recovery of each coincided with new insight into the nature of Providence and resulted in a major conversion of life style. Immediately thereafter, in 1709, Cuninghame joined the French prophets, whereas Cheyne renounced his previous life. Cuninghame resolved to work for the prophets in

---

[51] *CA*, 349.

[52] On 21 May 1709 Cuninghame wrote from Bath that he "had recovered to a miracle," and did not recognize himself "to be the same man I was some weeks ago;" see National Library of Scotland MSS 493, 73, and G.D. Henderson, *Mystics of the Northeast* (Aberdeen, 1934), 192.

[53] It is impossible, on the basis of extant material, to determine with accuracy when Cheyne first read Boehme, but he certainly knew his works by 1714–1715; and I suspect, on the basis of Cheyne's friendships and associations in Bath in 1709, that he knew Boehme's works by 1709. Cuninghame may have introduced Cheyne to Boehme's works when they met during that spring. For the dissemination of Boehme in England during this time, see S. Hutin, *Les disciples anglais de Jacob Boehme aux XVIIe et XVIIIe siecles* (Paris, 1960), chap. 2.

Scotland,[54] while Cheyne aimed to convert Englishmen to the "New Jerusalem" by the same doctrines of abstemiousness in diet he himself was rigidly following. Around 1709 or 1710 Cheyne may not have considered himself a "Quietist," but an observer of his daily life in Bath would have concluded he was one. Well-read in the works of Mme. Guyon, Bourignon and other Continental pietists, and possibly by now of Boehme, Cheyne believed that the millennium had begun, that recent political and social events were sufficient proof, and that he bore a special mission in its commencement. We do not know if he agreed with Whiston that the millennium would not begin until 1736 or 1766,[55] but Cheyne was confident that the important day could not be very far away. Besides, Cheyne's conversion had clearly occurred in 1706, in the very same months when the French prophets landed in England and when many were prophesizing that doomsday was close at hand. What evidence, all seeming to convene, could be more explicit from Cheyne's point of view?

During the next five years—1709-1714—Cheyne revised *Philosophical Principles* and practiced his body in rigid diet, regular exercise, plenty of sleep, pure air—non-naturals, as the eighteenth-century called them, the abuse of which had been a primary cause of his collapse. In 1711 the French prophets began to roam the West Country and to proselytize more actively than they had in London. Cheyne probably heard them in Bath or Bristol, even if he resisted them. During these years he also associated with Richard Roach (1662-1730), their foremost apostle who, like Cheyne and Cuninghame, had experienced a pattern of illness, healing, conversion, and redemption through new works.[56] Roach also published a diary which would have aroused Cheyne's sympathy if Cheyne could have read it. "Divines and Physicians, Literal and Mystical," Roach cryptically wrote, "There is a world of Science, Soul of the Science

---

[54] See H. Schwartz (n. 33), 157-58.

[55] The date had been announced in Whiston's 1707 Boyle Lectures, publicized in 1708 in his *Account of Scripture Prophecies*, and repeated as an accurate calculation in his *Literal Accomplishment of Scripture Prophecies* (1724).

[56] Roach, like Cheyne and Cuninghame, suffered a major illness in his early adulthood which he interpreted as Providential, as "an Internal Call to a more silent Attendance on the Powers of the Work of the Kingdom to come;" see the unpublished Roach Diaries, II-VI, *passim* and Schwartz (n. 33), 195-98, where they are discussed. Cheyne and Roach may have been brought together by Cuninghame sometime in 1709; some of their correspondence, still unpublished, was at Culladen, Scotland, in the Garden archives, until the house burned down in 1985.

unknown to the former."[57] Roach also scrutinized the Kabbala, and may have introduced Cheyne to the interpretations he, Roach, would publicize before his death in 1730 in *The Imperial Standard of Messiah Triumphant* and *The Great Crisis*. For all three men, millenarianism and medicine were related, and even if no one of the three was searching for a universal panacea[58]—as Fatio was—each had learned that extreme illness followed by healing was itself the highest form of revelation: the basis for a philosophical natural religion based on the body of man. Then, in 1713, the German Baron Metternich published an explication of Boehme under the guise of an attack on John Locke, entitled *Fides et Ratio—Faith and Reason*. Cheyne acquired it and sent it to William Law, the author of the popular *Serious Call to a Devout and Holy Life* (1728) which implored mankind to renounce the hustle and bustle of material life in preference for a quiet world of constant religious devotion.[59] By 1715 the second edition of Cheyne's *Philosophical Principles* appeared,

---

[57] Roach Diary, II, f. 304ᵛ.
[58] A salt compound based on *sal ammoniac*.
[59] Cheyne probably obtained the book from his old friend Dr. James Keith in London, the main link between Pierre Poiret in Leyden and Cheyne in Bath. The typical route for Cheyne's dissemination of Quietist literature was this: Pierre Poiret (Mme. Guyon's secretary and disciple who now wrote prolifically in semi-seclusion in Leyden) → the firm of J.H. Wetstein (the Swiss Protestant printer and bookseller in Amsterdam—Cheyne could not pronounce or write his name and continued to refer to him as "Western") → Paul Vaillant (the French Huguenot printer and bookseller in London) → Dr. James Keith (the Scot and London friend of Cheyne) → Cheyne (Bath). Cheyne then circulated these books throughout England, as is known from the correspondence of James Keith and Lord Deskford. In his diary for 28 May 1743 John Byrom, Law's loyal disciple, commented on this fascinating Anglo-Dutch network in his journal: "Dr. George Cheyne . . . was always talking about naked faith, pure love," and Byrom explained that Cheyne had been "the providential occasion of his [Law's] meeting or knowing Jacob Behmen, by a book" which Cheyne had sent to Law; see H. Talon (ed.), *Selections from Byrom's Journals and Papers* (1950), 221. The "book," Metternich's *Fides et Ratio collatae, ac suo utraque loco redditae, adversus J. Lockii* (Amsterdam: Wetstein, 1708), was translated into English in 1713 as *Faith and Reason Compared; shewing that divine faith and natural reason proceed from two different and distinct principles in man*. See also S. Hobhouse, "*Fides et Ratio*": the book which introduced Jacob Boehme to William Law," *Journal of Theological Studies*, XXXVII (1936), 350–68, where Cheyne's role is acknowledged. Cheyne's enormous activity as a transmitter of Quietist mystical literature from Holland to England, and from Jews to Christians, has been overlooked, even by the most erudite recent scholar of the Dutch book trade; see I.H. van Eeghen, *De Amsterdamse Boekhandel 1572–1795*, 6 vols. (Amsterdam: N. Israel, 1960–1978). In fact, he, together with Dr. Keith, was actually the main disseminator in the early eighteenth century, as Samuel Richardson, the printer-novelist well knew.

reasoning again "by way of Analogy" but now espousing a more mystical, if indeed somewhat neo-Platonist, theory of attraction than before. Creatures of the world were now direct reflections, or embodiments, of the Creator. Because of this similitude, Cheyne argued, one could reason exclusively by analogy and without hesitation from the material to the spiritual realm.[60]

Yet Cheyne's argument is not Shaftesburian. Attractions between living creatures are merely another form of attraction than that between the Deity and his material creation, but are no less valid or real. Therefore, spiritual love between man and fellow man is attraction of as noble a type as that between man and God. The 1715 revised edition also contained reflections on God and the "Divine Essence." Here Cheyne argued that forms of "divine things" exist as well as of material things, the material ones having been "Copied out" in the process of original genesis.[61] God's creatures, man included, become "Images, *Emanations, Effluxes,* and *Streams* out of his own *Abyss* of Being,"[62] a position that appears closer to the *Book of Urizen* than to the *Principia* or *Optics*. By 1720 Cheyne prepared another book championing Stoic abstemiousness entitled *Observations concerning the Gout*. This was a book less about gout than about the healthful effects of a lettuce, milk and seed diet, one promoting plenty of sleep, good air, and complete avoidance of luxury in diet.[63] It was well received by the medical community, which was so obsessed with gout in the 1720s that almost any book by an M.D. would have been viewed seriously. But since the book proclaimed nothing about cosmology or physico-theology, the Anglican Newtonians overlooked it or shunned it altogether.

V. *The Second Revelation*

But Cheyne relapsed. Again in 1723, now over fifty, Cheyne once

---

[60] But it is important to ask whether this assumption in itself, and without further consideration of the contexts and facts of Cheyne's life, renders Cheyne a Platonist or Neo-Platonist. Cheyne did, of course, write a short poem in rhymed pentameters "On Platonism," which deals with conventional Platonic love, but it refers to neither analogies nor causes nor a Platonic cosmology. See the manuscript collection of poems collected by Charles Parr Burney in the British Library, Burney MSS 390 fol. 8b.

[61] *Philosophical Principles* (1715), Part II, 46.

[62] *Ibid.*, Part I, 47.

[63] The book was in part autobiographical, as Cheyne was now "in a regular Fit of the Gout" (*CA*, 346). Perhaps the stinging criticism of the Newtonians in 1705–1706 had not yet been forgotten, for Cheyne avoided all metaphysical claims here.

more swelled to enormous size—"I exceeded 32 Stone," about 450 pounds—and grew so ill that "if I had but an Hundred Paces to walk, [I] was oblig'd to have a Servant following me with a Stool to rest on."[64] This time Cheyne was better prepared for dire calamity than in 1706, and could rely more on the resources of his acquired mystical millenarianism. Certain that misery is the mother of salvation, he bore up to his "perpetual *Sickness, Reaching, Lowness, Watchfulness, Eructation,* and *Melancholy*"[65] for almost two years, and diagnosed gout as the source of these melancholic conditions. Returning to a diet of "lettuce, little wine, and water best," this second protracted illness caused him to grow increasingly hermetic in his theory of diet. Contra Mandeville and Nicholas Barbon before him, Cheyne argued against the virtues of luxury. Yet like them, he considered luxury to be a psychological state as well as a physical reality (i.e. the presence of sugar in the poorest household). And he linked himself with others who related psychic health to daily diet. He would surely have encountered a kindred spirit if he had then read Thomas Tryon's works, the author of the book on the mystical divination of dreams.[66] But if Tryon advocated a similar rigid vegetarianism, he possessed little of Cheyne's mystical faith—"naked faith," as John Byrom later referred to it—nor was Tryon medically trained. Yet both men, to be sure, were of the hermetic tradition of Boehme: a lineage descended from Paracelsus to Boehme, and from Boehme to the baptists, pentecostalists, and other versions of English pietism that flourished in Cheyne's most formative years. Actually, Cheyne would probably have found himself in greater spiritual agreement with Thomas Byfield, the Anglican physician who turned prophet in 1707

---

[64] *CA*, 343.

[65] *Ibid.*, 346.

[66] See *Pythagoras his Mystick Philosophy reviv'd, or the Mystery of Dreams unfolded* (1691). Tryon, a constant reader of Boehme, sustained a "crisis of the spirit" in 1657 partly as a result of his reading of Boehme, after which time he recommended vegetarian diets similar to those later advocated by Cheyne. In the 1690s Tryon joined up with some of the London Philadelphians; a splinter group formed calling itself "Tryonists," reading the works of Madame Guyon, and practicing abstinence in diet; see *Memoirs of the Life of Mr. Thomas Tryon, late of London, Merchant* (1705), which appeared a few weeks after the publication of Cheyne's *Philosophical Principles* (1705) and on the advent of Cheyne's "great crisis." Cheyne refers to several Pythagorean cults (*CA*, 368), but I have found no evidence to suggest that he had heard of Tryon or the Tryonists or read their works. Benjamin Franklin recounts in his *Autobiography* how he became "a Tryonist" during his youth. Presumably, Franklin absorbed the vegetarian aspect and neglected the Behmenistic-Quietist strain of Tryon's thought.

after the arrival of the Camisards in England.[67] Byfield too came to Bath in search of health, where he may have sought out Cheyne to diagnose his case. While there, Byfield joined forces with the English prophets based in Bath-Bristol, and converted the vicinity into a stronghold of radical millenarianism.

In the midst of all this religious tumult, Cheyne was following his old pattern of publication accompanied by illness. In 1723 or 1724 James Leake, Richardson's brother-in-law whom the Earl of Orrery described as "the Prince of all the Fraternity of Booksellers" in Bath, opened a business on one of the parades, a few yards from Cheyne's house, and printed as his first book Cheyne's *Essay on Health and Long Life*: yet another Cheyne treatise work advocating abstemious diet, this time referring historically to the writings of Cornaro, Lessius, and other early vegetarians. It is impossible to know—at least Cheyne's memoirs offer no clue—whether this publication bolstered Cheyne's spirits sufficiently to cure him. But by December 1725 he was well enough to travel to London to consult with the most "distinguished physicians" alive about his ailments.[68] Cheyne's habit, then, of growing seriously ill just before and shortly after the publication of his books seems by now to have hardened into a confirmed pattern.

Geoffrey Bowles has called attention in the essay already cited to a correlation between Cheyne's theory of "attraction" and his attitude to the medical profession.[69] It is equally plausible that a correlation exists between the reception of Cheyne's books and his health.

---

[67] In old age Byfield published *Directions tending to Health and Long Life* (1717), a book advocating a modicum of the abstemiousness Cheyne insisted upon. Byfield was also the author of a number of medico-millenarian works such as *The Christian Examiner* (1720).

[68] See *CA*, 349. These included the luminaries one would expect: Arbuthnot, Noel Broxholme (Pope's physician in London), James Douglas, Richard Mead, and John Freind: Cheyne's old friend at Christ Church in Oxford who had been one of the first Pitcairnean proteges and whom Cheyne mentions with gratitude in the preface of *Philosophical Principles*. But Cheyne apparently did not consult John Freke, by 1723 Richardson's physician and a great friend of Dr. James Keith, Cheyne's main supplier in London of Quietist literature arriving from Wetstein's firm in Amsterdam. I have searched in vain for manuscript notes these physicians may have scribbled while treating Cheyne, on the grounds that such materials could illuminate the specific nature of Cheyne's ailment. My own diagnosis is that Cheyne suffered primarily from what we would call manic-depression, but that as he aged this psychiatric condition was aggravated by chronic cardiac arrest. I date the onset of cardiac-pulmonary arrest ca. 1722–1724, around the time of his second "crisis," when Cheyne was in his early midfifties.

[69] See n. 38 above.

If this approach is valid, it would have to include Cheyne's anticipation of the reception he would receive. Every time the Newtonians decimated him, his health declined. When no one took notice of *Philosophical Principles* in 1705, he grew dangerously ill. Now, in 1723, he again blistered into mania and fever while writing the *Essay on Health and Long Life*, only to be cured by the eventually favorable reception of the book. The *Essay* received more attention than any previous work by Cheyne, and within eighteen months was translated into several languages.[70] Gilbert Nelson, then an authority on gout, wrote approvingly of Cheyne, claiming that he was the only physician in England to be ranked with Sydenham on the subject.[71] Arbuthnot himself was willing to be deflected from other pressing professional work, and studied Cheyne's theories about vegetarian diet in *An Essay Concerning the Nature of Aliments* (1731). As these medical estimates and literary appraisals appeared, Cheyne improved; by 1729 he claimed "complete Recovery."[72]

Yet it falsifies the known facts to sketch a picture of praise without blame for Cheyne's reception. As the negative criticism mounted and continued to surpass the positive,[73] he began to see medicine and

---

[70] Clifton Wintringham translated it into Latin with extensive commentary. It also appeared in French and German. Seven years after Cheyne's death in April 1743, Edmond Litton, a self-styled disciple of Cheyne's synthesized its argument in *Philosophical Conjectures on Aereal Influences, the Probable Origin of Diseases* (1750).

[71] See G. Nelson, *The Nature, Cause and Symptoms of the Gout: as stated by Dr. Sydenham, Cheyne* ... (1728).

[72] *CA*, 352: "Upon the Whole, as in my *Nervous* and *Scorbutical* Disorder, I had continued my Milk, Seed, and Vegetable Diet, with proper Evacuations, for above two Years [1727–1729], before I obtain'd a compleat Recovery, so in this last Illness, I had observ'd the same Regimen near twice as long, before my Health was perfectly established."

[73] It had been building up for four years. In 1724 two anonymous books hostile to Cheyne appeared: *Remarks on Dr. Cheyne's Essay on Health and Long Life. By a Fellow of the Royal Society* and *A Letter to G.C., M.D., Occasion'd by his Essay on Health*. In 1725, Edward Strother, M.D., vigorously attacked Cheyne in *An Essay on Sickness and Health in which Dr. Cheyne's Mistaken Opinions in his late Essay are ... taken notice of*, and someone merely calling himself "Pillo-Tisanus" published *An Epistle to Ge—ge Ch—ne, M.D., F.R.S. Upon his Essay on Health*, which ridicules every aspect of Cheyne's writings, especially his "stilted style." Also in 1724, John Wynter, a somewhat jealous Bath rival, published a tepid appraisal of Cheyne's milk and seed diet in *Cyclus Metasyncriticus*, which Richardson's brother-in-law, James Leake, printed. Other works discussing Cheyne during the late 1720s are listed by F. Shum in *A Catalogue of Bath Books* (1913), 5–9. Negative criticism of this type continued to be published to the end of Cheyne's life. In three separate numbers of

millenarianism—together and apart—in a different light from the view he held during his first collapse. In 1729—his second medical *annus mirabilis*—Cheyne was fifty-eight, no longer young. According to Whiston, the millennium was now only seven years distant (1729–1736), or if Whiston altered his view by then, thirty-seven years (1729–1766). Unfortunately no evidence exists to learn whether Cheyne still extolled Whiston as he had in 1706—as a beacon of primitive Christianity—and the lack of any reference to Cheyne in Whiston's *Memoirs* complicates the matter further. But whether or not Cheyne was still reading authors of primitive Christianity, by 1730 he was certainly grieving the death of Richard Roach, perhaps the most inspired of the English prophets who has converted to the cause of the French.

As Cheyne's books continued to be reprinted and as the negative record began to accumulate,[74] his evangelical mission to connect medicine and millenarianism increasingly obsessed him. Doubt too crept in: perhaps he had not accomplished enough in the conventional medical sphere. Furthermore, as social and economic conditions suddenly changed in England after the disastrous South Sea Bubble, and as the tide of luxury dramatically increased, Cheyne believed that his energy was urgently needed to combat this appallingly widespread condition. Accordingly, sometime around 1730 he set about to write a treatise on scurvy, the only major disease he had not written about before. He noticed that it had peaked during the last two centuries, concomitant with melancholia. He also observed that there had been a drastic upsurge of dyspepsia in England—the main symptom of "flatulent melancholy"—during the decade of the 1720s, as well as an increase in suicide. By the mid-Twenties the medical profession was calling suicide, even more so than gin, "the English vice." Cheyne imaginatively combined all these current ideas into a single

---

The Champion (15 November 1739, 17 May and 12 June 1740), Fielding ridiculed Cheyne's ungrammatical style, although he dropped the charge when referring to Cheyne fifteen years later in *The Journal of a Voyage to Lisbon* (1755), "Sunday, July [14]." Such harsh criticism extended into the 1760s and 1770s, especially in unpublished correspondences and after Cheyne had long since been dead. For example, John Rutty, the Quaker physician, condemned Cheyne's diet to William Clark, the Wiltshire physician and author of an interesting treatise on psychosomatic illness; see Rutty's letter to Clark dated 8 August, 1773 in Rutty MSS, Society of Friends, Friends House, London, Case 32.

[74] Four years later, in 1733, he wrote in the preface of *The English Malady* (iii): "I have been slain again and again, both in verse and prose."

work, and in the same year (1733) in which Pope published *An Essay on Man* he brought out *The English Malady*, certainly his best known book today.

VI. Medicine and Millenarianism

Cheyne made clear in his preface, first of all, that he was writing for a particular audience. "Such a *Diet*," he insists at once, "is only proper for the *thinking, speculative* and *sedentary* Part of Mankind, and not for the *active, laborious* and *mechanical*."[75] Yet this "thinking Part"—clergymen, scholars, writers, artists, the whole intellectual establishment—constituted practically the whole group that was committing suicide with such astonishing rapidity. What had these types in common? A weak constitution, Cheyne concluded; one whose blood and, more significantly, whose nervous system, was either congenitally defective or imperiled through abuse. His own condition had been a case in point: from youth onwards he had observed a weak physiological constitution composed of "feeble Solids" and "excessive Juices."[76] Yet the nervous system—the constellation of nerves, spirits, and fibres—was the ultimate culprit; and Cheyne concluded that the only remedy, given that "none can choose his own Degree of *Sensibility*," was the spartan lifestyle he had been recommending since his visionary experience in 1706. The assiduous reader who was willing to peruse all 300 pages of *The English Malady* could discover how the nerves and fibres actually produced the melancholy about which so many Britons (including Hume) complained to their physicians and which drove many of them to suicide. Theoretically and methodologically viewed, *The English Malady* by no means endorsed "the mechanical philosophy," but it infused Newtonian and mathematical learning to a degree Cheyne had not used since 1715. Only a novice reader who had not followed Cheyne's bizarre scientific and personal career could reasonably have concluded in 1733 that Cheyne was still the dyed-in-the-wool iatromechanist he had once been. Yet he was not. If anything, his preface anticipates precisely the opposite charge: that he has now "turn'd mere *Enthusiast*, and resolv'd all Things into *Allegory* and *Analogy*, advis'd people to turn

---

[75] *The English Malady*, iii.
[76] *CA*, 325.

Monks, to run into *Desarts*, and to live on *Roots, Herbs,* and *wild Fruits*."[77]

The English Malady was an instant success. Within fifteen months it went into six editions. Cecil Moore, the literary historian, was so awed by its reception that solely on the basis of it he wrote of the mid-eighteenth century: it "deserves to be called," not the Age of Reason, Enlightenment or Exuberance, but "the Age of Melancholy."[78] An element of Moore's attitude was influenced by Cheyne's own explanation of the title: "the title I have chosen for this treatise is a reproach universally thrown down on this island by foreigners, and all our neighbours on the Continent, by whom spleen, vapours, and lowness of spirits are in derision the English Malady."[79] But *The English Malady* is not an apology for eccentricity or a justification of a dangerously high rate of English suicide. It is a cultural treatise embodying many of the unwritten assumptions of the age, and it synthesizes a whole range of current medical *topoi* (melancholy, spleen, vapours—the whole repertoire of then current psychosomatic illnesses) and controversial physiological assumptions (the nervous system in relation to the rest of the body and its behavior), as well as fundamental laws about the nature of man.[80] In view of Cheyne's ingrained iatromechanical and Newtonian beliefs, it is not surprising that many of the explanations in the book are mechanical and mathematical. But it would be a serious error to interpret *The English Malady* merely within the development of English mechanistic theory, especially because the deepest explanations—answers to the question, what is life?—are remarkably non-mechanistic. *The English Malady* also has historical value because it assembles so many prevalent mid eighteenth-century biases and discusses them within a social and topographical context, an instance of which is the effect of English climate on human health.

Viewed, however, from the perspective of millenarianism, *The*

---

[77] *The English Malady*, ii.

[78] C.A. Moore, *Backgrounds of English Literature 1700–1760* (Minneapolis, 1953), 179.

[79] *The English Malady*, i.

[80] Although a best-seller, *The English Malady* was virtually unknown in certain quarters for over a decade. For example, John Morris wrote in his *Observations on the Past and Present State of the City of London* (1751) that "hypochondriasis" and the "hysterical passion" were clearly the two main "forms of lethargy," then known, but he wrote unaware of Cheyne's analysis in *The English Malady*.

English Malady is less significant than the revelatory treatise appended to it: *The Case of the Author*, a fifty-page memoir delineating Cheyne's life, his various crises and his conversion to "more enlightening *Principles*."[81] Ten years later, in 1742, Cheyne told Richardson that he wrote this work to prevent his patients from believing he was "really mad." But this was recollection in hindsight, and it may be that Cheyne himself did not fully realize how well his *Case* formed a companion piece to *The English Malady*. Cheyne's memoir of his spiritual life provides a context for *The English Malady* and demonstrates how "nervous physiology"—one of his favorite scientific subjects—lies directly in the service of these "more enlightened principles." Here Cheyne argues, vulgarly, that we are our physiology, and that our constitution will predetermine most aspects of our behavior; yet he does so as justification of his own "naked faith." For more than anything else he wants to remind his readers that they possess nerves. But he also hopes to impress upon them the larger claim that health depends upon "Simplicity," and that every physiological type—whether a robust Fielding or a willowy Richardson—can improve his condition by adopting a spare diet.[82] "*Simplicity* is the greatest Contradiction to *Laziness, Foreign Studies,*

---

[81] This work is not the posthumously published compilation entitled *Dr. Cheyne's Account of Himself . . . (1743) His Remarks upon Pythagoras, Cornaro, Sir Isaac Newton, the famous Mr. [William] Law . . .* (1743), which was edited by John Campbell (1708–1775). Cheyne had read Campbell's *Voyage to the Levant . . . and the Abyssinian Empire* (1739) as a consequence of his belief that "our [best] diet is *Eastern*" (*Letters to Richardson*, 121). Early in 1743 Campbell had finished a translation of Johann Heinrich Cohausen's (1665–1750) Latin *Hermippus redivivus: or, the Sage's Triumph over Old Age and the Grave. Wherein, a Method is laid down for prolonging the Life and Vigour of Man*, and wished to publish extracts before his complete translation appeared in 1744. Cohausen may have used Cheyne's death in the spring of 1743 as the rationale for a brief compilation which he called *Dr. Cheyne's Account*, and which concludes with a sample of his forthcoming translation.

[82] Although Cheyne and Fielding never met, so far as is known, Cheyne took all sorts of personal liberty with Richardson, even reassuring him that he was physiologically *beyond* madness (*Letters to Richardson*, 94), and contending that Richardson's physiology had predetermined his literary destiny and medical condition: ". . . your constitution is not like Dr. [Stephen] Hales's: you are short, round, and plump; he is taller, and very thin and uses a good deal of Exercise" (ibid., 70). In *The English Malady* (366–367), Cheyne generalizes a monolithic law of physiological determinism: ". . . none have it in their *Option* to choose for themselves their own particular *Frame* of Mind, nor *Constitution* of Body; so none can choose his own Degree of *Sensibility*. That is given him by the *Author* of his *Nature*, and is already determined . . ." The consequences of this "law" have yet to be absorbed by students of the cults of eighteenth-century sensibility.

Negligence, Incuriosity and *Ignorance* in the Profession; but such a *Simplicity* . . . is worth a *Million* of these false and *foreign Art* sometimes us'd to rise in it; for it [Simplicity] is, in Truth and Reality, an *Eminence* of *Light* and *Tranquillity*."[83] Cheyne's final trope is characteristically mystical; it is the clue to his whole physico-theology. If others looked at the stars and heavens to discover "the Book of Revelation," he gazed inwardly at the body.

Yet a need to confess—to lay one's heart bare—is as crucial to the intentions of the author narrating this "case history" as are any observations about temperance and abstinence. This is why Cheyne locates abstinence within the Stoic or Quietist life as subservient to that "universal attraction" he thought he now (1733) understood better than ever. "For the Means us'd by *infinite Wisdom and Goodness* towards reclaiming his *wandering Creatures*, seem only to be either *Love or Punishment*: that those whom Love will not draw and allure, *Punishment* may drive and force."[84] Both types of revealed "attraction"—love and punishment—have strayed from any scientific model: Newtonian or otherwise. Now Cheyne belittles the progress of science and the revolutionary value of the Newtonianism he had formerly championed, postulating that the "physic" (i.e. medicine) of the early Christian fathers had achieved equally good results, "tho' not quite so soon perhaps as well by all our *Mathematicks, Natural Philosophy, Chymistry,* and *Animal Oeconomy*."[85] His tropes are consequently those of the anti-scientist who discovers who he "really is" by deconstructing his former scientific life; and there is very nearly something Sartrean and Barthean about Cheyne's concept of autobiography. Yet Cheyne proclaims himself to be no open enemy of "those *Divine Sciences*," and explains that luxury is the culprit. Luxury has outpaced science, as it were, and rendered its wisdom ineffectual in England. He concedes that Cornaro and Lessius, previous diet theorists discussed in *The English Malady*, lived in earlier and simpler times, when science and theology were not so intertwined. But saliently, they wrote long before the onset of the apocalypse. Their ideas of health, Cheyne reasons, were not colored by the onset of the millennium. As a consequence, they could not perceive man's ultimate needs so clearly as he could. Nor did physiologi-

---

[83] *CA*, 370.
[84] *Ibid.*, 367.
[85] *Ibid.*, 367.

cal necessity—there, again, was Cheyne's law of physiological determinism—cause them, as it forced him, to remain apart from society while contributing to it.[86]

Cheyne was now (1733) in his mid-sixties. He professes not to worry if death be close; all his goals have been accomplished and his mood is irenic. He has become the most dedicated spokesman of the age for the medico-millenarian analogy. Of this he seems practically certain.

VII. *Fame and Mysticism*

Cheyne's remaining years (1733–1743) displayed no evidence of mental decline but a rather marked intensity of belief in mystical religion. Amazingly, he had lost two-thirds of his weight, and remained thin and relatively well (relative to what he had been) until his dying day. This last decade, the 1730s, was the period, ironically, when his medical practice soared. Fashionable ladies—dowagers, duchesses, princesses—from everywhere sought him out in Bath where he was now a legendary figure. By 1734 he was treating the wealthy Countess of Huntingdon and continued in constant correspondence—"pious conversation"—with her.[87] Her own letters

---

[86] H. Schwartz (n. 33) perceptively inquires if "one might, applying Erik Erikson's developmental schema, associate kinds of millenarian ethos with stages of psychological development. For example, the ethos of judgment might be attractive to those who wish to resolve the issue of trust vs. mistrust, the ethos of cataclysm might appeal to those who must resolve the issue of initiative vs. guilt, the ethos of pentecost might be advocated by those resolving the issues of identity vs. identity confusion, and the ethos of the New Jerusalem might be taken up by those perplexed by the issue of intimacy vs. isolation" (261–262). Such a suggestion, no doubt, is fraught with peril, but it is interesting to notice how well Cheyne's career fits the schema of the last category. *Intimacy* vs. *isolation* continued to be the major dynamic issue of his adult life, even at the geographical level: whether to live in Scotland or England, whether to live in Bath far away from the booksellers and printers, or to expose himself to the excesses, luxury, and illness-producing conditions of London, etc. The only caveat is economic dislocation. In the Middle Ages and Renaissance, millenarian fervor, especially in its hysteric versions, was often the result of severe and sudden economic deprivation, even within one generation. Cheyne had certainly been "dislocated" in this sense: moving from his parents of middle income to the estate of the fabulously wealthy Earls of Roxburgh, and then on to the Newtonians in London and to poverty in Bath where his finances fluctuated as much as his health. Only in the last two decades of his life, from about 1730 onward, did economic stability manifest itself.

[87] See n. 14 above. In the winter of 1741/42, the Countess of Huntingdon wrote to her husband from Bath that she had been engaged "in most pious and religious conversation" with Cheyne, who had been "talking like an old apostle. He really has the most refined notions of the true spiritual religion I ever met with." See *Hastings MSS*, III, f. 32. Cheyne sent her many of Poiret's Quietist books.

to Cheyne portray her attitude as that of a worshipper in a temple. In Cheyne's brand of mystical millenarianism she discovered the reflection of her own ideas; simultaneously, as she obeyed her cult hero, her health mended.

By 1738 Cheyne was also deep in constant correspondence with Richardson—his "literary patient"—and trying to persuade him that extreme abstinence was the only salvation for someone physiologically as "nervous" and "delicate" as he was.[88] The source, Cheyne reasoned, lay in Richardson's "defective nerves." But Richardson's "nervous paroxysms" and "paralytic tremors," Cheyne recognized, were those of a creative artist; therefore they could not be treated as if Richardson were another aristocratic lady in Bath. Cheyne expended much energy and more ink to persuade Richardson in dozens of extant, and long, letters that his malady could be constructive—no less constructive than Cheyne's illnesses had been. Cheyne had something specific in mind, though it did not surface for three or four years.

While corresponding with Richardson, Cheyne published another book, *An Essay on Regimen* (1740), attempting to delineate "the principles and theory of philosophic medicin [sic] and [to] point out some of its moral consequences." This was the medico-moral analogy Cheyne had established long ago; only now it was extended more explicitly into a medical arena. A year before his death in 1743, he produced another long essay arguing that "disorders of the mind" depend "upon the body," and that care should taken to keep the body healthy.[89] This position was the reverse of the psychosomatic one gaining ground at mid-century: namely, the notion that diseases of the body were owing to mental distress. Yet, however receptive to psychosomatic theories of illness Cheyne may have been, by the end of his life he was more ardent than ever about the body as an instrument of divine revelation and as the source of the truest revealed religion. If there were such a state as "Enlightenment" in the England of the 1740s, this was Cheyne's most enlightened credo. Cheyne grew so fanatic about the matter that he could not imagine any "revelation" that circumvented the body, an intellectual stance that ought to cause Romantic scholars to be far more interested in him than they have been.

---

[88] *Letters to Richardson*, 104.

[89] *The Natural Method of Cureing [sic] the Diseases of the Body and the Disorders of the Mind depending on the Body* (1742).

Richardson knew his correspondent well and was aware of his bent. As late as August 1742—eight months before Cheyne's death—he continued to "bribe" Cheyne with gifts of "Boehme bound."[90] A few volumes would elicit the free medical advice Richardson direly needed. Sometimes, Cheyne, rather than Richardson, drove the bargain. By September 1742 Cheyne was imploring Richardson to print a "Catalogue of Books for the Devout . . . and Nervous."[91] Actually believing that it "would be of greater Use in England than any Book," Cheyne advised Richardson that he hoped to model it on "the Catalogue of the mystic Writers published by Mr. Poiret."[92] Richardson was not altogether unreceptive to the idea, but Cheyne could not have known he would be dead within a few months. When Richardson niggled and procrastinated, Cheyne conceived yet another "project in mystical religion." "Pray be so good," he begged Richardson, "to inform me if you know any Person having a Taste of Spiritual Religion that could translate a little French Book into clean English, entitled 'L'Essence de la Extract de Religion Chretiene.'"[93] Richardson apparently found a translator of whom Cheyne

---

[90] *Letters to Richardson*, 107.
[91] *Ibid.*, 111.
[92] I.e., Poiret's *Bibliotheca Mysticorum* (Amsterdam, Wetstein, 1708), which had been translated into French and which printed excerpts from the Baron de Metternich, the German adherent of Mme. Guyon who has already been mentioned. Later in the letter Cheyne states that he owns Poiret's "Catalogue of Mystic Writers," which he describes as "finely and elegantly painted in a small Octavo in Latin" (*Letters to Richardson*, 111). Cheyne then explains to Richardson where Poiret's book can be obtained, pointing to the specific network described in n. 59. The significant matter here is not the specific work by Poiret, but rather Cheyne's intentions in the project. For many years now, Cheyne had dreamed of continuing in the footsteps of Garden and Ramsey by disseminating Quietist literature throughout England. Now he hoped to obtain Richardson's assistance—it must not be forgotten that Richardson was first and foremost a prolific printer—in the somewhat underground Anglo-Dutch network already delineated. Cheyne's intention was not merely reaching the William Law to whom he had already sent many Quietist books. Now, in 1742, he also hoped to convert to Quietism naturalists such as the young Richard Symes, eventually the author of *Fire Analysed* (Bristol, 1771), and a large group of scientific disciples in the Bath-Bristol area. Thus, when Law published an *Appeal to All that Doubt* in 1742, the stage was set for Cheyne. Law's book introduced Behmenism unequivocally into natural philosophy. What remained was Cheyne's persuasion of Richardson to print an English translation of Poiret in a cheap single volume that could conveniently be sent through the post. As Cheyne was dying in March-April 1743, he continued to dream of the fulfillment of his plan. It was his last project, his private version of "rational Enlightenment," or as proximate to Enlightenment as he would come while on earth.
[93] *Letters to Richardson*, 124. This work is another of Poiret's Bourignonist compi-

did not approve. So this ultimate dream, like some of its awe-inspired predecessors, went the way of all flesh.

During this period at the end of his life Cheyne also corresponded with William Law, although many of their letters have disappeared, as Stephen Hobhouse, Law's recent knowledgeable student, has discovered. The subject they discussed most was religion and science: especially the diffusion of "mystical religion" among the growing numbers of naturalists. Cheyne was amazed at the number of young Newtonians who continued to carry on the work of their real and symbolic "father"; Law was intent, for obvious reasons, to prove that Newton himself had been a mystic of profound dimensions. Yet Cheyne wondered why Law claimed that Boehme *in particular* had been the source of much of Newton's science. On March 31, 1742 Cheyne put the question to Law in a letter, asking him to substantiate what Law had just claimed in his recently published *Appeal to all that Doubt* (1742): "... that he [Newton] had been a *diligent Reader* of that wonderful Author [Boehme], that he made large extracts out of him ..." Law replied by repeating his claim in the Appeal, and assured Cheyne that these "large extracts" had been among Newton's papers at the time of his death. Law's reply to Cheyne was not published in the lifetime of either man—Law died in 1761—but appeared in the September issue of the *Gentleman's Magazine* (p. 329), and was later republished by Christopher Walton, Law's Victorian biographer, in *Notes and Materials for an Adequate Biography of ... William Law* (1854). Cheyne may have been satisfied by Law's letter: at least he had no reason to deny what had been included among Newton's manuscripts at the time of his death in 1727. But it is also possible that Cheyne was too preoccupied with Richardson and his invalids at Bath, who he continued assiduously to treat, to pursue the intriguing question about Boehme and Newton.[94]

---

lations; it describes the life and works of Mme. Guyon and was printed by Wetstein in Amsterdam.

[94] The state of Newton's papers at the time of his death, and the precise number of manuscripts left, remains mysterious although his relation to Boehme has now been admirably studied by Betty J.T. Dobbs in *The Foundations of Newton's Alchemy* (Cambridge, 1975) pp. 9–12. Also important is Stephen Hobhouse's discussion of Cheyne as the link between Newton and Law in *Selected Mystical Writings of William Law ... and an Enquiry into the Influence of Jacob Boehme on Isaac Newton*, with a foreword by Aldous Huxley (2nd ed. rev., New York, 1948), 397–422. Walton's manuscript copy of his *Notes and Materials* is found in Dr. Williams' Library, London; for Cheyne see Walton MSS Book 1118 (I, i.38).

Throughout that summer of 1742—Cheyne's last—and during the next autumn he continued to search for a translator. Precisely why he relied so preponderantly on Richardson, and why he could not locate a translator by himself, must be something to preoccupy Cheyne's future biographers. Of greater concern here is the situation of the septuagenarian millenarian-dreamer knocking at death's door in this precise stance: still diffusing mystical but "more *enlightening* Principles" by scattering books throughout the British Isles, still compulsively imposing on Law, still enticing Richardson. According to so many commentators in his own day, Cheyne had been a brilliant medical mind, a caring doctor, a personality totally worthy of the notice he would no doubt receive in future ages. Yet time has somehow managed to obscure the very aspect which his contemporaries deemed to be so original to the Bath physician: his unique blend of medicine and mysticism, as even his bodily corpulence and exiguity demonstrated. It is, then, one matter to depict Cheyne in his own milieu and against the backdrop of his own times and quite another to rescue him now. If greater emphasis is placed on the second concern, then a different question ought perhaps to be put to the modern student. In this case the absolute historical portrait loses some of its thunder as we wonder—today—if Cheyne's career does not pose some major paradoxes for the intellectual historian of our times who happens to be interested in the eighteenth-century Enlightenment. Cheyne, Richardson, Newton, Law, Boehme, Pope, Poiret: what a strange lot of bedfellows! Surely, we wonder, this is a jumble worthy of commemoration in a polished neoclassical English couplet. But the constellation may reflect our own sense of "jumble" according to principles of "Enlightenment" we have inherited more than historical truth warrants. Perhaps our sense of *the* Enlightenment and its attributes requires some radical adjustment. This is the issue I want to discuss in conclusion, isolating it in relation to Cheyne's demise.

VIII. *Death in the Apocalypse*

Cheyne died in April 1743, having failed to convince the English public about a balanced diet, and valetudinarians like himself, about the terrific value of abstinence. His programme for scurvy—*the* disease of the seas at the time—had to await the late eighteenth century before gaining public recognition; and his plan for a balanced diet containing plenty of vegetables and nuts rather than meat and potatoes, has lingered into the twentieth century before partial adoption. His attack on luxury, it is true, impressed many of his patients, but "Estimate" Brown, Smollett, Goldsmith and others in the 1750s and 1760s were needed before the war against luxury could be formulated, let alone combatted.[95] When Goldsmith reported that Beau Nash "would swear, that his [Cheyne] design was to send half the world grazing like *Nebuchadnezzar*,"[96] we view the comic strain of Cheyne's programme. Indeed, there is a sense in which he must have appeared to many of his contemporaries as if he had been—or *ought* to have been—a caricature in a Smollett novel. Viewed solely as a type, he was a celebrated but decidedly eccentric physician who had become a best-selling author. But his contemporaries could not view him from within. If they had been able, they would have found a complex man who firmly believed that he had resolved intellectual dilemmas through a doctrine of "Universal Attraction" based on analogy. Furthermore from within, that he had faithfully served his Maker by carrying forward the supreme message about man's nervous body. And, despite the weight of a quarter of a ton, he had managed to live to seventy-two! As he told Richardson near the end of his life:

> I [who] have gone the whole Road had one of the most cadaverous and putrified Constitutions ever was known, and I thank God am returned safe and sound at 70 every way well ... and surely he knows the Road better who has gone to and come from the Cape of Good Hope, all the Surroundings, Rocks, Shelves, and Winds, than they who have only seen them in a Map.[97]

In other words, he had been a good physician but a better Christian, and by prioritizing the two in this way he had practiced what he preached: "medicine begins where philosophy ends." Despite his unorthodox Christianity it would be wrong to see Cheyne—whether

---

[95] As J. Sekora has demonstrated in *Luxury: The Concept in Western Thought, Eden to Smollett* (Baltimore, 1978), although he omits medical literature, the all-important messianic and millenarian tradition of luxury, and, perhaps more consequentially, neo-Stoic and neo-Pythagorean attacks on luxury by Cornaro, Lessius, Tryon, Byfield, and—of course—Cheyne. Sekora does not acknowledge to what an extreme degree luxury is a psychological rather than a physical state, and therefore why its religious strains and components are of crucial concern to the historian of luxury.
[96] A. Friedman (ed.), *The Life of Richard Nash* in *Collected Works of Oliver Goldsmith*, 5 vols. (Oxford, 1966), III, 364. For Cheyne in *The Bee*, see ibid., I, 400.
[97] *Letters to Richardson*, 81.

from without or within—as a hermit, even though he had retreated from city life to encourage the apocalypse. In my view it is equally incorrect to portray him merely as a zealot who repressed his earthly needs by rationalizing them in the name of millenarian enthusiasm.[98] Temperamentally, Cheyne was as social and clubbable as he was irenic and retiring. Socially, he was not so recalcitrant as his memoirs suggest: we know this from his medical activities in Bath. His personality was outgoing, permeated with a constant sunny cheerfulness he never abandoned. But he had been born with chronic obesity which played havoc with his physiological constitution to such a degree that he never expected to live to more than twenty or thirty. From youth onward his religious tendencies had been mystical, but when the crisis of 1706 broke, followed by the subsequent conversion-experience, something new in his apocalyptic and millenarian imagination jelled. Mentally and emotionally he was never again the same. The Cheyne who wrote to the ailing Richardson, "it is true you are not a Physician, but I hope you are a Christian,"[99] was the mature, ultimate Cheyne—anything but a Hogarthian or Smollettian caricature—who was persuaded he had found the way to Grace and eternal redemption:

> Our Saviour bids us fast and pray and deny ourselves without Exception, but for this there is no need for Revelation Advice. If you read but what I have written in this last in the Essay on Regimen in long Life and Health or Cornaro's or Lessius' little Treatise your own good sense would readily assure you; but you puzzle yourself with Friends, Relations, Doctors, and Apothecaries, who either know Nothing of the Matter, or whose Interest it is, or at least that of the Craft [,] to keep you always ailing . . .

Medicine and millenarianism, for Cheyne at least, could not impinge more on each other if they tried.

---

[98] Karl Marx—not the Marxist but the illustrious nineteenth-century professor of medicine at the University of Göttingen and the prolific commentator on Blumenbach—wrote a Lucianic "letter-to-the-dead" Dr. Cheyne, which James Mackness translated into English and published in *The Moral Aspects of Medical Life, consisting of the 'Akesios' of Professor Karl Marx* (1846), 34–46. Here Marx incorrectly addresses Cheyne as a fanatic "Quaker, who belonged to that respectable body of Quakers." Marx claims to have been profoundly moved by Cheyne's two most outstanding qualities: his "Quietist aversion to all personal strife" (36) and his "peace-loving disposition" (38). Neither quality perfectly tallies with the facts of Cheyne's diversified career, but the notion of an irenic personality at the root of his temperament is worthy of consideration.

[99] *Letters to Richardson*, 81.

IX. *Cheyne and the Cultural Map of His Times*

These conclusions about Cheyne's temperament and career may be valid, but they are inadequate in themselves unless Cheyne is properly related to the temper of his times. In this sense, it is irrelevant whether he was a major or minor figure. His activities as a representative man of the Enlightenment are far more crucial, and not merely his intellectual thought but his frenetic energy in dispersing Quietist literature from the Continent. It is necessary, then, to ask two or three large questions to understand precisely how he is a representative man and how he relates to the map of his time. Prominent among these topics is his relation to the overall science—especially to the "natural philosophy"—of the Enlightenment. Precisely how does Cheyne relate to eighteenth-century science?

Clearly, he was one of the more interesting early Newtonians: not only because he was, Arbuthnot notwithstanding, the physician closest to "the Wits"—he himself was something of a "scientific wit" whose numerous bestsellers made his name a household word among the "Hackney Scribblers" he described in the preface of *The English Malady*—but also as a result of his hermetical way of reasoning. Cheyne may not be a "scientist" when viewed from our perspective today, or when judged by our criteria of science; but he was certainly considered a "scientist" in his own time, although—as we have seen—a poor one by the Newtonians. The foundations of his system thrive on a hermetical concept of analogy that is neither logical nor accessible.[100] Rather than pitched at mathematical logic or secular accessibility, Cheyne's analogies were exercises to derive the love of God in a hostile, yet hardly void, universe. Yet Cheyne's life and works show positively no contradiction between science and theology, although it is perfectly clear that most historians of science would be more comfortable with his career if it had evolved in the early seventeenth, rather than the early eighteenth century. If it is true that in the seventeenth century a good scientist also had to be a good theologian, this law applies integrally for Cheyne, although he lived a century

---

[100] I use the vexed term hermetical as it has recently been developed by Dobbs in *The Foundations of Newton's Alchemy*, already cited and F. Yates in *The Rosicrucian Enlightenment* (1972). Unfortunately, there is no book such as K. Thomas' *Religion and the Decline of Magic* (1971) which deals primarily with England in the period of Cheyne's adult life (1695–1743), nor is R.S. Neale's *Bath: A Social History 1680–1850* (1981) of any help in these matters.

later. In this sense, though, the relation of his science and theology may compel contemporary students of the Enlightenment to ask some hard questions about the so-called "rational century" or "Age of Reason." It is true that Cheyne stands apart from many of his medical brethren—the Arbuthnots, Cheseldens, and Olivers—who were less interested in theology than he was, and that he appears instead to be a harbinger of Hartley and Priestley.[101] But the point is not at all that Cheyne was born too early or too late; but rather that he, like Fatio, was "stricken" by the French and English prophets, and that this seizure impelled him to integrate "mathematics" and "naked faith" in a way that scholars have yet to describe. Perhaps there is an even larger point to be gathered. Cheyne was not alone in his mystical millenarianism. He had his brand, just as Pitcairne, Fatio, Byfield, and so many others had theirs. Yet Enlightenment scholars have remained largely oblivious to this huge underbelly of their so-called Age of Reason.

Moreover in the relation of science and theology, Newton was not the messiah for Cheyne who would have agreed with those in the 1730s who interpreted Pope's famous couplet in the *Essay on Man*, about "showing Newton as we show an Ape," as a satiric barb. And he probably would have argued that it was directed specifically at those of his scientific brethren (FRS?) who gadded about portending that the messiah had arrived in the name of Sir Isaac Newton. As Cheyne gradually retreated throughout his life from a system that may crudely be called "Newtonian metaphysics," he substituted a set of poetic analogies derivative from—pure love. At least nothing in the empirical universe could even begin to corroborate these similitudes. They formed the basis of a metaphysics that increasingly denied the basis of physics. But this is precisely why Cheyne is so interesting, and why the *literati* were so attracted to him. In this sense Cheyne's career violates the paradigm referred to earlier about "a good scientist also having to be a good theologian," yet it shows a man continually striving to wed science and theology.

In this evolving drama Newton is represented as an anti-hero who

---

[101] Cheyne was in fact more self-reflective about his use of analogy than any other millenarian thinker I have encountered in the early eighteenth century. His writings abound with comments about his self-consciousness in the use of analogy, and even his rhetorical tropes are worthy of scrutiny when he is in this reflective mood. See, for example, *The English Malady* (1733), ii.

continues to lose ground to the more potent Boehme. Even Pitcairne recedes, although Cheyne could never reject the Symbolic Father. Newton had been a pillar of Cheyne's early intellectual life—but not because he was any type of "Saviour". Furthermore, there is no evidence whatever that Cheyne read Newton's posthumously published prophecies, neither the *Observations upon the Prophecies of Daniel and the Apocalypse of St. John* nor the manuscript about the conversion of the Jews,[102] nor is there any evidence that Cheyne was curious about this aspect of Newton's thought. Besides, even if Cheyne had read these works, it is doubtful that his quasi-Behmenistic attitude to the laws of universal attraction would have changed. Newton, for Cheyne, was too whimsical in his wedding of science and religion, perhaps as a consequence of the way he was lionized by the whole of England. Cheyne had enjoyed no such instant success; he argued that the millennium was here, that there could be no doubt it had started. He had been old enough in the 1690s to witness, and then to remember, its first appearances. He had personally watched the events of 1706 and reasoned that they coincided with unprecedented brilliance in the mathematical sciences. Newton's appearance as the most perfect mathematician the world had ever known seemed to be evidence of the Deity's providential intentions, even though Cheyne was personally (and obviously) less awed by Newton's achievement than were most Englishmen; and he viewed the rapid succession of several mathematical geniuses—Pitcairne, Newton, the Bernouillis—as an important millenarian clue.

What remained, Cheyne believed, was to integrate medicine—"queen of the sciences"—into this state of mathematical perfection.[103] Finally in the scientific sphere, Cheyne's role in the development of medicine is clearer than is his precise millenarian niche. I would even go so far as to contend that it is perilous to omit him from any "Whig history" of eighteenth-century medicine: for this is one

---

[102] See F. Manuel, *The Religion of Isaac Newton* (Oxford, 1974), 99–104. Manuel comments on p. 35 that Cheyne's "new-found principle of Reunion with God, analogous in the system of intelligent beings to the principle of attraction in the material universe, was too saturated with religious Neoplatonism for his [Newton's] taste." True, but Manuel seems unaware that Cheyne's pietism led him to far more byzantine beliefs than mere Neoplatonism.

[103] The idea that mathematics and medicine, in the Greek sense both Apollonian activities, represented the pinnacle of the sciences was a commonplace of seventeenth and eighteenth-century thought. See Gideon Harvey, *The Vanities of Philosophy and Physick* (1699).

category in which he shines constantly. In what we today approvingly call holistic medicine, he may be the most important spokesman of the century. He not only developed a theory but advocated a therapy as well.[104]

We must also ask what Cheyne's career reveals about the theology of the period. This issue is far less equivocal than the scientific one because the emphasis of recent eighteenth-century studies has been on the century's so-called ever-increasing secularism. Historians have been willing to concede to the occasional appearance of Quietism, chiliasm, and millenarianism as a backdrop on the stage of ordinary life in the period; but few historians other than historians of religion have acknowledged these appearances as the period's underbelly. Yet Cheyne's career demonstrates that more radical enthusiasm existed—even among "the wealthy and the great," as Pope might have said—than has been thought. The important question, then, about Cheyne's theology is not precisely of what version it was, but rather how it related to that of his contemporaries, and how it grew hand-in-hand with his scientific and medical hypotheses. Clues must be drawn from his life-long attachment to the Aberdeen Quietist group centered around George Garden and James Keith, as well as from Cheyne's tropes which thrive on a principle of analogy and which suggest a symbolic rather than scientific imagination.[105] Yet Cheyne does not fit the labels currently used by historians: Platonist, Quietist, Chiliast, Philadelphian, Behmenist, French Prophet, English Prophet. In a sense he was all, yet paradoxically none of these; and his personal theology, to the degree that it can be isolated, was a blend of these. But he cannot be cavalierly labelled by any of these tags without explanation of his life and his particular constellation of

---

[104] Cheyne continued to argue that *both* body and mind—in this priority—had to be sound for health to obtain. In the *Essay on Health and Long Life* he comments: "When I see a gloomy, melancholy, heavy, stupid, thoughtless, joyless creature, much more a whimsical, anomalous or libertine ... I conclude him in a bad state of health, under a dangerous bodily disease, or under a perpetual mal-regimen, which will soon terminate in one, whatever appearances be to the contrary, and, sooner or later, I have been always confirmed in the justness of this opinion ... For I am convinced that calmness, serenity, cheerfulness, and common-sense ... are the constant attendants and only infallible symptoms of perfect bodily and intellectual (or of *sana mens* in *corpore sano*) health."

[105] The analogical frame of mind and the type of imagination stimulating it has been ignored for scientific thinkers in the period 1680–1780. Here Cheyne is a natural candidate who ought to be included in the continuum of thinkers pronouncing about the natural world from Newton and Whiston to Priestley and Erasmus Darwin.

beliefs. For example, if one must label, then it is equally accurate to consider him a Neo-Pythagorean or Neo-Stoic, for Cheyne certainly practiced aspects of Pythagorean and Stoic religion in his daily life. Perhaps the point to be gathered without belaboring it is that we have been coerced into dividing the religious sensibility of the early eighteenth-century into opposed camps of traditional versus dissenting religions, while neglecting what I am calling "the underbelly of religion:" the great *diversity* of types of radical enthusiasm. Moreover, we are willing to acknowledge the influence of Shaftesbury as a Platonist and Stoic, but not of a Cheyne, altogether different though his influence was. Our new sense of the widespread activities of the French prophets in England will eventually change this bipolar thinking, but it may be a decade or two before this recent research is assimilated into eighteenth-century studies.[106]

The final matter pertains to Cheyne's peculiar brand of millenarianism: to his sense of life in the apocalypse as well as to Christ's role in man's eventual redemption. But only his peculiar biography, its startle of ups and downs, can begin to account for the contours of his piety. At the moment of greatest crisis in his life, Cheyne turned to the early Christian Fathers and to Madame Guyon and her followers rather than to the traditional Church. Like the Quietists with whom Cheyne associated, he extolled natural and revealed religion in place of the teachings of Jesus, attitudes that earned him the reputation of enthusiasm, and even of Arian heresy. This is why he was "indicted for heresy" shortly before his death in *The Arraignment of George Cheyne ... for ... logical heresies*.[107] But Cheyne was not an Arian, despite his one-time worship of Whiston. He was a

---

[106] A clear example is found in literary historiography of the period. Even the most serious scholars of English literature who toil today in this period write as if there had been only the extremes of traditional and dissenting religion. This situation may perhaps change when the work of H. Schwartz (n. 33) is assimilated. Schwartz's monograph, *Knaves, Fools, Madmen, and that Subtile Effluvium* (Gainesville, 1978) is also important in this context, but it does not exhaust this response, pro and con, to the French prophets. Much more work remains to be done.

[107] The work is pseudonymously signed by "T. Johnson," and is ultimately disappointing, despite its title, because the "heresy" focuses on Cheyne's grammar rather than his mysticism: "... the English language has had more Violence done it by a very great and eminent Physician, George Cheyne ... [who] hath so mangled and mauled it, that when I came to examine the Body, as it lay in Sheets in a Bookseller's Shop, I found it an expiring heavy Lump, without the least Appearance of Sense" (34).

millenarian fanatic, or more accurately, a medico-mystical millenarian. His portrayal as such has not been made, pre-eminently because his early students (Marx, Greenhill, G.D. Henderson) knew almost nothing about his medical career, and conversely, because his close ties to all types of enthusiasts have been overlooked by those (Viets, C.A. Moore, R. Schofield, G. Bowles) who have studied only his scientific career. Cheyne, of course, has been connected to William Law, then the leading British exponent of Boehme, but not to the Quietists, chiliasts and millenarians from the Cevennes, or to their English converts whose influence on British soil, as well as on Cheyne's career, was far more extensive than has been thought. Cheyne's career demonstrates the trend I am attempting to delineate: the effect of radical millenarianism on early eighteenth-century England has been neglected to such a degree that most scholars of its literature and science write and think as if it never occurred.[108] Contemporary Newtonians, for instance, explicate much about Fatio, but say little about his role in the radical millenarianism I have been describing.[109] This Quietist-mystical context is the one in which Cheyne belongs, with one exception: the neo-Stoical cults of the period.

Elsewhere I have written that neo-Stoicism is the least understood intellectual development of the Restoration and early eighteenth century.[110] And in this series we heard Professor Funkenstein brilliantly attempt to describe the Cambridge Stoics (Stoa) rather than the inaccurately labelled Cambridge Platonists. Likewise for Cheyne, aspects of his radical theory of abstinence derive from Stoic and sometimes neo-Pythagorean attitudes, rather than from neo-Platonic beliefs.

---

[108] Yet another example is found in the commentators on *A Tale of a Tub* (1704) who discuss this complex satire as if it had been written in a religious milieu that consisted only of Anglicans and Puritan dissenters, without appreciating the cults of mysticism and millenarianism that flourished while Swift was writing (1696–1704). Another instance is found in secondary writing about Swift's published predictions (e.g., *Predictions for the Year 1708: A Famous Prediction of Merlin*, 1709; etc.), which fail to understand the millenarian context of these prophecies. Swift's adult life from 1690 to 1710 needs to be reconsidered against this background.
[109] See F. Manuel, *A Portrait of Isaac Newton* (Cambridge, Mass., 1968), 274, who merely notes this about Fatio: "By the time Newton became President of the Royal Society, Fatio had fallen into disfavor, though he lingered on the sidelines for a few years."
[110] See G.S. Rousseau, "Science," in *The Context of English Literature: The Eighteenth Century*, ed. by Pat Rogers (1978), 192.

But Cheyne usually does not name his sources, as a consequence of which his commentators have overlooked his relation to the Stoic and Pythagorean cults of the time.[111] I do not want to engage in unnecessary hermetical classification; I see no reason to classify Cheyne as a "Stoic medico-millenarian." But I think it is important to stress the affinities he has with neo-Stoic thinking, and I would want to add that he came by his Stoicism through reading of the early Christian fathers and the Quietists, and when prompted by near-fatal illness and chronic suffering, rather than by reading of the so-called Cambridge Platonists.

In conclusion, Cheyne's radical millenarianism is ultimately paradoxical. On the one hand he advocates extreme abstinence in diet; on the other, he tries to convert a Richardson with all the ardor of a Christian missionary in China: his approach is anything but stoic or passionless. Every restraint Cheyne espouses in diet is contradicted by apparent excess in mystical proclivity. His career is replete with other paradoxes as well. He begins to write, as we have seen, as an avowed mechanist (iatromechanist) and ends as an animist, although this shift, too, has not been studied in the light of his religious beliefs. All the Stoic fervor about relinquishing the needs of the self are contradicted, it would seem, by his intense search for a professional identity in an age (the early eighteenth century) when the physician could appear in almost any typology; his blend of personal interests and misfortunes would not readily fit any profession. A perfect example of these paradoxes is found Cheyne's unrelenting need to take stock and confess: whenever he studied himself he uncovered layer upon layer of Providence that had tended to favor him.

I agree with Robert Schofield that Cheyne's "progress from kinematic mechanism toward vitalistic materialism, by way of Newtonian dynamic corpuscularity, was ... occasioned by religious consider-

---

[111] Scholars such as H. Metzger (n. 38) and F. Manuel (n. 102) considered Cheyne a Neoplatonist for four main reasons: (1) they were unaware of his central role in the Anglo-Dutch dissemination of Quietist literature; (2) they were apparently unaware of his involvement with the leaders of the French prophets; (3) they overlooked or were unaware of his ties to the mystical Garden-Ramsey group and to the type of millenarianism it fostered; (4) they wrote with little appreciation of Cheyne's health and bizarre personal life. In bewilderment, then, they grasped at the label Neoplatonist in the hope that this catch-all would sum up the many conflicting tendencies they despised. All they knew for certain was that Cheyne had fallen out of favor with the Anglican Newtonians.

ations."[112] But this explanation does not extend far enough. It omits consideration of these all-important religious contexts in relation to his personal and professional life. Moreover, Cheyne's death in the early 1740s has been said to make of him a transitional figure: his career—the argument goes—lies on "the boundary" of a vast continental shift between apparently opposed sets of values.[113] But these are not merely the differences of Neoclassicism and Romanticism, Mechanism and Vitalism (Animism), or Mechanism and Organicism. Cheyne's mysticism deserves to be studied precisely because of the way in which it accommodates iatromechanism, Newtonianism, and animism. A close look at his theology demonstrates its affinities not only with animism, but with a pantheism of the type the Romantics, especially Coleridge, were to invoke. The Cheyne who at the end of his life espouses a pantheism in which every living creature embodies the specific attributes of the Godhead, is hardly the same thinker who wrote mechanistically about fevers or analogically about "philosophical principles." Inconsistency is a venial sin for a confirmed mystic; intellectual growth is not. But Cheyne's was intellectual growth incapable of adequate explanation unless his millenarianism is also described.

The Cheyne who wrote just before his death that "Man is a diminutive *Angel*, shut up in a Flesh Prison or Vehicle,"[114] has more in common with Blake's visionary physics and Coleridge's pantheism than with his own early thought. Does this alteration make of him a "Romantic thinker?" The Cheyne who argues as he approaches his Maker that man's creative powers are somewhat analogous to God's—are "Something *analogous* to Creative Fecundity"[115]— sounds more like Wordsworth on the creative imagination than the mechanistic Pitcairne or the mathematical Newton he served at the start of his career. Does this hermetic reasoning of Cheyne's render him a transitional figure in the shift from Neoclassicism to Romanticism? The Cheyne who laboriously anatomizes the mystical revelations he has experienced surely deserves to be considered as more than merely "one of the early Newtonians." Yet he has consistently

---

[112] R. Schofield, *Mechanism and Materialism, British Natural Philosophy in an Age of Reason* (Princeton, 1970), 62.
[113] Ibid., 61–63.
[114] *The Natural Method of Cureing [sic] the Diseases of the Body* (1742), 79.
[115] *Essay on Regimen* (1740), 270.

been described as no more than another early Newtonian. The Cheyne who was anonymously extolled by a rhyming scribbler in the 1730s as having tamed "the Sacred Art ... the Fetter'd Science,"[116] was someone far more prone to romantic agony and temperamental pantheism than any labels such as neo-Platonist or early Newtonian suggest. Again, paradoxically, the same Cheyne who finally claimed to have understood himself so well, seems never to have comprehended to what an extent he had been one of England's staunchest anti-luxury campaigners—perhaps *the* fiercest opponent of luxury anywhere.[117] Yet our most recent scholarly survey of luxury never—not even once—mentions Cheyne's name.[118] Finally, the Cheyne who wrote so prolifically about nervous diseases seems never to have realized to what an extent the very diet of abstemiousness he was proposing would directly lead to nervous tension.[119] An age that practically ate itself into the grave will certainly not grow calm and steady if nine-tenths of its daily diet is suddenly removed by the likes of a Cheyne.

Perhaps my subtitle indicates the ultimate paradox: "immortal Doctor Cheyne." Immortal he has hardly been, for most scholars today do not know who he was. Yet in his own day one could flirt with the idea that history would keep his name alive because he managed, despite his colossal weight, to live on for so long. A type of myopic immortality, then, was granted to him by his contemporaries, perhaps for the wrong reasons.

Biographical and Iconographical Note on the Portrait of Dr. Cheyne:

The portrait reproduced above is the only one known to have been painted of George Cheyne. Sometime ca. 1735 Cheyne sat for Johan [sic] Van Diest (ca. 1680–1760), son of the Dutch landscape painter

---

[116] *Gentleman's Magazine*, VIII (1738), 136, anonymous poem.

[117] Vicesimus Knox, the physician and commentator who wrote at the end of the eighteenth century, seems to have comprehended Cheyne's extraordinary contribution to countering the immense gluttony of the epoch, as well as the degree of hostility shown him by his contemporaries. See *Personal Nobility* (1793), 90.

[118] See Sekora (n. 95).

[119] Why did so many nervous diseases proliferate after mid-century? The situation *vis-a-vis* nervous ailments grew so serious by the 1780s that James Makttrick Adair, the physician with whom Burns the poet took walking tours, replaced Cheyne at Bath as a "nervous doctor" and wrote book after book about the reduction of food intake as a direct cause of depression and anxiety.

Adrien Van Diest (1656–1704). The resulting portrait was later engraved by the prolific engraver John Faber the Younger (1695?–1756). Van Diest resided in the vicinity of Bristol-Bath during the period 1730–1750 where he was employed for a while by Ralph Allen; he was known to practically all the members of the circle which gathered around Allen at Prior Park and which included Pope, Bolingbroke, Henry Fielding, John Wood the author of an *Essay on Bath*, Lords Burlington and Bathurst, Bishop Warburton, general painters and landscape architects, and Drs. Oliver, Pierce, and Cheyne (see B. Boyce, *The Benevolent Man: A Life of Ralph Allen of Bath*, Cambridge, Mass., Harvard University Press, 1967, 38–39). Together with Pope, Van Diest advised Allen on the statues to be built in the Library at Prior Park and he may have painted them. Pope also seems to have hired Van Diest to paint in his grotto, but the work was never completed. Nor was the portrait of Pope by Van Diest to which the poet himself alludes in his correspondence: "Vandiest [sic] has made an Excellent Picture of Mr. [Nathaniel] Hook, which I hope will fall to your [Allen's] Lott. I will sit to him too, when we meet at your house" (*Correspondence of Alexander Pope*, ed. G. Sherburn, 5 vols., Oxford, Clarendon Press, 1956, IV, 239). Nathaniel Hooke (d. 1763) was a lifelong friend of Pope's and a very close associate of Dr. Cheyne's. According to Warburton, Hooke was also "a mystic and Quietist, and a warm follower of Fenelon and Mme. Guyon." In the latter capacity Hooke undertook an English translation of Michael Ramsay's *Cyrus*, and employed Dr. Cheyne's half-brother William Cheyne (1704–1767), Vicar of Weston-near-Bath, as his amanuensis (see *Spence's Anecdotes*, ed. J.M. Osborn, 2 vols., Oxford, Clarendon Press, 1966, I, 455–456). Cheyne, who had been a boyhood friend of Ramsey's while both men were youthful members of the mystical circle rallied around George Garden in Aberdeen, was sympathetic to the translation. He permitted Hooke to live in his house in Bath while translating, as Pope acknowledged several times in his correspondence and as was widely known by Allen's circle in Prior Park: "this elegant translation was made at Dr. Cheyne's house at Bath" (Joseph Warton, *An Essay on the Genius and Writings of Pope*, 2 vols., 1782, 4th ed., 129) and also according to Spence: "Mr. Hooke was then at Bath for his health, and Dr. Cheyne's [half] brother was so good as to write for him. Hooke walked about the [Cheyne's] chamber and dictated to him, so that it was a sort of

[Cheynean] exercise as well as study" (*Spence's Anecdotes*, I, 455). The mezzotint version of Cheyne's portrait is lettered "sold at the Great Toy Shop at Bath" at a location close to Cheyne's house. There is also a later copy (in reverse) of the print by J.M. Berngroth.

MARGARET C. JACOB

FREEMASONRY AND THE UTOPIAN IMPULSE*

By the early eighteenth century in England millenarian beliefs and apocalyptic predictions had all but disappeared from elite culture. In that widening gap between the high culture of the educated and prosperous, and the "low culture" of the illiterate, the menial and the economically marginal,[1] the time available to the few became infinite, and possibly even enjoyable, while the masses probably still clung to beliefs in abrupt pauses or final conflagrations which their prophets assured them would alter the human condition and destroy the wicked and oppressive.[2] As high culture came to presume an infinitude of earthly time, the new scientific thought, particularly as it was applied mechanically to material needs, simultaneously encouraged the belief that human progress was possible, or even inevitable and unending. In early eighteenth century England the utopian *genre* of literature—related as it can be to profound frustration with existing reality—responded to the new conceptual framework of earthly time by largely, and somewhat ironically, disappearing. The impulse to search for perfection in this world suddenly appears in a new form; it infused the private and ritually organized social gatherings of the now secular and affluent seekers after a progressive heaven on a self-perpetuating earth.

Freemasonry, that most neglected yet quintessential expression of its age, permitting this fraternal search for human perfectibility within the confines of its select gatherings. After the founding of the

---

* The author wishes to thank the Research Foundation of the City University for a grant to research this topic during the summer of 1981, and to revise it in 1983 on the basis of further research.

[1] See Peter Burke, *Popular Culture in Early Modern Europe* (New York, 1978); Natalie Davis, *Society and Culture in Early Modern France* (Stanford, California, 1975); David Rollinson, "Property, Ideology and Popular Culture in a Gloucestershire Village 1660-1740", *Past and Present*, no. 93, 1981, 70-79.

[2] Cf. Hillel Schwartz, *The French Prophets. The History of a Millenarian Group in Eighteenth-Century England* (Berkeley, California, 1980); and Clarke Garrett, *Respectable Folly, Millenarians and the French Revolution in France and England* (Baltimore, 1975), pp. 210-23. And for background, Michael Mullett, *Radical Religious Movements in Early Modern Europe* (Boston, 1980).

Grand Lodge in London in 1717, the hundreds of lodges that sprang up there and in the provinces also published a substantial number of sermons or lectures which had first been preached in the lodges and which were in turn deemed worthy of publication by the assembled brethren. This valuable source for British masonic history, especially when combined with other types of masonic publications, has never received proper scholarly attention.

This literature provides the historian with access to gentlemen, tradesmen, and some aristocrats, who were, as it reveals, among the first Europeans to embrace the new secular religiosity that an infinity of time on earth implied. Their fraternal oaths and ceremonies complemented their openly proclaimed belief in religious toleration, science, and strong, constitutional government. In sermons as well as constitutions, those principles are seen as the foundation of true masonry, while within each lodge brothers are exhorted to build the perfectly harmonious society. The masonic utopia can only exist in secular time, and among the prosperous, the meritorious, and the educated; it specifically excludes servants and bondsmen, the illiterate, and "the profane". Those sorts of men—and initially all women—were incapable, it was argued, of embracing either the wisdom found in the masonic mysteries, or the convivial egalitarianism of the lodge. They were excluded from the social affirmation of commonly-held beliefs and values which, it was believed, could only be found in fraternal unity.

The masonic vision of true wisdom also excluded, by definition, the illuminations of the saint. For the freemason knowledge must be achieved socially, as well as secretly, and so the unique insights proclaimed by the enthusiast as a result of his or her special communication with God are simply irrelevant to the experience and discipline of the lodge.

The abandonment of the millennium and the embracing of time to be found only in this world occurred quite abruptly within English, and particularly Anglican, high culture, approximately between 1680 and 1720.[3] That shift in sensibility signals an acceptance of the tem-

---

[3] M.C. Jacob and W.A. Lockwood, "Political Millenarianism and Burnet's *Sacred Theory*", *Science Studies*, 2, 1972, pp. 265–79; E. Tuveson, *Millennium and Utopia: A Study in the Background of the Idea of Progress*, New York, U. of California, 1964; and Margaret C. Jacob, *The Newtonians and the English Revolution* (Ithaca, New York, 1976), pp. 122–27; R. Crane, "Anglican Apologetics and the Idea of Progress", *Modern Philology*, 31, 1934, pp. 273–301, 349–82.

poral and secular, and hence of a political and social order ordained by and for human beings, that is central to modern thought. For some men such a sudden shift could only be sanctioned by new ritual; they created and led a fraternity that in the course of the century captured the imagination of thousands of educated and enlightened Europeans, from Montesquieu, Helvétius and Franklin, to Mozart, and quite probably, Robespierre.

That this new masonic rhetoric dramatically reflected a new glorification of the secular, and even adorned it with utopian possibilities, should hardly surprise the student of late seventeenth century English political history. The abandonment of millenarianism occurred primarily in the 1690s after the establishment in 1689 of constitutional monarchy and parliamentary government. In that same decade we find the first evidence for the existence of a purely "speculative" lodge, i.e. one not composed of working, or operative, masons, and it was established among London gentlemen of decidedly Whiggish inclinations.[4]

That lodge was headed by Sir Robert Clayton, lord mayor of London, scrivener, and an extreme Whig. His friends included John Wildman, the former Leveller, and John Toland, who later in his career made much out of what he may have learned about secret fraternizing from Clayton and his friends. Unique among non-aristocratic Europeans, these beneficiaries of the Revolution Settlement possessed unprecedented access to political power through parliament and the press. They had established the means by which their power, and the polity, might be rendered both permanent and stable. They could begin to think about the permanence of temporal institutions through which those fantasies of progress might someday be enacted.

One element making possible that political stability, upon which material progress might rest, was the clear subordination of church to state. After 1689 the commands of heaven, as understood by some clerical interpreters, implored the gentlemen of land, finance and commerce, as well as all lesser folk, to bend their self-interest in the

---

[4] Margaret C. Jacob, *The Radical Enlightenment: Pantheists, Freemasons and Republicans*, London, Allen & Unwin, 1981, p. 79, 118; Henry Horwitz, *Parliament, Policy and Politics in the Reign of William III*, Manchester, Manchester University Press, 1977, p. 20; for eighteenth century mention of that lodge, J. Scott, *The Free-Masons Pocket Companion*, Glasgow, 1765, p. 66; and A.S. Frere, *The Grand Lodge, 1717-1967*, Oxford, Oxford University Press (for the United Grand Lodge of England), 1967. Cf. Guildhall MS. 5992 for Clayton's support of the fraternity in 1677.

service of religion and society, but never to abandon it. Their worldly occupations received affirmation from the reasonableness of latitudinarian Christianity. Whether they bothered to listen or not to this newly subordinate and acquiescent clergy, secular-minded men like Clayton, could comfortably imagine themselves the creators, the priests if you like, of a new social order.

But late seventeenth century Whiggery, as we well know, possessed a radical underside with intellectual roots in the revolutionary and republican tradition of the Civil Wars and Interregnum. The political and secular philosophy that legitimated the Revolution Settlement to the enfranchised of town or shire always carried with it the possibility of further transformations, the reform of existing institutions, however glorious and legitimate their settlement might once have been. And in the eighteenth century that language of reform would never entirely lose its revolutionary associations, its republican tendencies, that echo heard long after the late 1640s and 50s when the language justifying revolution and regicide had first been spoken on the streets, in the taverns and the ale-houses. Throughout the century oligarchic Whigs sought to disown this radical inheritance; but it kept coming back to haunt them—in the 1690s and well into the reign of Anne, in the 1760s and the Wilkesite agitation, in the 1790s among the supporters of the Continental revolutions, to be found in Derbyshire as well as in London.

Because of that intellectual inheritance, whenever progressive gentlemen gathered to celebrate the secular—regardless of their individual affiliations as Whigs or Tories, or more simply, their propensity to the grandeur of the court or the virtue of the country—their attachment to order and harmony, to commerce and industry, to fraternity and equality among themselves, could threaten to confront society as a whole, to measure existing institutions against those private ideals. The rhetoric of eighteenth century masonic literature gives us new insight into the complex interaction between the ideologies of court and country. They were more intimately related than is sometimes supposed; and where we find a mind that was wholly secular and progressive those ideologies existed within it simultaneously, in a precarious and largely unhappy, but necessary, compromise. The advocacy of reform in one area—public behavior, domestic architecture, the application of science to industry, the increase of fraternizing between tradesmen and aristocrats—inevitably implied reform in all areas. The utopian and reforming aspects of masonic idealism, particularly as they were elaborated upon by Continental devotees, provides one intellectual bridge between the republican and democratic inheritance of the English Revolution and the reform movements and democratic revolutions of the later eighteenth century.

After 1689, as the Manuels note in their monumental study of European utopian thought, few specifically utopian tracts exist in English prose.[5] It is all the more interesting, therefore, to turn our attention to a body of literature with distinctively utopian features, one ignored by the Manuels. Because masonic literature speaks so consistently of the perfectibility of earthly time and place in the future, and despite the problems raised by its having been first addressed to a secret fraternity, it may well be the largest body of eighteenth-century nonfiction that can be safely classified as utopian, without, of course, implying that only that category is sufficient by which to classify it. But the context wherein this literature developed, before any analysis of it, requires introduction.

English masonic orators generally delivered their addresses in the back rooms of taverns or alehouses. They spoke to brothers who had assembled, at least monthly and often fortnightly, to honor the Grand Architect, and through ritual and ceremonial garb, aprons, gloves, etc., to express their identification with the values of work and merit, as once practiced, they believed, by working guildsmen, most of whom had long since left the fraternity. Whatever their private political affiliations or reservations, these brothers in the official Masonic lodges all swore allegiance to the *Constitutions* of 1723 published by the Grand Lodge. That document glorified constitutional monarchy, extreme religious toleration, even by implication for Jews, and the new science, and it contained not a single statement that could be described as millenarian or even vaguely eschatological.[6]

English masonic literature from the eighteenth century can include everything from mythical histories, constitutions, speeches and sermons delivered at lodge meetings, to pocket manuals, songs and tracts

---

[5] Frank E. Manuel and Fritzie P. Manuel, *Utopian Thought in the Western World*, Cambridge, Harvard University Press, 1979, pp. 413–14, 431. And see R. Crane, "Anglican Apologetics and the Idea of Progress", *Modern Philology*, 31, 1934, pp. 273–301, 349–82.

[6] For a copy of the *Constitutions*, see Margaret Jacob, *The Radical Enlightenment: Pantheists, Freemasons and Republicans* (Boston and London, 1981), appendix, pp. 279–87.

written in defence and praise of the order. All display remarkably similar themes: the joys of fraternity, conviviality and mutual benevolence; the exaltation of virtue and merit as the sole criteria for status within the lodge, coupled rather contradictorily, with frequent allusions to the large number of gentlemen and aristocrats, even kings, who proudly share in the masonic mysteries. Also stressed is the importance of privacy and secrecy, and the essential role of the liberal arts and sciences, particularly geometry, in improving and civilizing mankind.[7] Uniformly these writers claim to represent an ancient, generally Egyptian and Hermetic wisdom, rediscovered and augmented by the new useful learning of their age; with supreme optimism freemasons always find knowledge to be beneficial and progressive. The lodges eschew bigotry and superstition, yet they take care to exclude those whom masonic literature and ritual describe as "the prophane". And while also excluding women from this sacrosanct world, the English freemason, although increasingly less committed as the century wears on to sexual exclusivity in the lodge, glories in the joys of family and domestic life.[8]

The most commonly repeated theme found in masonic literature is predictably the joys of fraternal benevolence and social harmony. In 1779, for example, the Kent vicar and freemason, James Smith, preaching before his lodge, employed language drawn from the Newtonian tradition to illustrate the necessity and power of benevolence: "attraction binds the universe as benevolence binds men", he confidently asserted.[9] In similar language and in the same period, Daniel Turner, an Anglican minister in Norwich, urged his brothers to practise philanthropy which "is not confined to name or sect. Like the power of attraction, which reaches from the largest to the smallest bodies in the universe, it unites men from the throne to the cottage."[10]

---

[7] One of the more convenient places to get at this literature is in Rev. G. Oliver, *The Golden Remains of the Early Masonic Writers*, London, 1847, 4 vols. For songs see C. Brockwell, *A Collection of Freemason's Songs. To Which Is Prefixed A General Charge to Masons*, London, 1904.

[8] On the question of women, see Jacob, *The Radical Enlightenment*, pp. 207–08, and "Freemasonry, Women and the Paradox of Enlightenment", in *Women in the Enlightenment*, Haworth Press, under the auspices of The Institute for Research in History, New York, 1984.

[9] Rev. Brother James Smith, *A Sermon preached at the Chapel in Deal ... 1779 before the Provincial Grand Lodge of Kent ...*, Canterbury, 1779, p. 5.

[10] G. Oliver, *Golden Remains*, I, p. 267; see also Rev. Thomas Davenport, *Love to*

Newtonian science, as propagated by the early Newtonians, had been made to lay great emphasis upon order, stability and the rule of law. It in turn encouraged masonic fantasies about the possibility of creating perfect harmony in human society, if only within the confines of the lodge. Yet the Newtonian model also explicitly proclaimed a rigid spiritual hierarchy within nature, and by implication within society: spiritual forces, "active principles", rule over "brute and stupid" matter. Not surprisingly, masonic aspirations for stability and perfectibility were threatened whenever it appeared necessary to change the world outside the lodge in order to achieve those aspirations. Beginning in the 1760s, as we shall see, that threat, and the quandary it presented, became acute.

The prevalence within masonic literature of these metaphors of harmony and stability drawn from Newtonianism must owe something to the active role played by Desaguliers in the establishment of British freemasonry. As an Anglican clergyman and active scientist, his commitment to the fraternity earned him the enmity of his church congregation who complained to their bishop about his frequent absence. Undeterred, Desaguliers kept his true interests which lay simultaneously in the spread of freemasonry in Britain and the Netherlands, and the application of science to industry through the promotion of scientific education among the entrepreneurial classes. Both represented the progressive spread of learning, the domination of nature by the specially enlightened. His exact role in the dissemination of freemasonry onto the Continent remains unclear, and its elucidation by future research would tell us much about that institution's early history in northern and French-speaking Europe.[11]

The rapid spread of freemasonry on the Continent, as well as outside of London, also owed much to a host of Whig grandees, grand masters such as the Duke of Richmond and Lord Waldegrave—both of whom served as British ambassadors—the Earl of Chesterfield, and William and Charles Bentinck, who eagerly brought their mode

---

God and Man Inseparable. A Sermon preached before ... the Society of Free and Accepted Masons ... 1764, Birmingham, 1765.

[11] C.H. Collins Baker and Muriel I. Baker, *The Life and Circumstances of James Brydges, First Duke of Chandos,* Oxford, 1949, p. 152. For a portrait of Desaguliers see B.L. Stowe MS. 755, f. 139 and the manuscripts of the Royal Society, RBC. 11.161 and 168, correspondence books, and RBC. 18.53. In addition there are Desaguliers' MSS at the British Library.

of fraternizing wherever their travels took them.[12] Yet equally important were the ordinary gentlemen and tradesmen who paid their dues, and among whom the records reveal a noticeable number of Dissenters, Huguenot refugees (as was Desaguliers), merchants and shopkeepers, court placemen, scientific practitioners, publishers, printers, and even, known republicans.[13]

When these English freemasons showed their utopian side they dwelt upon certain especially pleasing and salutary aspects of their benevolent, progressive, and as they imagined it, ancient creed. One of the most commonplace expressions of that sort of sentiment appeared in the standard almanac used year-in and year-out by the practising freemason. *The Free Mason's Pocket Companion* first appeared in 1735, and then proceeded through a multitude of editions and translations. This masonic manual—on the Continent these manuals were called catechisms—provided its owner with a copy of the 1723 *Constitutions*, gave lists and addresses of known lodges in London and the environs, masonic feast dates, songs, and a short, largely mythic history of the progress bestowed upon humanity by the fraternity. It informed its readers that the growth of freemasonry augurs "the pleasing Prospect of having even in our own Days the Arts of the fam'd Augustan Age revive amongst us . . ."[14]

In this masonic credo the easy equation is made between the building of public and especially domestic mansions and the revival of learning. Indeed the ancient Romans had enjoyed such a revival, but it was destroyed by the Goths who "with very little knowledge of geometry" gave us the ugliness of the Gothic. The Renaissance in

---

[12] For Waldegrave and the use of his ambassadorial residence for a lodge meeting which was raided by the Parisian police, see Waldegrave MSS., at the home of Lord and Lady Waldegrave, Chewton Mendip, Somerset; and my *The Radical Enlightenment*, p. 110, and E.A. Boerenbeker, "The relations between Dutch and English Freemasonry from 1734 to 1771", *Ars Quatuor Coronatorum*, v. 83, 1970, pp. 149–92.

[13] Margaret C. Jacob, *The Radical Enlightenment*, chapter 4; but an important exception exists for Welsh freemasonry, see Philip Jenkins, *The Making of a Ruling Class*, Cambridge University Press, Cambridge, 1983; and his "Jacobites and Freemasons in 18th Century Wales", *Welsh History Review*, 9, 1979, pp. 392–406.

[14] W. Smith, *The Free-Mason's Pocket Companion*, London, 2nd edition, 1738, pp. 6–11; cf. a German translation, *Fründliche Nachricht von den Frey-Maurern*, Franckfurt-am-Mayn, 1740, and *Histoire des Francs-Maçons contenant Les Obligations et Statuts . . . 1747*, introduction signed by le Frère de la Tierce. In addition to these manuals there were annual almanacs published in some countries and the largest collection of these with which I am familiar can be found at the library of the Grand Lodge of The Netherlands, 22 Fluwelenburgwal, The Hague.

Italy, "more especially the great Palladio", revived the Augustan style of architecture and Inigo Jones brought it to England. The masonic architects are portrayed at every turn as the harbingers of this cultural revival, and the Palladian mansions of the new oligarchy—the Earl of Burlington is mentioned by name—symbolize a total cultural revival. The freemasons gloried in the transformation of the royal style of the seventeenth century into the court and hence oligarchic style of the eighteenth.[15] While it is hard for us to imagine places such as Houghton Hall, its garish interiors housing Sir Robert Walpole and his crowd, as a sure sign of cultural vitality, yet so the freemason was told by his trusted *Companion*.

The Palladian style, particularly as it appeared in the new mansions of the great, thrilled the masonic imagination. It was pagan and ancient, ornate yet symmetrical, and most of all these huge edifices and landscaped gardens encompassed by vast landed estates symbolized the private and domestic realm of patronage, prosperity and power. Out of those private enclaves came the foundations of an order and stability that imitates the cosmic order decreed by providence and confirmed by scientific observation. A masonic poet of 1739, with more enthusiasm than literary talent, rejoiced:

> But *Order* and *Simplicity* alone,
> Which in fair nature's works so fair are shown,
> Which now the schemes of Architecture fill,
> Can claim just wonder, or display just skill.
> By these old Greece and Rome their schemes did raise,
> And shone the patterns of succeeding days:
> By these their gen'rous modern sons are known
> A Kent, a Flitcroft, and a Burlington.[16]

Other masonic literature is even more explicit in this glorification of the lavishly domestic. An early but anonymous masonic tract, like many others, accepted an essentially Hobbesian view of the original human condition but mitigated it not by the establishment of a contract but by the institution of civilizing domestic units built by masons:

---

[15] T.P. Hudson, "The Origins of Palladianism in English Eighteenth-Century Architecture", D.Phil. dissertation, Cambridge University, 1974, pp. 146–47, 296–98.

[16] [Anon.] *Masonry: A Poem. To which are added several Songs*, Edinburgh, 1739. Cf. Edward Oakley, *A Speech Deliver'd to the Worshipful Society of Freemasons . . . 1728* and bound with *Cole's Constitutions*, ed. by William J. Hughan, Leeds, 1897; almost entire speech on the Palladian.

> The race of man in full possession of wild and savage liberty, sullen and solitary, mutually offending and afraid of each other; hid themselves in thickets of the woods, or dens and caves of the earth. In these murky recesses, these sombrous solitudes, the Almighty Architect directed Masonry to find them out and pitying their forlorn and destitute condition, instructed them to build houses, for convenience, defence and comfort.[17]

But the construction of homes is only the beginning of human progress as measured in masonic terms; a plenitude of riches is the ideal—the heart of the utopian fantasy. That same anonymous writer continues:

> some of our brethren from their exalted situation in life, rolling in their chariots at ease, and enjoying every luxury, pleasure and comfort, may with strict propriety be considered as standing on the basis of earthly bliss, emblematic of the greater square, which subtends the right angle. Others whom Providence hath blessed with means to tread on the flowery meads of affluence, are descriptive of the squares which stand on the sides which form the right angle.[18]

But what of those who cannot hope to achieve such extraordinary wealth in their lifetimes as to stand as squares supporting the masonic edifice—are they to be banished from the masonic paradise? While exulting in the splendor of his oligarchic betters, our early masonic writer reserved a special place for the commercially industrious:

> Those, who by application to peculiar arts, manufactures, and commerce, from their several productions not only add to the wealth of the nation, and to the happiness of the exalted, but have the heartfelt satisfaction of administering to the wants of the indigent and industrious, may with strict justice, be compared to the angles which surround and support the figure ...[19]

The lodge differs from the domestic unit only in that it admits men of a variety of ranks, from the exalted to the industrious and even occasionally to the now "indigent", once "industrious". All may

---

[17] "On the rise and progress of Freemasonry", in Rev. G. Oliver, *The Golden Remains of the Early Masonic Writers*, London, 1847, vol. I, pp. 32–34. For attacks on Hobbes coming from later in the century see Wellins Calcott, "On the Advantages of Society" in G. Oliver, vol. II, p. 34, and the Rev. Dr. Dodd, "Eulogium on Freemasonry", *ibid.*, p. 205: "indeed the history of mankind might well be considered as the history of social life; perpetually and invariably tending more and more to perfection".

[18] *Ibid.*, vol. I, pp. 44–45.

[19] *Ibid.*, p. 45.

join in the intimacy of its secret proceedings. Indeed just as the domestic sphere teaches obedience to authority, order and charity, so too the masonic lodge, in the words of one of its founders, seeks to civilize, "to subdue the passions, to promote morality, charity, good fellowship, good nature, and humanity."[20] The lodge is to the cultivation of social virtue as the home is to private virtue. The Rev. R. Green, a masonic preacher from Durham but lecturing in 1776 in Newcastle, summed up the meaning of the lodge succinctly: it is "a place of safe retirement where we may securely enjoy generous freedom, innocent mirth, social friendship, and useful instruction."[21] As a result of these advantages the freemason distinguishes himself from the rest of humanity by his gentle manner and moderate language, by his dedication to the work ethic and to the cultivation of the mind.[22] As the 1759 edition of the *Pocket Companion* remarked, the freemason is also a model citizen because he is "submissive to superiors, courteous and affable to equals, kind and condescending to Inferiors ..."[23]

But the placid assessment of true citizenship masked the dissension that had developed by mid-century within the masonic lodges over the issue of fraternal equality. By 1750 brothers had begun to criticize the social exclusivity of some lodges and to demand a more genuine egalitarianism. Very little of a scholarly nature is known about the resulting "Scottish" freemasonry, except that it had little to do directly with Scotland, but it did signal a split within the fraternity which left historical traces on both sides of the Channel. The first known lodge to admit men and women as equal members and officers met in The Hague in 1751, and its records make specific reference to "Scottish" freemasonry. The official British masonic lectures and songs found in the reprint of the *Constitutions* done in that same year acknowledge "the Contentions amongst Men" and beg the brethren "to avoid all discourse that may divide you into parties". The Hermetic tradition, with its pantheistic inclinations is, nevertheless, praised at great length, and one overtly anti-clerical song is given.

---

[20] *Ibid.*, p. 49, from "A defence of Masonry, occasioned by a pamphlet called Masonry dissected ... A.D. 1730", by Dr. Anderson.
[21] "On the Masonic Duties" in G. Oliver, ed. *Masonic Institutes by Various Authors* bound with *The History of Masonic Per-Secutions*, New York, 1867, p. 389.
[22] *Ibid.*, p. 390.
[23] *The Pocket Companion and History of Freemasons ...*, London, 1759, p. 330, written by Isaac Head, a prominent masonic writer.

Another *New Song* for the year intones

> For Truth's sake a Lord is of equal Degree,
> With a man that is own'd for Mason and Free.[24]

In addition I strongly suspect that the appearance, also in 1751, of the English translation of Toland's *Pantheisticon*, with a specific reference to freemasonry in the margin, is related to these rumblings within the fraternity over the true implications of equality and fraternity.

Later in that decade, a utopian fantasy entitled *The Temple of Virtue: A Dream* employed obviously "Scottish" rite language to elucidate its moral message. Written by David Fordyce, this dream vision takes the reader on an imaginary journey to the "temple of virtue" (the name, incidentally, that the lodge for men and women in The Hague used for the place where it met). *En route* there is a cautionary side-trip into the "land of vice wherein could be found the cave of poverty, inhabited by its mistress accompanied by a set of dismal figures, dejection, lamentation, meanspiritedness, suspicion, dishonesty, and despair."[25] The escape from the cave of poverty is made possible through contemplation and work which take the wayfarer along "a secret path" into the temple of virtue "built of a transparent stone ... of a quadrangular form ... its portal supported by a double row of pillars of the Dorick order."[26] Both men and women are admitted into this temple, and their virtues, which are represented symbolically in the temple by deities, such as the gods of "Industry and Commerce", include domesticity and modesty (especially, but not exclusively for women), a willingness to protect the modest "against the oppressor's Wrong", and scientific acumen.[27] By the

---

[24] *The Antient Constitutions and Charges of the Free-Masons with a True Representation of their Noble Art in several Lectures or Speeches*, London, printed and sold by Brother Benjamin Cole, 1751, pp. 3, 5, 9, 63. On Scottish free-masonry see J.M. Roberts, *The Mythology of the Secret Societies*, London, Secker-Warburg, 1972, pp. 94–100; C.H. Chevalier, "Maçons ecossais au XVIIIe siècle" in *Annales historiques de la révolution française*, v. 41, 1969, pp. 393–408; and see note 8.

[25] James Fordyce, *The Temple of Virtue. A Dream*, London, 1759, pp. 23–25. I am grateful to Margaret Hunt for bringing this tract to my attention. The 1759 *The Pocket Companion* reprints a sermon by Isaac Head, *A Charge deliver'd to a constituted Lodge ... Histon, Cornwall ...*, April 21, 1752, wherein it is argued that the great part of mankind is not fit to be members, pp. 329–30. *The Temple* was seen into print by Fordyce's brother and bears his name.

[26] *Ibid.*, p. 47.

[27] *Ibid.*, pp. 63–64.

end of the treatise the virtue celebrated is patently country in its ideological association, and the journey ends with a thinly disguised paean of praise for Pitt and "his most ardent love of liberty."[28]

The Temple of Virtue is a somewhat impatient tract. The search for virtue is being encumbered by court corruption (p. 70), luxury, greed, and tumult. The successful pilgrim who has finally been permitted to join "virtue's priests" has become increasingly alarmed along the way by the behaviour of those inhabitants of "the mansions of luxury"— however Palladian their taste—whose vices and circumstances may differ profoundly from those found in "the cave of poverty", but who are nonetheless dangerously distracted from the search for true virtue. The secret and spiritual path to virtue has disclosed that "the prophane", the corrupt and the decadent, can only be banished through concrete political reform.

The social turmoil caused in the 1760s by Wilkes and his followers, not a few of whom were freemasons,[29] sent the masonic leadership scrambling for the lecterns to remind the faithful that perfection within the lodge requires order and stability. In 1763 Thomas Edmondes, Esq. addressed his fellow masons in the old and prestigious Horn Tavern Lodge to which Montesquieu had once belonged, and praised his brothers for standing above "the turbulent disquietudes, and vitiated principles of most of the unselected and uncivilized part of mankind."[30] Two years later in Taunton, John Withmash reminded his brothers that "there are two grand pillars of the masonic art ... its professed design to promote civilization and to adorn human life with every scientific and moral accomplishment." To achieve these goals, however, the freemason must honor God and King and be subordinate to his superiors.[31] In 1764 an anonymous grand master lecturing near Birmingham admitted that "in all ages of the World, we find a record of unruly Members of every State; grasping at Power to which their virtues or abilities were by no means equal, and which too often overthrew the Constitution they attempted to defend .... This Observation affords a moral lesson to members

---

[28] *Ibid.*, p. 71. In case the reader is in any doubt as to who is intended, an anonymous and contemporary hand has written in "Pitt" on the B.L. copy.

[29] See my *The Radical Enlightenment*, pp. 175, 263.

[30] Thomas Edmondes, Esq., G.W., *An address delivered at the Stewards Lodge, held at the Horn Tavern, Fleet Street, London, November 16, 1763*, p. 17.

[31] G. Oliver, *op. cit.*, vol. I, pp. 178–79 and 193, from "On the Government of the Lodge. Delivered before the brethren of St. George's Lodge, No. 315, Taunton", 1765.

of private societies, as well as Kingdoms and States . . . ." He asserted, however, that "Masons have ever made faith to the government".[32] In 1764 the Rev. Davenport, also lecturing in Birmingham, warned masons to be careful whom they admit to the society; "there was never a time when our fences needed to be more strictly guarded."[33] It is not accidental that these sermons were given in a city where Wilkesite agitation was particularly intense.

Yet in that same sermon and almost by way of compensation, the Rev. Davenport called for the admission of women into the lodges, or at least for the creation of lodges for women such as existed, he claimed, in Germany and France.[34] Indeed the very sermons from this later period which exalt order and hierarchy also most clearly demonstrate the tensions inevitably produced by masonic idealism with its utopian vision of equality and harmony for all. An anonymous oration of 1772 demanding that freemasons never "poison their minds with Republican Principles" nevertheless warns of the dangers of corruption in a language that clearly implies the need for some kind of reform:

> when [the law] is dispensed with at Pleasure, when it is pressed against its true Intention into the service of prerogative on the one hand, or privilege on the other; when magistrates are put into office to serve a party by the partial administration of it . . . in a word when an honest cause is overturn'd by artifice, the torturing of witnesses, the disguising of truth . . . then the law . . . loses its nature and efficacity."[35]

This masonic speaker is sure, he says, that this would never happen in England, but many of his fellow orators were not so sure about how well the larger society measured up, or should measure up, against the demands of masonic idealism.

In 1770 John Codrington preaching in Exeter reminded his brothers

---

[32] *A Charge delivered at the Constitution of Lodge No. CXXX at the Swan in Wolverhampton* . . . October, 1764. By the . . . Grand Master, Birmingham, 1765, p. 6, 9.

[33] Rev. Thomas Davenport, *Love to God and Man Inseparable* . . . 1765, p. 15–16. On freemasons and radicals see John Money, *Experience and Identity: Birmingham and the West Midlands, 1760–1800*, McGill University Press, Montreal, 1977, pp. 137–40.

[34] Rev. Thomas Davenport, *Love to God and Man Inseparable. A Sermon . . . before . . . Free and Accepted Masons . . . 27 December 1764*, Birmingham, 1765, pp. 15–16.

[35] Rev. J.C., a Brother, *A Sermon preached at Bury St. Edmund's . . .*, Bury, printed and sold by Brother W. Green, 1773, p. 11–12.

that they must never be involved in plots and conspiracies. But he tempers that obligation with the assertion of cherished masonic ideals: men of merit even "of the most indigent circumstance ... we rank as brethren on a level" and freemasons must free themselves of bigoted notions about religion—"humanity is the soul of all religions."[36] Indeed the divisions between men are wholly artificial and Codrington proclaimed:

> The whole world is but one great republic, of which every nation is a family and every particular person is a child. To revive and spread abroad those ancient maxims drawn from the nature of man, is one of the ends of our establishment. We wish to unite all men of an agreeable humour and enlightened understanding, not only by the love of the polite arts but still more by the great principles of virtue; and from such a union, the interest of the fraternity becomes of all mankind.[37]

A few years later, at the height of the American Revolution, the Rev. James Smith lecturing in Kent proclaimed that

> by nature the whole race of mankind however different they may be in their modes of living, in their size, or their complexions, from the most polished courtier down to the savage Caffer ... from the fair Dane to the sooty Negroe ... however unlike these are to each other, however unknown, still they are brethren ... as all men are by nature brethren, so consequently all men are by nature equal ...[38]

This man of democratic sentiment, whom we met earlier through his use of Newtonian imagery in this sermon, speaks not only of the force of attraction binding the universe and the need for order and harmony, but also of the equality of all men, and attempts somewhat frantically to hold these notions in an increasingly fragile equilibrium:

> a good Mason ... is properly said to live upon the level with all men. Yet Freemasons are by no means Levellers ... order and subordination ... are requisite for the welfare of every society ...[39]

---

[36] *On the design of Masonry. Delivered in the Union Lodge, Exeter, # 370 ... 1770*, in G. Oliver, *Golden Remains*, I, pp. 197–99.

[37] *Ibid.*, pp. 208–09. But Codrington cautioned against admitting women, "not that we do not pay a natural and due regard to that most beauteous part of the creation ... but because their presence might insensibly alter the purity of our maxims and our manners we are afraid ... that love would enter with them" (p. 213). He denied that they were incapable of keeping secrets.

[38] *Rev. Brother James Smith, A Sermon preached ... in Deal ... 1779 ...*, Canterbury, 1779, pp. 8–9.

[39] *Ibid.*, p. 10.

Spoken but a few years before the outbreak of the first of a wave of democratic revolutions on the Continent, this sort of masonic rhetoric, which offered the private lodge as the cosmopolitan ideal for society as a whole, simply restated boldly what had always been at the heart of the masonic utopia. Then tandem with the proclamation of luxury and affluence as ideals came the almost naive belief that the meritorious actually deserved to prosper. To say, so simply and so straightforwardly, as Codrington did in 1770, that "we are all upon a level, and ... merit is the only just distinction" may well have encouraged those who regarded themselves as meritorious and who resented the distinctions and prejudices that inhibited their progress. Such utopian sentiments could justify demands for concrete social reforms, for the translation of that private masonic ideal into public action: the abolition of privilege and corruption, the institution of true fraternity and equality for all men, even for all women and also for slaves. The masonic presence in those revolutions, however moderate and undoubtedly non-conspiratorial it may have been, must be understood by reference to this utopian rhetoric, and hence in relation to the legacy of the English Revolution in all of its phases.

But the reforming and utopian tendencies within eighteenth century British freemasonry generally never obscured the more typical and widespread masonic dedication to harmony, moderation, conviviality, and social cohesion within the lodge. This stoical, even complacent serenity (however epicurean might be the fraternizing that accompanied it) directly imitated the harmony and order of the universe as revealed, of course, by science. In a well-known piece of masonic propaganda intended for a French audience, but of English origin and possibly even translated by Desaguliers, this harmonic and microcosmic relationship of the lodge to the larger macrocosm is developed at some length.[40] This is a particularly forceful piece of masonic propaganda written after a series of police raids on lodge meetings in Paris and in the wake of the Papal condemnation of 1738. The *Relation apologique et historique de la société des Franc-Maçons* argues that nature itself authorizes the masonic lodge, and it in turn is the

---

[40] *Relation apologique et historique de la société des Franc-Maçons par J.G.D.M.F.M.*, Dublin, Patrice Odonoko, Libraire et Imprimeur [undoubtedly a false imprint], 1738. In G. Oliver, D.D., *The Revelations of a Square*, London, 1855, pp. 61–62, it is claimed that Martin Clare was responsible for this tract and that it had great approval among the London lodges. Clare was indeed very active in the 1730s.

place where science is learned under the guidance of Isis or Minerva, and nature is mastered. Scientific lessons are actually given at the lodge meetings, "in many cases a discovery about nature or a demonstration of one of her phenomena has been more delicious than the best wine. The gaity [however] never exceeds the bounds of reason, politeness and modesty."[41]

Although forced to compete with feasting and conviviality, science does manage to teach the freemason a lesson that is the essence of his religiosity: the universe is composed of many things yet there is a unity amid this multiplicity, and that unity "is God, eternal, immense and wise .... He is the All of which each being is a product ...."[42] Science sanctions theism, nothing more and hopefully nothing less. This apology intended for a Continental and largely Catholic audience, like so many other pieces of masonic literature, calls forth a single creed, one that could be embraced by a variety of Christians, as well as by Mohammedans and Jews.[43] This universalism makes sense not only as propaganda but also as a true reflection of early masonic history.

In those years pantheists like John Toland had played a significant role in the spread of freemasonry onto the Continent. Toland's advocacy of an almost complete religious toleration derived not from any sort of Christian charity but rather from an extreme heterodoxy. In 1714 he praised the Jews because they "honor one supreme being, or First Cause, and obey the Law of Nature."[44] As one of the first eighteenth century writers to take up the cause of religious toleration for the Jews, Toland is resuming a campaign that, as Christopher Hill has shown, must be associated with the utopian yet millenarian impulse of the seventeenth century revolution. In Toland's hands the cause finds a new advocate and one who, as a pantheist, deified nature and hence the world of ordinary mortals. Toland had no need of an apocalyptic moment to justify, or to permit, his radical reforms, yet

---

[41] *Ibid.*, pp. 10–17, 28. Bracketed word added by this author.

[42] *Ibid.*, pp. 32–33, "Ce qui est tout en toutes choses est Dieu, éternel, immense et sage. C'est en ce Tout que nous sommes, que nous vivons & que nous avons le mouvement. C'est par ce Tout que chaque Être est produit ...."

[43] *Ibid.*, p. 62. But anti-Semitic comments do occasionally occur in masonic literature, e.g., Rev. John Hodgets, "On Brotherly Love. Delivered at the Constitution of the Harmonic Lodge", Dudley, 1784, in G. Oliver, *Golden Remains*, I, p. 243.

[44] John Toland, *Reasons for Naturalizing the Jews in Great Britain and Ireland* ... London, 1714, in *Occasional Papers. English Series No. 3. Pamphlets relating to the Jews in England* ..., California State Library, San Francisco, 1939, p. 64.

he did require a new religiosity, possibly even a new, yet civil, religion. As he proclaimed in the *Pantheisticon* which included the ritual for his followers, he was seeking a religion "more mild, more pure and more free", and in the tradition of Milton, Toland also proclaimed himself one of those who "study the safety of the republic."[45]

The tradition of religious toleration so much a part of masonic idealism may well have derived in large measure from pantheists and republicans like Toland whose links with the order have now been reasonably well established. Although Jewish membership in masonic lodges was always quite small, in 1731 we can identify a London lodge where six out of twenty nine members were in all probability Jewish.[46] The records of Amsterdam freemasonry, where a pantheist and follower of John Toland served for many years as grand master of its main lodge, also contain names that are almost certainly Jewish.[47]

That curious ritual devised by Toland for his Socratic Brotherhood was sent by him to The Netherlands as early as 1711, and was then published in Latin in 1720 as part of his *Pantheisticon*. Although official freemasonry never adopted it, we can see its appeal to liberal men (and even women) of a variety of religious backgrounds. Indeed its philosophical assumptions depart so far from Judeo-Christian orthodoxy as to praise "the male and female Votaries of Truth".[48] Small wonder then that in the course of the eighteenth century, despite the efforts of Anglican clergy to the contrary and especially in places where clerical influence within the lodges was very limited, freemasonry became a European institution that embraced not simply Christians and Jews but also deists, pantheists, materialists and libertines, from M. and Mme. Helvétius to Casanova. In what other social setting of the age could heresy be made so convivial, and so safe?

Indeed conviviality preoccupied the masonic publicists; as their literature makes abundantly clear, wine, song and great culinary

---

[45] John Toland, *Pantheisticon: or the Form of Celebrating the Socratic Society*, London, 1751, pp. 57, 100.

[46] John Shaftesley, "Jews in English Freemasonry in the 18th and 19th Centuries". *Ars Quatuor Coronatorum*, v. 92, 1979, pp. 34–38.

[47] The Grand Lodge of The Netherlands, MS "Kronick Annales", where Salomon Noch is listed among the original founders of the first Dutch lodge, 8/19 November, 1734; cf. Jacob Katz, *Jews and Freemasons in Europe, 1723–1939* (Cambridge, MA., 1970), pp. 8–22.

[48] *Pantheisticon*, London, 1751, p. 65.

feasts occupy a central place in every masonic evening. One of the first identifiably masonic tracts is Henri Sallengre's amusing *Essay in Praise of Drunkenness*, translated from the French by the freemason, Robert Samber, and dedicated by him in 1723 to the London freemasons, whom Samber includes in a list of great tipplers. That sort of celebration of over-indulgence was counterbalanced by a masonic literature advocating moderation, one that almost obsessively discusses the acceptable limits to be observed by the imbiber.[49]

It is as if the masonic affection for private luxury, fed by the unprecedented affluence and prosperity to be found among the eighteenth century English bourgeoisie, induced a certain discomfort among its very participants. This is not to say that in general we find in this literature anything like the sustained attack on decadence and corruption, on greed and commercial interests, that was so much at the heart of "country" sensibility. Indeed the masonic acceptance of commerce and glorification of the industrious and prosperous entrepreneur left room only for the occasional reflection on the dangers of luxury and over-indulgence. The freemason coveted affluence; he wanted prosperity, but without decadence. His is the conscience of those Whig gentlemen who wanted to live like the court and reap its benefits, while managing somehow to avoid the inevitable slide into licentiousness and corruption. So the masonic publicists emphasize the ritual and fraternal aspects of food, drink and song; they seek to make them into symbolic expressions of masonic unity, harmony and moderation. Yet masonic drinking songs give ample evidence that the bacchanalian thrived in various lodges and may even have provided an occasion for the safe expression of ideals which in that context were certainly harmless. Take for example this verse:

> Let Monarchs run mad after riches and power,
> Fat Gown-men be dull, and Philosophers sour,
> While the Claret goes round, and the company sings,
> We're wiser than Sages, and greater than Kings.[50]

In contrast to that harmless ribaldry, most masonic literature lays great emphasis on decorum, civility and table manners, literally on

---

[49] For a good example see *The Antient Constitutions and Charges of the Free-Masons*, London, printed and sold by Brother Benjamin Cole, 1751, pp. 25, 37.

[50] [Anon.] *Masonry: A Poem. To which are added several Songs*, Edinburgh, 1739, p. 23. For a brief discussion of Whig ideology see J.G.A. Pocock, "Gibbon and the Shepherds: The Stages of Society in the Decline and Fall", *History of European Ideas*, vol. 2, no, 3, pp. 194–96.

forks, plates and napkins.[51] One of the primary functions of the lodge was to make all its members, regardless of birth, into well-mannered gentlemen who help instill public order. For the freemason society alone is the source of man's greatest happiness,[52] and as a result, he has a particular obligation to foster socially acceptable virtues.

There is some limited evidence that membership in the London lodges did modify the public behavior of brothers and hence contribute to the increasingly more ordered forms of public recreation that became common in the later decades of the eighteenth century. For instance, the epilogues and prologues given in London playhouses and specially intended for masonic audiences make frequent references to the virtuous and peaceful behavior of the assembled lodge members.[53] Their deportment was apparently in noticeable contrast to the near riotous assemblies for which the everyday audiences of the playhouses were well known.

Those masonic evenings in the London theatres were frequently accompanied by a special charity collection for a brother or his widow fallen on hard times. Charity to the deserving poor or the needy brother formed an important part of masonic ideology, if not practice. In advertising the benefits of membership to a Continental audience, that anonymous French tract of English origin, about which I spoke earlier, claimed that the order always took care of its own, even to the point of providing free medical care for members when a lodge was lucky enough to possess a fraternal doctor.[54] There may be some truth to these charitable claims, although further research into the British archives—some of which are still not available to non-masonic scholars—would be necessary before we could know if the lodge truly functioned as a hedge against the uncertainties and

---

[51] *Relation apologique*, p. 57. And for an attack on masonic drunkenness, see Peter Farmer, *A New Model for the Rebuilding of Masonry on a Stronger Basis than the former*, London, 1730, p. 14, and on sodomy, p. 22.

[52] [Anon.] *Shibboleth: or, Every Man a Free-Mason. Containing a History of the Rise, Progress, and Present State of that . . . Order. By a Pass'd Master*, London, 1765, p. 44.

[53] Harry William Pedicord, "White Gloves at Five: Fraternal Patronage of London Theatres in the Eighteenth Century", *Philological Quarterly*, v. 45, 1966, p. 277. I am grateful to Paul Fritz for this reference. For an early discussion of manners see Martin Clare, *An Address Made to the Body of Free and Accepted Masons . . . December, 11, 1735*.

[54] *Relation apologique*, p. 64.

insecurities characteristic of an increasingly pervasive market society. Certainly masonic loyalty could be palpable and could extend even to the victims of crime if their assailants were masonic and if, as I suspect, the good name of the order was threatened. In the 1730s members of the Horn Tavern lodge gave assistance to a woman who had been raped by one of their members, yet they did not abandon him even after he was imprisoned for the crime.[55] For political crimes such as fomenting revolution, the masonic *Constitutions* specifically forbade expulsion of a brother although it did insist that "the loyal Brotherhood must and ought to disown his rebellion . . . ."[56]

The masonic literature of the eighteenth century, both British and Continental, offered the lodge as the foundation for earthly happiness. It provided an ethical system that emphasized fraternity and equality, as well as the value of liberty; it could also furnish a sufficiently broad religiosity to accommodate both the Christian and the heterodox or the anti-clerical, yet it never encouraged social alienation. In general masonic writers urged ordinary men to identify with the great and the prosperous, to emulate their comforts and luxuries yet never to forget the necessity for industry, virtue and learning. An extremely popular fraternal song, first published in 1763 but almost certainly older, summed up, in three part harmony, the essence of this idealism:

> Comus, away, away, with all thy revel train
> Begone ye loud, ye wanton and ye vain
> Come pensive Science, come pensive science
> Bring with thee Commerce and Arts, Commerce and Arts
>   Commerce and Arts and Industry
> Come Patriot virtue, Patriot virtue, also bring
>   and Loyalty who loves his King . . .

Of freemasonry, it proclaimed:

> Thy social influence extends beyond the narrow sphere
>   of Friends
> Thy Harmony and Truth improve the Earth our universal love.[57]

---

[55] Rev. Arnold W. Oxford, *No. 4. An Introduction to the History of The Royal Somerset House and Inverness Lodge*, London, 1928, p. 16.
[56] Margaret Jacob, *The Radical Enlightenment*, appendix, p. 280.
[57] Thomas Hale, *Social Harmony. Consisting of a Collection of Songs and Catches*, [London], 1763, pp. 13–14.

Late in the century as an expression of that universalism, some Continental lodges actually began to admit women, first in 1751, and then most commonly in France during the 1770s and 80s. The egalitarian ideology of freemasonry possessed an inexorable logic. In that sense the utopian impulse inevitably led to social and quite possibly political reformism, however much the gentleman freemason, satiated by drink and conviviality, might want to avoid such troublesome exertions.

That we can detect quite early in masonic history a politically radical underside, one which is particularly evident on the Continent later in the century, should come as no surprise given what we now know about the idealistic content of masonic rhetoric.[58] At every turn the clerical and social institutions of the various *anciens régimes* frustrated even the most harmless desire for social equality based upon merit or the institution of a religion of humanity. Yet within the lodge the emphasis on education, personal virtue and decorum must have given dedicated brothers a sense of their own worth and ability, a sense further reinforced by the hierarchy based upon merit established among themselves and by the claim that freemasons had a unique purchase on ancient wisdom. Given the opportunity, they might indeed try to transform those private utopian impulses, however rhetorical and secretive their original expression may have once been, into a concrete social reality. But such a transformation would inevitably entail a massive reform and alteration of the old order, a break with the past so abrupt as to constitute a new and secular form of apocalyptic action, although the paradise sought bears little relation to the reality finally attained.

---

[58] On this theme see J.M. Roberts, "Liberté, egalité, fraternité: sources and development of a slogan", *Tijdschrift voor de studie van de verlichting*, 4, 1976, pp. 329–70, and in the same issue, 5, 1977, Hugo de Schampheliere, "L'Egalitarisme maçonnique et la hierarchie sociale dans les pays-bas autriciens", pp. 433–504; cf. Peter Christian Ludz, ed., *Geheime Gesellschaften* in *Wolfenbütteler Studien zur Aufklärung*, Heidelberg, 1979, with particular attention to German-speaking secret societies in the latter part of the century. The repudiation of the Enlightenment and the French Revolution can be tied to a revival in the apocalyptic; see Nicholas Rupke, "The Apocalyptic Denominator in English Cultures of the Early Nineteenth Century" in Martin Pollock, ed., *Common Denominators in Art and Science*, Aberdeen, Aberdeen University Press, 1983, pp. 36–37, 42.

AMOS FUNKENSTEIN

THE BODY OF GOD IN 17TH CENTURY THEOLOGY AND SCIENCE

1. *The Body of God*

Thomas Hobbes, trying as always to be blunt, insisted that to call God—or spirits—immaterial entities is like speaking of them as bodiless bodies, a contradiction in terms. We may be committed to assert their existence not by an act of reason, but only by decree of a sovereign.[1] Spinoza's *Deus sive natura*, the one and only substance, must possess infinitely many attributes. Of these, only two are known, namely thought (*cogitatio*) and extension. Now Spinoza, following Descartes, regarded extension as the constitutive attribute of bodies, the only "clear and distinct" idea we have of a body if regarded by itself.[2] According to Henry More, God and other spirits, albeit incorporeal, must nonetheless be extended things. Extension is as necessary a predicate to the divine as are perfection or suisufficiency.[3] More developed his doctrine against Descartes' mechanical outlook: Only if spirits are extended could real forces be introduced into the universe. But he knew—if not from other sources, then from Descartes' response—that he could easily be misconstrued as claiming that God has a body.[4] And Newton called space—the empty, infi-

---

[1] Thomas Hobbes, *Leviathan* I,4; III,33; IV,45 (ed. C.B. MacPherson, Penguin Books, 1968), pp. 108, 426, 428–30, 661; cf. Watkins, *Hobbes System of Ideas* (London, 1965), pp. 68, 157, 164. In order to enhance the role of the sovereign, Hobbes emphasizes the discrepancies in Scriptures; cf. L. Strauss, *Spinoza's Criticism of Religion*.
[2] B. Spinoza, *Ethica more geometrico demonstrata* II def. 1 (ed. Gebhardt, *Opera*, Heidelberg, 1925), p. 88; Descartes, *Principia Philosophiae* T. I,2 sec. iv (ed. C. Adam and P. Tannery, *Oeuvres de Descartes*, VIII, Paris, first ed. 1908, 1973).
[3] Henry More, *The easie, true and genuine notion ... of a Spirit*, sec. XXII (London, 1700; ed. F.I. McKinnon, *Philosophical Writings of Henry More*, Oxford, 1925), p. 213; further elaborated below, pp. 171–175.
[4] *Oeuvres de Descartes*, V (Paris, 1903), pp. 269–70: "I am not in the habit of disputing about words, and therefore if somebody wants to say that God is, in some sense, extended because He is everywhere, I shall not object. But I deny that there is in God, in an Angel, in our soul, and in any substance that is not a body, a true extension."

nite, homogenous, absolute Euclidean space—*quasi* a sense organ of God (*sensorium Dei*), without which there could be no real forces in nature, without which therefore we could not say of God that he acts upon his creatures, nor that he intuits them, let alone that he is "everywhere" (*ubique*).[5]

These and similar positions are not occasional odd formulations, metaphors chosen at random, but rather systematic pronouncements. They cross the dividing lines between rationalists and empiricists, pantheists and deists, theosophic speculations and discursive reasoning. They form a genuine family of ideas which I shall call, for the sake of brevity, "the body of God." You may object that the term distorts the intentions of Spinoza and More, Newton and Raphson. "The body of God" smacks of anthropomorphic images, which all of them rejected emphatically. Spinoza did not say of God that he has *a* body; his God *is* body. Every idea corresponds to, or is the extension of, a material constellation: *ordo rerum idem est ordo et connexio idearum*.[6] The soul is but an ideational expression for a material constellation. The sum total of all bodies and their constellations (*facies totius universi*) is an infinite mode of God.[7] God, the *natura naturans*, is the idea of unity and coherence of all laws of nature.[8] More and Newton distinguished between corporeality, which God lacks if he is to penetrate all things, and dimensionality, which every entity *qua* entity must have. Spirits, according to More, are unlike bodies in that they are not impenetrable. Yet they are blessed with a fourth dimension—spissitude—which bodies lack.[9]

Yet these very distinctions prove that the absolute medieval commitment to an idea of God purged radically from all material connotations, however abstract and remote, was broken in the 17th century.

---

[5] I. Newton, *Optics or a treatise of the reflections, refractions, inflections and colours of light*, Query 28, 31 (London, 1730).

[6] Spinoza, *Ethica* II prop. 7 (ed. Gebhardt), p. 89. It should be noted that this correspondence theory accounts also for confused and indistinct ideas: inasmuch as they correspond to indistinct boundaries between bodily constellations. All single bodies are but a relative unity, inasmuch as their proporation of motion (m·v) remains constant. Rivaud, "La Physique de Spinoza," *Chronicon Spinozanum*, 4 (1924–1926), pp. 24–27.

[7] Spinoza, *Epistulae* (ed. Gebhardt, *Opera*, III), p. 120. The *facies totius universi* is the universe "seen as" one body.

[8] E.M. Curley, *Spinoza's Metaphysics: An Essay in Interpretation* (Cambridge, Mass., 1969), pp. 45–81, 119–58.

[9] Below, p. 172.

Medieval theology in most of its varieties viewed with intense suspicion any doctrine which took God's presence in the world too literally. So much was this true that not only physical predicates, but also general-abstract predicates such as goodness, truth, power and even existence were at times considered an illicit mode of speech when predicated of God and his creation univocally.

In the latter sense, nearly all important philosophical discussions on the nature of God sinned against the classical, medieval-thomistic tradition. Not only More or Spinoza was guilty: To all of them, including Descartes, Malebranche and Leibniz, God shared with his creation some genuine predicates literally and unequivocally. The body of God is only a special case of what may be named the transparency of God in the 17th century. Why, then, did God acquire a mundane reality in the 17th century, sometimes even a body of sorts? And why was it denied to him in the Middle Ages? Why was the medieval tradition broken in one way by Descartes, and in an almost opposite way by More?

A precise answer to these questions may sharpen our understanding of both theology and science in the 17th century. Partial aspects of our theme—notably the divine status of absolute space[10]—have often served to prove the influence of theology on science, or vice versa. By restoring the original context and complexity of the body of God we wish to prove more than the mere interaction between theology and science. At stake were the epistemic foundations of both, the very reasons why both constituted the same kind of safe *knowledge* in the cultural configuration of the 17th century

2. *The God of the Philosophers*

Whether with or without extension, the "God of the Philosophers" in the 17th century differed *toto coelo* from his medieval ancestor. Descartes, More, Newton and Leibniz share an image of the divine which is sometimes clothed in a scholastic terminology, yet always betrays the break with tradition. They learned to speak of God and

---

[10] Notably A. Koyré, *From the Closed World to the Infinite Universe* (Baltimore, 1957); cf. M. Jammor, *Concepts of Space: A History of Theories of Space in Physics* (Cambridge, Mass., 1954), pp. 26–32, 39–48; E. Grant, *Much Ado about Nothing, Theories of Space and Vacuum from the Middle Ages to the Scientific Revolution* (Cambridge, 1981), pp. 221–30.

all other entities *univoce*, *i.e.*, unequivocally. I do not necessarily mean that 17th century thinkers always claimed to know *more* about God than medieval theologians. To many of them God remained a *deus absconditus* of whom little can be known. What I mean to say is that they claimed what they knew about God, be it much or little, to be precise knowledge, "clear and distinct" ideas.

Why was the ontological proof of God's existence discarded in the Middle Ages, and why was it so widely acclaimed in the 17th century?[11] If successful, it proves God's existence from his very notion by demonstrating that an adequate notion of God excluded, by necessity, non-existence. All medieval theologians after Anselm denied that we possess a notion of God adequate enough to sustain the ontological proof. According to Thomas, God is indeed a *notum per se ipsum*—but only to himself, not to us.[12] Our knowledge of him is inevitably a-posteriori, from the consideration of his creation. Duns Scotus admitted the validity of the proof, but only hypothetically: *if* the notion of an *ens perfectissimum* could be proven to be free of contradictions—but it cannot—*then* God's existence would follow from his very definition.[13] Ockham even went so far as to relativize all other proofs for God's existence: They may prove, from the study of nature, that *a* God exists, but not necessarily one God, nor indeed the God of revelation.[14]

But Descartes, Spinoza, More, Cudworth and Leibniz revived the onto-theological argument because they believed in the capacity of the *lumen naturale* to form an adequate and precise, even if incomplete, notion of God. The historians of philosophy find interest in the revival of Anselm's proof because of the changes in the argument and

---

[11] On the rejection of the ontological proof in the Middle Ages and the causes for its revival in the 17th century, see D. Henrich, *Der ontologishce Gottesbeweis: Sein Problem und seine Geschichte in der Neuzeit* (Tübingen, 1960), pp. 1–22; Henrich's distinction between the forms of the ontological proof has been shown to be implicit in Anselm's *Proslogion*: N. Malcolm, "Anselm's Ontological Arguments," *The Philosophical Review*, 69 (1960), pp. 41–62.

[12] Thomas Aquinas, *Summa Theologiae* I q.2 a.1; *De veritate* q.10, a.12; *Contra Gentiles* I, 10–11; cf. O. Paschen, *Der ontologische Gottesbeweis in der Scholastik* (Auchen, 1903). Thomas distinguishes between *per se notum simpliciter*, which God is, and *per se notum quoad nos*, which God is not.

[13] Johannes Duns Scotus, *Opus Oxoniense* I d.2 q.2 nn.8; cf. P.L.M. Puech, "Duns Scotus et l'argument de saint Anselme," *Nos Cahiers* (1937), pp. 183–99.

[14] Ockham, *Quodlibeta* I q.1 (in P. Boehner, *Ockham, Philosophical Writings* [Edinburgh, 1957], p. 126): Neither the proposition "the unicity of God can be proven" nor its negation can be proven demonstratively.

because of the central role it played in ontology until, and even after, it was demolished by Kant. To the historian of ideas it offers a unique indication of a changed mentality. For lack of a better name, I shall refer to this change as the nominalistic revolution.

In part, this change originated among the staunchest opponents of the ontological proof during the later Middle Ages. Already Duns Scotus—much like Descartes—insisted that some divine attributes, such as existence or willing, have the same meaning whether applied to God, to man, or to lifeless objects.[15] Scotus reacted against the Thomistic doctrine of *anologia entis*,[16] according to which what we say about God and God's relation to the world is only by way of analogy to terms within nature or to their relation, and therefore always equivocal. The emphasis on unequivocal knowledge—*i.e.*, usage of terms—was even stronger among the so-called terminists or nominalists of the 14th century, notably Ockham. Our terms, they insisted, must be either denotative or connotative. The former name singular, discrete entities (subjects) and their absolute properties directly, the latter indirectly (*in obliquo*). Only the former can be said to exist, and do not need for their existence or for their immediate cognition (*notitia intuitiva*) the mediation of universals. Connotative terms, such as relations, are only valid to the measure in which they are coextensive with a set of singular entities: No two terms can both refer to the same group of objects and their absolute properties, *i.e.*, be coextensive, and yet have different meanings.[17] God, too, was a singular entity with real relations to the world.

Once the Thomistic theology of equivocation was abandoned, knowledge of god *sola ratione* had to be either very little, or include many aspects common to God and to other entities besides existence. The medieval nominalists chose the first position, the 17th century (in which nearly all philosophers were nominalists!) the second. God wills in the same way we do, according to Descartes, namely without bounds. Note that, for Descartes, infinity is a "clear and distinct" idea from which the notion of finitude is derived, rather than vice

---

[15] All *transcendentalia* are predicated univocally of God and His creation, whereby *unum, verum, bonum* are *passiones entis unicae*, others *disiunctae*: *Expos. in Metaphysicam* IV, summ. ii c.2 n.9.

[16] Below, pp. 163–4.

[17] E. Moody, *The Logic of William of Ockham* (New York, 1935), pp. 53 ff.; G. Martin, *Wilhelm von Ockham, Untersuchungen zur Ontologie der Ordnungen* (Berlin, 1947), pp. 221–27; Gordon Leff, *William of Ockham*.

versa.[18] God is extended in the same sense that other spirits or bodies are, according to More, except that God's extension is infinite and unchangeable. Leibniz, and his 18th century followers, went even further: Simple, univocal attributes never contradict each other, by definition. Every one of them is a perfection, and adds *reality* to the entity of which it is predicated.[19] Every real entity possesses *some* perfections, and God possesses them all. God, therefore, is the *summa realitatum*, the sum total of all realities and therefore the embodiment of a well defined entity (*omnimodo determinata*). He must therefore—this was their version of the ontological proof, and their answer to Scotus' objections—exist. It was this version of the ontological argument which Kant sought to demolish.[20] He showed that the *ens realissimum* is only a hypostatization, and even personification, of a necessary ideal of reason: namely the idea of unequivocal, complete determination of every thing. But this *durchgängige Bestimmung* is only a regulative ideal of reason, never a patterning precondition of all possible experience.

If, as we argued, what was said in the 17th century about God was said of God and the world unequivocally, then we ought to examine theology in terms of physics. Two forceful impulses determine the outlook of nature in early modern science. I shall call these impulses, in turn, the drive for unequivocation and the drive for homogeneity. The former seeks simplicity *a parte nominis*, the latter seeks simplicity *a parte rei*. Scientists since the 17th century wanted their scientific language to be unambiguous: Therefore, they desymbolized nature, or, in the words of Foucault,[21] exchanged similitudes for precise comparisons of "sameness and difference." No more did natural phenomena symbolize and reflect each other: Only language was to refer to things and to constellations of things in a system of artificial, unequivocal signs. On the other hand, scientists in the 17th century also

---

[18] *Oeuvres* III (ed. Adam and Tannery), p. 426: "Infinitum non a nobis intelligi per limitationis negationem." For other, similar as well as contradicting, references cf. E. Gilson, *Index Scholastico-Cartésien* (Paris, second ed., 1979), p. 143.

[19] A. Maier, *Kants Qualitätskategorien* (*Kant-Studien*, 65 [Berlin, 1930], pp. 10–23, 34–38), traces the history of the problem down to the Kantian separation of the category of "reality" (*Realität*) from that of existence (*Wirklichkeit*).

[20] I. Kant, *Kritik der reinen Vernunft* (*Gesammelte Schriften* [Berlin, 1911], pp. 680–84). Cf. My article "The persecution of Absolues: On the Kantian and Neokantian Theories of Science", *The Israel Colloquium for the Philosophy and History of Science* I, to appear soon.

[21] M. Foucault, *Les mots et les choses* (Paris, 1966), p. 67.

wanted nature to be in itself homogenous. The same laws of nature should apply to heaven and earth alike. No more should each region of the universe obey, as in Aristotle's physics, different mathematical models—such as the natural motion in straight lines in the sublunar realm, and the circular motion in the celestial region.

These two impulses—towards unequivocation and towards homogeneity—are separable logically as well as historically, *i.e.* in their origin. The main flaw in Foucault's ingenious thesis is the confusion between them. Aristotle's physics—which was, *mutatis mutandis*, also the physics of medieval schoolmen—was as unequivocal as any of the 17th or 18th century biologists quoted by Foucault. Comparison and definition (*per genus proximum et differentia specifia*), not similitude, described nature exhaustively and unequivocally. In order that the classification of entities in the universe be exhaustive and unequivocal, Aristotle commits himself to a grave, though seemingly innocuous, metaphysical assumption: namely, that no specific difference can ever appear in more than one genus. In other words, he knows *a priori* that there can never be a thinking stone or a piece of metal with social inclinations.[22] Nature, however, was not homogenous: Aristotle's universe was a hierarchy of *natures*. The Stoic universe, on the other hand, was homogenous, but it was also full of hidden meanings, of similitudes, in that each being reflected all others. Never, *e.g.*, have magic and astrology been given a better theoretical foundation than in the Stoic doctrine of universal sympathy. The Scholastic universe was Aristotelian; the cosmos of the Renaissance philosophies of nature was rather Stoic. I intend first to trace briefly the fortunes of both impulses, towards unequivocalization and towards homogeneity, since antiquity, and to do so at the example of the problem we started with—the body of God.

3. *A Short History of God's Corporeality*

Why did medieval Christian theology abhor all corporeal predicates of God? The answers which come immediately to mind are imprecise and insufficient. It is true that the Church inherited from Judaism the

---

[22] Aristotle, *Topica* VI,6; cf. S. Nacht-Eladi, "Aristotle's Doctrine of the Differentia Specifica and Maimon's Law of Determinability," *Iyyun, A Hebrew Philosophical Quarterly*, 4 (1953), pp. 203–18; C. Prantl, *Geschichte der Logik im Abendlande*, reprint Graz 1955 I p. 232–36.

fear of idolatry, and of anthropomorphic images. Paganism was not only a historical reminiscence in the Middle Ages: It lived subterraneously in the country-side. It is also true that, from Jewish and Hellenistic soteriological religions, the Church inherited the contraposition of sinful flesh to the pure spirit. Christianity defined itself as "Israel in the spirit." Yet neither of these impulses had to be lost by necessity if God were to have a body. Patristic theology, much as 17th century philosophy, was aware of a variety of Greek philosophical interpretations of God's body which stripped it of any definite shape (μορφή) but left a material substance (φυσις) only, a substance more refined than any ordinary body and therefore befitting spirits. Why were all of them eventually rejected?

Lest we be accused of musing about abstract possibilities, consider, e.g., Tertullian's defense of God's body: "Nothing is, unless it is a body. Whatever is, is a body of sorts. Nothing is incorporeal, unless that which is not."[23] The language reminds us of Hobbes or, more to the point, of the atomists. "Who can deny that God is body, even though he is spirit? Spirit is also a body of its own kind."[24] Tertullian evidently opposes the extreme pneumatization of Christology among the Alexandrian exegetes. The abrogation of a body to God may lead to the denial of his affections—anger, compassion, justice—without which God would not be able to communicate with men. "I state: God could not enter the walks of man, unless he assumed human senses and affections."[25] In order to accommodate himself to the *mediocritas humana*, he must appear human; God lowers himself to the human level so as to raise man to his level (*adequatio*).[26] But, in order that incarnation be possible, God must possess, it seems, some physical properties to begin with: a most subtle body. Why did Tertullian's defense of the corporeality of the spirit—so close, in fact, to the etymology and image of the word spirit both

---

[23] Tertullian, *De anima* 7: "Nihil enim, si non corpus. Omne quod est, corpus est sui generis: nihil est incorporale, nisi quod non est." This is a Stoic maxim; cf. E. Zeller, *Die Philosophie der Griechen*, III,1 (Leipzig, fourth ed., 1909, Darmstadt, 1963), pp. 119 f.; J.M. Rist, *Stoic Philosophy* (Cambridge, 1969), pp. 153 ff.

[24] Tertullian, *Adversus Praxen* 7: "Quis enim negaverit, deum corpus esse, etsi deus spiritus est? spiritus enim corpus sui generis in sua effigie." The soul, too, is material (*De anima* 6).

[25] Tertullian, *Adversus Marcionem* 11,27,1 (CCSL 1, 505).

[26] Ibid. (CCSL 1, 507); A. Funkenstein, *Heilsplan und natürliche Entwicklung. Formen des Gegenwartsbestimmung im Geschichtsdenken des Mittelalters* (Munich, 1965), pp. 25–27.

in the Bible (רוח, נשמה) and in Greek (πνεῦμα)—why did it not strike more roots in Christian theology?

Let us review the alternatives—the main Greek models for defending the divine corporeality after the devastating critique of anthropomorphic images by Xenophanes. Both models, the Stoic and the Epicurean, influenced Tertullian and influenced again the 17th century defenses of God's body.

At the center of Stoic thought, be it logics, ethics, or physics, stands the endeavor to explain what a context, *i.e.*, a contextual unity, is: how the whole is formed by its parts yet transforms its parts. The relation between parts and the whole has replaced the constitutive role which, in the Aristotelian and Platonic systems, was occupied by the relation of the *general* to *the particular* (Dilthey).[27] Like the universe of Aristotle, the cosmos of the Stoics was a finite material continuum.[28] But unlike the Aristotelian universe, theirs was not structured by a hierarchy of forms, such that a chain of specific differences and proximate genera could give an exhaustive description of the world if we assume that a specific difference never appears in more than one genus. Qualities are, in the Stoic interpretation, not fixed forms but rather active *forces*.[29] Forces account both for the variety and for the unity of the cosmos. The cosmos (again in contrast with Aristotle) is embedded in boundless space. Forces account for the contextual unity of each body, because each discrete continuum of matter is held together by the "tension" (τόνος) of its interdependent parts.[30]

All forces are instantiations of *one* force, the whole universe is a quasi animated, organic whole. The force which permeates and unifies all is both divine and material: the Pneuma (The very choice of πνευμα over νοῦς indicates their materialistic bend.). It is God, because it governs the world planfully and holds it together by invisible bonds of sympathy. It is matter, because a principle of integration is inseparable from that which it integrates; it permeates matter through

---

[27] W. Dilthey, *Weltanschauung und Analyse des Menschen seit Renaissance und Reformation, Gesammelte Schriften*, 2 (Stuttgart-Göttingen, seventh ed., 1964), p. 316.

[28] M. Pohlenz, *Die Stoa*, I (Göttingen, second ed., 1959), p. 76; II, p. 43 (The Stoic distinction between ὅλον and Παν: Only the later is infinite). S. Sambursky, *Das physikalische Weltbild der Antike* (Zurich, 1965), pp. 337 f.

[29] Plutarch, *De Stoicorum repugnantiis*, in H. von Arnim, *Stoicorum Veterum Fragmenta*, II 1053F–1054A (Leipzig, 1921); Pohlenz I, p. 71; Sambursky, p. 189.

[30] Sambursky, pp. 187 ff.; Pohlenz I, p.76; II, p. 43.

and through and must therefore be itself matter—active matter, subtle enough to permeate all things. Indeed, two bodies—the pneuma *qua* mater and the body it inspires—can occupy the same place and be fused into a continuum.[31] The early Stoa identified the Pneuma with fire and air.[32] The whole universe is, in a manner of speech, God's body, in which each part reflects and signifies the whole. The Stoic universe is full of hidden meanings.

In their own way, the Stoics systematized one of the oldest impulses of Greek philosophy since the Ionian φύσικοι—to show that the world is "full of gods,"[33] to deify nature by depersonalizing the gods. The course of early Greek religion may well have been the opposite.[34] Against the deification of nature, the Atomists—especially since Epicurus—were even willing to defend anthropomorphic images such as the human shape and habits of the gods. The later Atomists defended anthropomorphism in order to empty the world from the presence or indeed the governance of the gods, and in order to emancipate man from fear of them.[35]

Atomism, we remember, was a universal heuristic principle which permits no exceptions. Not only the world around us, as seen or otherwise perceived, is composed of atoms and clusters of atoms. No entity can be thought of except atoms and space. The earliest developed their doctrine in a dialectical reference to the one and only "Being" of Parmenides. Their atoms were miniature versions of his undifferen-

---

[31] Alexander of Aphrodisias, *De mixto* 216:14 (ed. I. Bruns, *Scripta minora* [Berlin, 1887]); Sambursky, p. 198; Pohlenz I, p. 72; II, pp. 41–42; cf. Plotinus, *Enneads* II,7.

[32] The closest Presocratic predecessor was perhaps the doctrine of Diogenes of Apollonia; on him and his theology, W. Jaeger, *Die Theologie der frühen griechischen Denker* (Stuttgart, 1953), pp. 188–95; G. Murray, *Five Stages of Greek Religion* (Garden City, N.Y., third ed., 1955), pp. 87–88.

[33] Kirk-Raven, pp. 93–97; F.M. Cornford, *From Religion to Philosophy* (New York, 1957), pp. 134–36 (Physis as the Divine).

[34] Murray, pp. 8–37, esp. 25 ff.

[35] That Epicurus included in his attack against the traditional gods also the astral gods and the world-soul of the philosophers (Plato, Aristotle, the Stoics) has been shown by A.J. Festugière, *Epicurus and His Gods* (English trans., Oxford, 1952), esp. pp. 73 ff. In this context we ought to see the atomist argument, the only one in antiquity known to me against the sphere as the most perfect figure and, hence, the form befitting divine and besouled entities: "Admirabor eorum tarditatem qui animantem immortalem et eundem beatum rotundum esse velint, quod ea forma neget ullam esse pulchriorem Plato: at mihi vel cylindri vel quadrati vel coni vel pyramidis videtur esse formosior" (Cicero, *De natura deorum* 1.10.24 (Vellius) (ed. Plasberg, Stuttgart, 1959). Cf. below, n. 41.

tiated, indestructible, unchangeable, one being; except that, contrary to Parmenides, the atoms were many and of different shapes so as to account for differentiation and motion, and they had therefore to be embedded in space, in a "non-being endowed with a kind of being."[36] The soul, too, cannot be thought of except as atoms of a more rarified, refined matter, which enables them to move very quickly everywhere in the body. As for the gods, Democritus at times tends to identify them with their image in vision or dreams.[37] Epicurus postulates real, existing gods who emit, or radiate, a continuous effluence which impresses itself upon our (likewise material) spirit because our spirit is materially akin to their picture (εἴδολον, *simulacrum*). It follows, at least according to Epicurus, that the gods are exactly what they appear to be in visions and dreams: human-shaped. Yet their body is composed of atoms so fine that they can never interact with grosser bodies or ordinary worlds. The abode of the gods, physically as well as methodologically, is therefore the *intermundia*—the spaces between the infinitely many, more solid universe like ours. There the gods lead a suisufficient, happy and eternal life, a paradigm for us to emulate and adore. Not only do they have a shape and a body: It is a human-shaped body, for no shape is nobler or more beautiful; and they must even feed it, although their kitchen is better than the best of ours.[38] The gods must, then, be many, suisufficient, inactive, and withdrawn totally from our world if the universe is to be conceived as devoid of any τέλος or plan, so that human freedom and dignity are preserved.[39]

It is evident why Epicurus' theology could never be modified to suit Christian needs. "Epicurean" is a synonymous word for those who deny God's providence. That they do so by ascribing a human shape to God adds insult to injury. Why was the theology of the Stoa rejected by Christian theologians? It had much to recommend itself to

---

[36] Dielz-Kranz, *Fragmente der Vorsokratiker* 67A6 = Aristotle, *Metaphysica* A4, 985b4. Cf. G.W.F. Hegel, *Vorlesungen über die Geschichte der Philosophie* (ed. E. Moldennauer and U.M. Michael, *Werke* 18 [Frankfurt, 1971], p. 355): "Was in Wahrheit bei den Eleaten vorhanden war, spricht Leukipp als seiend aus."

[37] E. Zeller, *Die Philosophie der Griechen in Ihren geschichtlichen Entwicklung*, repr. Darmstadt 1963 I,2 p. 1157–64; U.K.C. Guthrie, A History of Greek Philosophy, Cambridge 1965 pp. 478–83.

[38] Ibid. III, 1 pp. 441–52.

[39] For a general discussion of the emancipatory aims of Epicurean theology, cf. C. Bayley, *The Greek Atomists and Epicurus* (Oxford, 1928), p. 83; L. Strauss, *Spinoza's Critique of Religion*, New York 1965 pp. 37–52.

Christianity: The Stoic universe is much more teleological, guided by providence, than Aristotle's. In fact, through Philo's Logos and other channels the Stoa did exert some influence on Christian thought.[40] More undoubtedly revived many elements of Stoic theology. But why were the Stoics, unlike Plato, never called "ours" by Christians, never seen—as Plato was—as a "preparation of Christ" (παιδαγογος εἰς Χρἰστον)? The first answer is because their gods and God expressed a naked, immediate deification of nature. The deification of nature was seen as the real essence of paganism by both Christians and Jews. They viewed the difference between crude anthropomorphism and the identification of the gods with natural forces—or even one force—as a difference of degree only. Indeed, Aristotle admits that much,[41] and so did the philosophical allegorisis of myth in which the Stoics excelled. But there is a deeper reason yet. There is one instance in which Christian religion assumed something very close to a divine body, the body of Christ. It is a heavenly body, yet a body—not unlike the body of Epicurus' gods. The Middle Ages came, after painful controversy, to the decision that Christ's body is really present in every piece of the Eucharist.[42] The doctrine of real presence, of transubstantiation, sometimes used the Averroistic distinction between determinate and indeterminate extension: The latter is the subject in which the accidents of bread and wine inhere after transubstantiation. This very distinction was resumed by More and Newton to explain the distinction between dimensions, which God lacks, and extension, which he must possess.[43]

Admitting the physical, equal, homogenous presence of God everywhere—with or without a material substrate—amounted to a relativization of Christology (God would be in each of us equally) and would make the sacraments and the hierarchical Church superfluous. Again, I do not speculate upon merely theoretical possibilities. The nascent University of Paris was intoxicated with a sense of intellectual freedom just gained. It seemed to the new European intelligentsia as if all ideas might be tried on for size—at least if investigated without dogmatic claims, *disputandi more, non asserendi more*. Amalrich of

---

[40] H. Wolfson, *Philo*, Cambridge/Mass ª1948 passim, esp. II, 439 ff.

[41] *Met.* A 8, 1074/b1; cf. F.M. Cornford, *From Religion to Philosophy*. Repr. New York 1957.

[42] J. Pelican, *The Christian Tradition: A History of the Development of Doctrine* III, Chicago-London 1978 pp. 184–204.

[43] Cf. Jammer, *Das Problem des Lammes*, Darmstadt 1960.

Bene—following, perhaps, the pantheistic cues of Johannes Scotus Erigena—maintained that God is the *forma mundi*, the true essence of all things. This could still be given an innocuous, even Aristotelian interpretation; but look at the consequences. Amalrich and the Amalricans denied the merit of any positive religion. God is in all of us, and only those who know it are better off. Only true philosophy saves, and it saves Jews, Christians and Moslems alike. "What is more absurd," says their opponent, "than that God is stone in a stone, Godinus in Godinus, that Godinus should be worshipped—not only adored—because he is God. Until now we believed in the incarnated Son of God: now they preach the ingodinated Christ."[44] (Godinus was a popular Amalrican preacher.)

Amalrich's contemporary, David of Dinant, maintained even that God is the *materia-mundi*—the very stuff underlying all substances, spiritual as well as material.[45] The details of these doctrines are hard to discern, and their exact driving forces remain obscure because of their persecution and intended obliteration. But both Amalrich and David evidently belonged to those who were led by their pantheism to believe "*quod sermones theologi fundati sunt in fabulis.*"[46]

How close pantheism, anti-hierarchical leanings and pagan leanings really were even in the countryside we learn from a few rare outbursts. A case in point is the vulgar pantheism of a half-literate village miller in the 15th century, recently discovered in Venetian inquisitorial acts.[47] The man went around preaching, with a missionary zeal, that the Church, its hierarchy and doctrines are a self-serving fraud. We all are God in the same measure; the universe is one huge piece of cheese, spirits and angels the worms in it. Salvation can come through this knowledge only. Against such latent paganism throughout medieval Europe, it was prudent to abstain from any creative interpretation of God's shape or body.

---

[44] *Contra Amaurianus* XXIV,5–6 (most possibly by Garnerius of Rochefort, ed. Clemens Baeumker, *Beiträge zur Geschichte der Philosophie des Mittelalters* [Münster, 1926], p. 24).

[45] F. Überweg and B. Geyer, *Grundweiss der Geschichte der Philosophie*, II (Basel-Stuttgart, 1960), p. 251.

[46] H. Denifle et E. Chatelain, *Cnartularium Universitatis Parisiensis*, Paris 1889–1897 I, 552 (no. 152).

[47] Carlo Ginzburg, *The Cheese and the Worms: The Cosmos of a Sixteenth Century Miller* (Baltimore, 1980), pp. 4–5, 52–71, 102–08. The history of popular pantheism is still, to a wide extent, uncharted land. The history of philosophical pantheism was summed up by W. Dilthey, ibid.

True, the deification of nature was seen as the quintessence of paganism. Yet God's presence in the world—his ubiquity—was a most fundamental part of Christian theology. Referring to God as the creator and governor of the world—as efficient cause—did not suffice to satisfy the sense of his presence. It could be taken neither too literally nor too allegorically. Patristic and medieval theology was inevitably led towards an interpretation of the world as a sign, symbol, picture of God: A true symbol, in the words of Durkheim, manifests a *participation mystique* with that of which it is a symbol; it is both one with it and different from it: it is much more than a linguistic metaphor. Nature reveals God's *symbolic* presence.

> omnis mundi creatura
> quasi liber et scriptura
> nobis est et speculum.[48]

Nature was seen as a system of symbols, of signatures of God; and so was history. Events, persons and institutions of the Old Testament were prefigurations of the New Testament; Cain and Abel were prefigurations of the Synagogue and the Church, as were Leah and Rachel; Adam was a prefiguration of Christ, the second Adam. Deciphering these hints of the Old Testament to the veracity of the New Testament over and beyond the *sensus historicus vel literalis* was the task and duty of the *spiritualis intelligentia*.[49] Nature and history were the mirror of the divine—not only through his acts in and on them, but also through his symbolical presence.

Sound theology had to put some strictures to the symbolizing propensity. If nature is to signify God's presence, then not in equal measure and degree, for otherwise—in the words of Bayle's later critique of Spinoza—God in the form of Turks would be fighting against God in the form of Christians. Medieval Scholasticism sought after

---

[48] Alanus ab Insulis, PL 210, 579A; on the history of the commonplace "book of nature," see E.R. Curtius, *Europäische Literatur und lateinisches Mittelalter* (Bern, 1948), pp. 323–29; Hans Blumenberg, *Die Lesbarkeit der Welt* (Frankfurt am Main, 1981), pp. 47 ff., esp. p. 51.

[49] On the history of the method cf. H. Grundmann, *Studien über Joachim von Floris* (Leipzig, 1927), p. 37; E. Auerbach, "Figura," in *Scenes from the Drama of European Literature* (New York, 1959), pp. 11–56; A. Dempf, *Sacrum Imperium* (Munich, second ed., 1949), pp. 229–68. On the influence of the eminently Christian mode of exegesis on Jewish medieval exegesis, cf. A. Funkenstein, "Nachmanides' Symbolical Reading of History," in *Studies in Jewish Mysticism*, ed. J. Dan and F. Talmage (Cambridge, Mass., 1981), pp. 129–50.

a balanced, restricted expression for the symbolic sense of nature and history. Thomas Aquinas offered such a balanced theory with his doctrine of *analogia entis*.

If as we claimed, Aristotle's natural science was unequivocal, how could it serve, as it did, the Thomistic doctrine of analogy, which interprets divine names as equivocal? It is because of the balance it maintains between absolute equivocation and univocation; because it did as much to curb, to restrict the sense of God's symbolic presence as it did to promote it. At the heart of the doctrine lies the distinction between *significatio* and *representatio*, meaning and similitude.[50] Words, as was known since Aristotle, name objects, but acquire their *meaning* through the mediation of concepts. A concept (and therefore the word declaring it) *represents* the object of which it is a concept by virtue of its resemblance (*similitudo*) to it. Resemblance need not mean texture or shape; it consists of a one-to-one correspondence of elements in the picture and the depicted—and may well be a similarity of proportion only (αναλογια in the original, mathematical sense). To use a modern example, if a computer transmits, or remembers, my face by indexing every milimeter of it with a unique sequential number, then the proper sequence of numbers in the memory of the computer is as much my "picture" as the final photography. In this way, concepts are also pictures and can be said to represent objects. Now since pictures do not always address the same elements in that which they depict, a picture of a picture of an object need not also be a true picture of the original object: The relation of similitude can, but need not be, transitive. In the case of divine names, similitude is indeed intransitive. Concepts, Thomas maintains, represent objects by way of defining them; concepts resemble their objects. Objects may also resemble objects. Every entity, inasmuch as it possesses a perfection, resembles God—albeit incompletely.[51] The world is an *imago dei*.

---

[50] Thomas Aquinas, *Summa Theologica* I q.13 a.1; ibid., a.2: "*Significant* enim sic nomina Deum, secundum quod intellectus noster cognoscit ipsum. Intellectus autem noster, cum cognoscat Deum ex creaturis, sic cognoscit ipsum, secundum quod creaturae ipsum *repraesentant*." On the Thomistic doctrine of analogy, the book of H. Lyttkens, *The Analogy between God and the World* (Upsala, 1953) is still indispensable. Of the fourfold employment of analogy, we are interested in the first sense: the analogy of proportionality—which is also the original sense of ἀναλογία. The construct of a "picture of a picture" is my interpretative device, not Thomas'.

[51] Ibid I q.13 a.5; cf. I q.4 a.3: "licet aliquo modo concedatur quod creatura sit similis Deo, nullo tamen modo concedendum est quod Deus sit similis creaturae." On other aspects of the *imago dei* doctrine, cf. B.J. Lonergan, *Verbum, Word and Idea*

Because this is so, I can say of God that he is "powerful." The concept of power involved in such predication is gained from a powerful mundane being, say a lion or a king or the wind. Because the power of a lion is but an incomplete reflection of its cause and paradigm, namely God's power, my divine predicate is, as it were, a picture of a picture; it signifies a substantive quality of God without being able to represent it. Analogy in this matter is neither univocal nor utterly equivocal: It is an exercise in critical, restrained equivocation, in which we must always be careful to distinguish between the unequivocal primary signification of a term and the derivative, analogical usage. Terms by which we describe nature have a direct, unequivocal meaning; only as an additional dimension, clearly separable from the first, can such a term refer to God by virtue of the fact that things themselves are vestiges, images, of God in much more than a merely causal sense.[52]

The same considerations apply to God's (or Christ's) symbolic vestiges in history, those systems of prefigurations I mentioned before. The distinction between *significatio* and *representatio* is also at the heart of Thomas' exegetical doctrine. In contrast to a long preceding tradition, Thomas emphasizes that the Scriptures (i.e., the language in them) must be understood on a plain, literal level only, and that they do not have any additional meaning. The things, events, or persons which the Scriptures talk about, and they only, have a symbolic meaning, a *sensus spiritualis*.[53] Neither our discourse concerning nature nor that concerning history ought to be equivocal. The hidden significance of things (*res*) can and must be separated from the immediate meaning of words (*voces*). Theology and physics can and must be separated.

---

in Aquinas (Notre Dame, 1967), pp. 183 ff., esp. pp. 212–15.

[52] Ibid., I q.13 a.2.

[53] Ibid., I q.1 a.10: "auctor sacrae scripturae est Deus, in cuius potestate est ut non solum voces ad significandum accommodet (quod etiam homo facere potest) sed etiam res ipsas ... illa autem prima significatio, qua voces significant res, pertinet at primum sensium, qui est sensus historicus vel litteralis. Illa vero significatio qua res significatae per voces iterum res alias significant, dicitur sensus spiritualis qui super litteralum fundatur et eum supponit." Cf. H. de Lubac, *Exégèse médiévale*, II,2 (Lyon, 1964), pp. 272 ff., 285 ff. This expressed the renewed interest in the *veritas Hebraica*. For a formulation similar to Thomas' cf. Alexander of Hales, *Summa Theologiae*, pars II inq.3 tr.2 sec.39 (vol. IV [Quarrachi, 1948], pp. 760 ff). The link between Thomas' exegetical theory and the doctrine of analogy has, as far as I know, not been discussed in the literature.

The Nominalists of the 14th century objected to any equivocation, whether restrained or not. They aimed, as we said, at an absolute trans-parency of any scientific language. Theirs was a program of semantic reduction (that is, simplification) of the world-view in the name of both logics and theology.[54] In a world of independent entities, each of which could exist *toto mundo destructo*, connotative terms, such as terms for relations or aspects, never refer to anything real beyond the entities involved in them; and if two of them are coextensive and exclusive, one would be redundant. Take, *e.g.*, the impetus-theory of later medieval physics. It answers the question why a projectile continues to move *cessante movente*, such as a stone when I throw it. This seems to contradict the Aristotelian axiom that everything which moves moves by another, contiguous mover. Rather than, as Aristotle thought, the air surrounding it, the impetus-theoretician assumed a force which passes from the moving to the moved body. Ockham rejects all answers hitherto given.[55] The question, he argues, is a non-question: It rests on a semantic confusion. It looks for two causes—the cause for motion and the cause for the continuation of motion. But the term motion, a connotative term, does not refer to anything real in and of itself. It refers to a body and to a sequence of places (*ubi*) which the body passes. "Motion" and "continuation of motion" are one and the same notion; one cause suffices: If a body moves, it continues to move *ipso facto*.

Indeed, the terminists could not but object to any attempt to see god symbolized in nature, because nature was, in their eyes, so utterly contingent upon God's will. The entities in the universe, their *ordo ad invicem*, were changeable at any time; the order of salvation was not necessary—let alone the Aristotelian cosmos (which the nominalists never challenged *de facto*). Had God wanted it so he could, *de potentia eius absoluta*, place the whole universe in the (not logically impossible) infinite space and let it move rectilinearly and indefinitely; or he could have created many universes in Space exactly like ours; or could even, rather than sending his son to save us, have saved humanity through a stone or a donkey—*aut lapis, aut asinus*.[56] Of the

---

[54] Above, n. 17.
[55] William of Ockham, *Sententiae* 2,26 (Lyon, 1495 = Boehner, *Ockham's Philosophical Writings*, pp. 139–41; A. Funkenstein, "Some Remarks on the Concept of Impetus and the Determination of Simple Motion," *Viator*, 2 (1971), pp. 329–48, esp. pp. 337–40.
[56] William of Ockham, *Centiloquium Theologicum* conc. 6; A. Funkenstein, "The

many logically possible universes, ours is neither the best nor otherwise of a particular, discernable, aim or significance so as to represent God's image. The nominalists had to reject the doctrine of analogy because they desymbolized nature.

The universe of the Terminists was unequivocal to the extreme. But was it also homogenous? On the contrary: For one thing, most of them accepted Aristotelian physics as a matter of fact, only to add that it is not logically necessary. Moreover, their universe was split into as many orders as there are entities, each of which can exist without the others: "*omnis res absoluta, distincta loco et subjecto ab alia re absoluta, potest existere alia re absoluta destructa*"[57] (or even, *toto mundo destructo*). Against the conceptual reduction of our language about nature attempted by the Terminists there stands the speculative reduction of nature itself by Renaissance philosophers of nature. Telesio, Cardano, Campanella or Bruno did not share the Terminists' obsession with precision of language. Their philosophy, so they believed, was not the scholastic preoccupation with words and definitions,[58] but a *philosophia realis*, a turning to nature itself. What most of them really turned to, or returned to, was the universe of the Stoa.

We shall limit our discussion of Renaissance philosophies of nature to one example—to Bernardino Telesio.[59] His system is, in many ways, a *tertium comparationis* between the Stoic universe and the universe of Henry More. Like the Stoics, he wished to replace the Platonic or Aristotelian "forms" (*i.e.*, essences) with real *forces*—all of which are reducible to attraction and repulsion, or to head and

---

Dialectial Preparation for Scientific Revolutions," *The Copernican Achievement*, ed. R. Westman (Los Angeles, 1975), pp. 178–87, 194–95.

[57] William of Ockham, *Quodlibeta* IV, p. 6 (Boehner, *Ockham's Philosophical Writings*, p. 26); *Sent.* prol. q.1 HH; E. Hochstetter, *Studien zur Metaphysik und erkenntnislehre Wilhelms von Ockham* (Berlin, 1927), pp. 56–57.

[58] Pierre Gassendi, *Exercitationes Paradoxicae adversus Aristoteleos* I,14 (ed. B. Rochot [Paris, 1959], pp. 45 f.): "Postremo, ut coarguantur verba magis curare, quam sensus, efficere ut cum Seneca exclamare merito liceat 'nostra quae erat Philosophia facta Philologia est, ex quo disputare docemus, non vivere."

[59] Bernardino Telesio, *De verum natura juxta propria principia, Tractationum philosophicarum* I (1586). On him, see E. Cassirer, *Das Erkenntnisproblem in der Philosophie und Wissenschaft der Neueren Zeit* I (1922, repr. Darmstadt, 1974, pp. 232–40). A similar link between sensualism, materialism and dynamism characterizes most Italian new philosophies of nature: Cardanus, Campanella, Bruno. Bacon, we are reminded by J.H. Randall, called him *primus novorum virorum*—first of the moderns; *The Career of Philosophy*, I (New York, 1962), p. 202.

coldness (as had Empedocles at one time). These forces operate on one homogenous, actual yet passive matter; the actuality of matter was already stressed by the nominalists. Each body represents a balance of these forces and seeks to preserve that balance: Each body possesses an instinct of self-preservation.[60] The center of heat is the sun, the center of cold the earth; but the harmony in the universe is the outcome not of one pre-established goal, but the outcome of each animated body—indeed, all bodies are animated by force—acting in its own self-interest. This is one of the earliest occurrences of an anti-teleological, political, ethical, as well as natural, principle of the "invisible hand of nature."[61] The soul is only a finer, more subtle matter than the rest of the body; hence epistemology could be reduced to a sensualistic account, eliminating the *species intelligibiles* of the schools. And, since matter is not mere potentiality, time and place must be distinguished from it as absolute receptacles. The war between the Aristotelian adherents of form and the new adherents of force was fought in Italian universities in the generation before Galileo, and at times with bare fists.

The animated universe of the Renaissance was homogenous in the sense that the absolute distinction between coelestial and terrestrial matter was eliminated, and the number of elements reduced to two or less. It was also a universe which, like its Stoic ancestor, was much more ambiguous than the Aristotelian-scholastic. The very notion of a "force" in Telesio's system expresses little more than the affinity of like bodies to each other, their "similitude;" in a universe which is held by bonds of sympathy, every thing becomes a "sign" of others and the world is full of hidden connections. How much easier such a universe became susceptible to pantheistic reading we see not only in Ficino or Bruno, but even in the thought of Cusanus: The world is an explication, a self-expression of God—God contracted himself into the world[62] ("contraction" is a term he probably borrowed from

---

[60] Telesio, *De rerum natura* IV, xxiv, p. 728; cf. also H. Höffding, *History of Modern Philosophy*, Repr. New York 1950 pp. 92–102.

[61] On its early history in modern social thought cf. W. Euchner, *Egoismus und Gemeinwohl. Studien zur Geschichte der bürgerlichen Philosophie* (Frankfurt am Main, 1973), pp. 74–76, 104–15; on its medieval roots and predecessors cf. A. Funkenstein, "Periodization and Self-Understanding in the Middle Ages and Early Modern Times," *Medievalia et Humanistica*, V (1974), pp. 3–23, esp. pp. 13–14.

[62] Nicolaus Cusanus, *De docta ignorantia* II,4, ed. P. Wilpest, *Nikolaus von Kues Werke*, Berlin 1967 I pp. 44–46.

Scotists, who viewed the individual form as a "contractio" of all other forms inhering in a subject). God, it seems, began to regain his body.

Did the Protestant Reformation help God to regain a body? We argued earlier that Christian fears of pantheism derived not only from fears of the deification of nature, but, in a more specific way, from the fear of diluting the meaning of God's (and Christ's) particular, real presence as managed by the priestly hierarchy. Protestant theology lost that fear: It abandoned, to various degrees, the Catholic doctrine of sacraments with its reification of the presence of God at particular times and places. Protestantism had much less to fear of pantheistic or panentheistic doctrines: Indeed they occur more often. Jacob Boehme's thought may have been richer or deeper than the vulgar pantheism of the poor village miller Menocchio mentioned before. But the main difference between them was that Boehme was not burned at the stake. On the other hand, Protestant theology also encouraged, at least on the level of exegesis, unequivocation: It called for a return to the *sola scriptura*. Socinianism went even as far as renouncing the trinitarian doctrine because it was at best an equivocal metaphor, and certainly not derivable from the Scriptures *literaliter*.

It seems to me that only in the 17th century did both trends converge into one world picture: namely, the nominalists' passion for unequivocation with the Renaissance sense of the homogeneity of nature, the sense of *one* nature to replace the many Aristotelian *natures*. Protestant theology may have acted as a catalyst to the fusion. Both trends may seem, in retrospect, to be two sides of one coin, as two complementary aspects of one principle of economy—the economy of thought and the economy of nature. Yet, historically they evolved almost antithetically. Once both ideals converged, the vision of a unified science could and did emerge, a *mathesis universalis* in which theological arguments are also physical arguments and vice versa.

4. *Descartes and More*

The universe which became, in the 17th century, both unequivocal and homogenous inspired a fusion between theology and physics to an extent unknown earlier and later. Theological and physical arguments became nearly indistinguishable. This circumstance brought with it advantages as well as disadvantages to both theology and physics. Some of the most pressing theological problems of the Middle Ages dissipated with the commitment to new physical systems, as, *e.g.*, how to translate the immortality of the soul or *creatio ex nihilo* into Peripatetic terms. The eternity of the world and the conception of the soul as the organizational principle of the body were an integral part of Aristotle's physics and psychology, yet were unacceptable theologically. Early modern physics could easily sustain a genuine cosmogony and eschatology, *i.e.*, a conception of the universe as coming to be and about to pass away at the end of days. In exchange, however, for problems solved, the 17th century faced new problems which grew precisely out of the need to invest certain theologumena with a precise physical meaning. Descartes' physics is a case in point.

Descartes' vision of a homogenous material universe governed always and everywhere by the same unequivocal, *i.e.*, mathematical, laws held in its spell even those thinkers who recognized its flaws. The flaws in the system are innumerable; they result mostly from the very same circumstance responsible for its fascination. In his eagerness to mathematize physics through and through, Descartes recognized only one indispensable attribute of matter, namely extension. Bodies are nothing but extended things (*res extensae*).[63] Thus there could be no different meaning to space and matter: The material world is one infinite continuum, and in fact all of matter is one substance. Motion means nothing else than that a body changes from the vicinity of some bodies to the vicinity of others; it is a relative concept altogether.[64] How, then, can Descartes assume the conservation of the quantity of motion whenever two bodies collide, let alone the conservation of a fixed quantity of motion throughout the universe? How can motion be both relative and an absolute universal constant?

Furthermore, Descartes' famous rules of motion seem to assume the impenetrability of colliding bodies.[65] Now, motion of bodies in Euclidian geometry—say, in proofs of congruency—always assumes that bodies pass through each other (lines, areas) or coincide with each other. Impenetrability can certainly *not* be derived from the geometrical characteristics of bodies as extended things. Moreover, the assumption of solid bodies speeding towards each other with no ob-

---

[63] Above, n. 2.
[64] *Principia Philosophiae* II,25 (Adam-Tannery, *Oeuvres*, VIII,1, p. 53): "dicere possumus [motus] esse translationem unius partis materiae sive unius corporis ex vicinia eorum corporum, quae illud immediate contingunt et tanquam quiescentia spectantur, in viciniam aliorum."
[65] Ibid. II,37–53 (pp. 62–71).

stacle between them contradicts the image of matter as a continuum. For the very same reason, Descartes' two laws of inertia are also counterfactual conditional: No body is separable from other bodies so that it can move uniformly and rectilinearly; wherefore Descartes speaks only of the "tendency" of bodies to so move "inasmuch as they can"—if "considered by themselves."[66] Indeed, the only sensible way to interpret Descartes' laws and rules of motion, including the postulate of impenetrability, is by taking them as counterfactual conditionals which function as limiting cases. Descartes' physics is altogether hypothetical—and so, by his own admission, is his cosmology: *if* we assume that God imparted a constant quantity of motion to the universe and then left it to its own devices, *then* matter will form a vortex from which a system of planets will emerge such as ours.[67] To make things worse, God is not even needed; all we need is the quantity of motion—even from eternity. Newton's outcry, "hypothesis non fingo," may be directed not only to a particular theorem within Descartes' physics; it pertains to all of it.

Moreover, Descartes' physics seems to eliminate real forces from nature. If motion and direction are sufficient to determine force, and motion is transferred from body to body according to conservation laws, then there is no significance to Galileo's discovery that acceleration rather than motion is caused by a particular force, namely gravity.[68] It is ironical that Descartes, who first formulated the inertial principle properly, never made proper use of it, while Galileo, who never formulated it as a universal law, employed it with great yield.

If forces were removed from matter, all the more so were spirits and God. These are substances *sui generis*. The only attribute characterizing spirit is cogitation (what Descartes has in mind comes closest

---

[66] Ibid. II,37 (p. 62): *quantum in se est*; (p. 63): *seorsim spectatem*. Why did Descartes split the inertial principle into two—one governing motion (i.e., the *quantitas motus*), the other governing direction? Leibniz thought that, in this way, Descartes hoped to secure a structure by which spirits could influence minute bodies, not by changing their motion but merely by changing their direction. But this is more likely to be an afterthought, a side benefit (if indeed it solves the difficulties of mind-body interaction, which I do not believe). Rather, (m·v) is, to Descartes, always a skalar; throughout the "rules of motion," change of direction obeys another logic than change of motion.

[67] See Funkenstein, "The Dialectical Preparation" (above n. 56).

[68] But see, against this common interpretation, A. Gabbey, "Force and Inertia in the Seventeenth Century: Descartes and Newton," in *Descartes: Philosophy, Mathematics and Physics*, ed. St. Gaukroger (Brighton, Sussex, 1980),pp. 230–320. Descartes' specific term for force, he argues, is *determinatio*.

to the phenomenological "intention"). But, if so, how can spirits act upon matter—as indeed our soul acts upon our body? And how does God act upon matter? What does it mean, literally, that he implanted certain rules and a quantity of motion in matter? By what mode of causality is this conceivable? And finally: Descartes insists on a voluntarism more radical than that of the most radical nominalists. God is first and foremost omnipotent and self-caused; all his other attributes depend on his will. If he so wanted, he could even invalidate our "clear and distinct" ideas, even eternal truths are contingent upon his will.[69] But what does it mean that God could make $2 + 1 \neq 3$? Does it merely mean that God could abstain from creating matter, since matter is reified mathematics? Could he also make $2 + 1 = 4$? Eventually, the sharp separation between matter (extension) and spirit (cogitation), the source of so many troubles in Descartes' system, is also justified on the grounds that it constitutes a "clear and distinct" idea. Could God invalidate it too? Or could he create a world in which spirits are extended?

These and similar questions are theological as well as physical. They stem from the unique Cartesian fusion of theological and physical arguments such that the most fundamental laws—the inertial law and conservation of motion—are derived from the first law of physics—the constancy of God. God is constant, *i.e.*, does not change without sufficient reason.[70] God's presence in the world is likewise understood unequivocally. It is neither material nor symbolical: It is *meta*physical only in the sense that all other beings depend, at any moment of their existence, on God's will to preserve them. It is a relation of logical implication.

Henry More developed his positions in a constant dialogue with and against Descartes. Much emphasis is given to his insistence on the absolute nature of empty space.[71] We shall see that this is only a derivative concern of his. His fundamental, never modified or qualified position asserted the extended nature of spirits. Against Descartes he insists that spirits are extended. The presence of spirits (and ultimately of God) in the world was not only metaphysical, *qua* substances, but also physical: With bodies they share dimensionality. It

---

[69] Cf. A. Funkenstein, "Descartes, Eternal Truths, and the Divine Omnipotence," *Studies in the History and Philosophy of Science*, 6 (1975), pp. 185–99.
[70] *Principia Philosophiae* II,36 (Adam-Tannery, *Oeuvres*, VIII,1, p. 61).
[71] Cf. above, n. 10.

seemed to More that most of Descartes' problems were solvable in this manner: through the psychophysical interaction (*commercium mentis et corporis*), the assertion of absolute motions and hence the introduction of real forces into matter—a way to deal with impenetrability as a real rather than as a hypothetical condition of bodies—in an unequivocal divine mode of causation. Seen from this vantage point, More's concerns and solutions were not very far from those of Leibniz.

Spirits and bodies are *res extensae*. It is fair to say (though against More's objections) that spirits and solid bodies are bodies in most senses of the word—they occupy places and can interact amongst each other as well as amongst themselves. The difference between spirits and bodies lies in the nature of the forces they represent. Bodies, though breakable, are impenetrable; spirits, though indivisible, are penetrable. Spirits can penetrate bodies as well as each other; they can also contract and expand.[72] Upon reflection, we see the reason why More regards both properties as one: when spirits penetrate each other, their intensity grows; so also, if a spirit contracts. Contraction, he may have felt, is a kind of self-penetration. Stoic physics stated very similar states for the Pneuma and used the analogy of rebounding waves. More called this property "spissitude,"[73] and added that it may be conceived as a fourth dimension. Bodies in and of themselves lack spissitude. But since, in nature, all bodies are permeated by spirit of some kind, the ability of a complex body to maintain its size indicates a tired, constant spissitude.[74] Every change within a body is accounted for by the spirit penetrating it; which is only another say of saying that there are real forces which account for absolute motions. Spirits are forces.[75] Once they are admitted into

---

[72] Henry More, *The immortality of the Soul, so farre forth as it is demonstrable from the knowledge of nature and the light of reason*, I, ii, 11 (London, 1669); ibid., p. 20. R. Zimmermann, "Henry More und die vierte Dimension des Raumes," *Kaiserliche Ak. d. Wissenschaften*, Philosophisch-hist. Kl. 98 (1881), pp. 403 ff. It certainly resembles the Stoic τόνος.

[73] Henry More, *An antidote against atheism*, I,iv,3 (London, 1652, published in *Collection of several philosophical writings* [London, 1662], p. 15); Koyré, *From the Closed World to the Open Universe*, pp. 127–30. We remember the capacity of mutual penetration of spiritual and passive matter from the Stoa.

[74] The distinction between fixed and changeable spissitude, or between plastic and mechanical forces, is not unlike the Leibnizian distinction between dead and live force (*vis viva*)—a circumstance of which Leibniz may have been aware in his praise of More.

[75] Forces, properties, spirits are often interchangeable terms. By mechanical power

the realm of nature, one can ascribe to matter as such all the properties ascribed to it by Descartes: It is incapable of self-motion, has no force of its own, its motion as such is always relative, and it may therefore obey Descartes' geometrical rules.

Such are the contours of the doctrine which More developed over fifteen years. It shows its affinity with the Renaissance philosophies of nature (notably with Telesio's) as well as with Stoic physics. Yet, in contradistinction with both, he attends not only to the homogeneity of his (and their) animated universe; he also wishes the notion of force, spirit, and matter to be "clear and distinct," *i.e.*, unequivocal. In so doing, he may have solved some of Descartes' most pressing problems, but in turn he created new problems. He may have solved, *more suo*, the psychophysical dilemma of Descartes, but his God has difficulties of his own.

Like Descartes' God, More's is the Spirit-in-Chief. All other spirits or forces depend on him. Some spirits lack reflection and purposefulness, such as the (Stoic) *anima mundi*; some have it; God is the vertex in the hierarchy of spirits (or ideas). In the sense that God is a spirit, More admits, though not without initial hesitations, that he is extended; contrary to other spirits, however, his extension is infinite: it is space itself. Now this forces us to deny of God what he ascribed to spirits—namely spissitude. God cannot expand or contract. He, like space, is always the same.[76] The only way to avoid interpreting this circumstance as a deficiency or imperfection is as follows. Contrary again to Descartes, spirits and God are not absolutely discrete substances. God is rather the spirit of all spirits, their source and place. His is an emanational theology, not unlike the Kabbalistic speculations which he admired: God is veritably the אין סוף (*infinitum*), both identical with and different from the powers (ספירות) of which he is the source. More's relation to the Jewish (and Christian) Kabbala corroborates, I believe, my interpretation. He criticizes its anthropomorphic symbolism of God's body (אדם קדמון).[77] Nor does

---

he means Descartes' "quantity of motion;" spirits possess "plastic power."

[76] Henry More, *Enchridium Metaphysicum sive de rebus incorporeis . . . dissertatio* I,vi,5 (London, 1671), p. 42. It would be more precise to say: God's spissitude is so immense, he is "all penetrating" and therefore the capacity to expand or contract, which other spirits have, cannot be ascribed to him any more than the capacity of self-annihilation.

[77] B.P. Copenhaver, "Jewish Theologies of Space in the Scientific Revolution: Henry More, Joseph Raphson, Isaac Newton and their Predecessors," *Annals of*

the "empty space" of Lurianic Kabbalism impress him: He criticizes it as being finite and a result of the contraction (צמצום) of the original infinite light, *i.e.*, God (אור אין סוף).[78] Only derivative spirits, we remember, contract: God does not. But he is impressed with the emanational structure and process of the divine forces, with the vision of God as a balanced harmony of interacting and counteracting aspects. More's concept of the divine amounts to the concept of a harmonious sum total of all mechanical and purposive forces in the universe. Such a God could not but be reasonable.[79] He is the very embodiment of πρovoία, much as was the Stoic Pneuma. It contrasts again with Descartes' God, in whom will had primacy over reason.

Let me sum up. The medieval sense of God's symbolic presence in his creation, and the sense of a universe replete with transcendent meanings and hints, had to recede if not to give way totally to the postulates of equivocation and homogeneity in the 17th century. God's relation to the world had to be given a concrete physical meaning. Descartes did so by maintaining the medieval sense of God's utter transcendence: The only relation of God to the world which could thus be rescued was that of causality, a relation which Descartes exploits to the extreme. More, on the other hand, rather translated the pansychism, or even pantheism, of philosophies of nature in the Renaissance into a "clear and distinct" language. God thus acquired a body of sorts, or at least a *"sensorium."* It may be of some significance that Descartes, a Catholic, avoided even the semblance of endowing his God with a body while More, the liberal Protestant, did not.

It is clear why a God describable in unequivocal terms, or even given physical features and functions, eventually became all the easier

---

Science, 37 (1980), pp. 489–548, esp. pp. 515–29; *Adam Kadmon*: pp. 527–29; *Tsimtsum*: pp. 523–26.

[78] Copenhaver, "Jewish Theologies", as against, e.g., Jammer, *Concepts of Space*. It is worth while to remember that, even among Jewish Kabbalists who followed the Lurianic Kabbala, it was fiercely disputed whether to understand *tsimtsum* literally (*leifshuto*)—and conclude that, therefore, God cannot be literally "filling all the world" (*memale kol almin*)—or whether *tsimtsum* should be taken metaphorically (*snelo leifshuto*) so as to save God's real presence in the world. Cf. M. Taitelbaum, *Harav miladj umifleget Habad*, 11 (Warsaw, 1913), pp. 62 ff., 78.

[79] A. Lichtenstein, *Henry More: The Rational Theology of a Cambridge Platonist* (Cambridge, Mass., 1962). In this respect, More's main tenets come close to those of Leibniz.

to discard. As a scientific hypothesis, he was later shown to be superfluous; as a being, he was shown to be a mere hypostatization of rational, social, or psychological ideals and images. Our detective story thus comes to its end. We have seen how and why God lost his body in Christian theology, how and why he regained it in the 17th century. Once God regained transparency or even a body, he was all the easier to kill. The story of his slow philosophical death—from Kant through Feuerbach to Nietzsche—is as fascinating as the story we told of his lost and found body. But it is another story.

ARTHUR QUINN

ON READING NEWTON APOCALYPTICALLY

"That strange agglomeration of incongruities, the seventeenth century mind"—I can't remember exactly when I first thought to apply this phrase of Aldous Huxley specifically to the preeminent seventeenth-century mind, Isaac Newton.[1] But it was certainly after a brief visit I made to the Warburg Institute of London in the academic year of 1966–67. Until that time I had been interested only in the scientific ideas of the great man—in particular, I was interested in making his ideas about atomic forces, especially as they were received and developed by his followers, as little incongruous as possible.[2] As fate would have it, I was visiting the Warburg the very afternoon Ratansi and McGuire were reading to a seminar the manuscript of their now well-known paper, "Newton and the 'pipes of Pan'."[3]

I was startled to hear presented conclusive evidence that Newton not only believed in the *prisca theologia* but also perceived his own natural philosophy to represent the recovery of that primal wisdom. I can still remember the immediate response to that presentation by Frances Yates, who had done probably more than anyone else to show the importance of such occult traditions in early modern thought.[4] Clasping her hands, she said she had always known of the influence of the occult on the development of modern science but she had never until this very moment dreamt that Newton himself was, as she put it, "one of us."

Well, I wasn't convinced that Newton was one of *them*. But this paper did suggest that his persistent interest in theological and alchemical matters could be better integrated with his famous achievements in physics and mathematics than was previously thought possible. How exactly this was to be done became for me then, and

---

[1] Aldous Huxley, *The Devils of Loudun* (New York, 1952), p. 39.
[2] Eventually, thanks to a pleasant summer spent as a fellow at the Clark Library, this line of research was worked into publishable form as "Repulsive Force in England, 1706–44," *Studies in the History of the Physical Sciences* 13 (1982): 109–28.
[3] J.E. McGuire and P.M. Ratansi, "Newton and the 'pipes of Pan'," *Notes and Records of the Royal Society of London* 21 (1966): 108–42.
[4] Notably her *Giordano Bruno and the Hermetic Tradition* (London, 1964).

remains for me now, one of the most interesting questions in Newton studies.

The "pipes of Pan" paper seemed to kill once and for all the old positivist handling of this question, which claimed that although Newton might have shared many of the theological preoccupations of his age, his modernity consisted in his ability to keep these separate from his scientific pursuits. Privately he might have had metaphysical aspirations, but publicly he allowed his inquiries to be strictly governed by the principles of the Scientific Method. Perhaps in his later life he allowed this distinction between procedures and metaphysics to blur a bit; if so, this was only a symptom of his intellectual decline.

This was what Ratansi and McGuire had seemed to render untenable by finding the *prisca theologia* at the heart of the *Principia*. But nothing ever dies in historiography. And the positivist interpretation has recently been given new life in Richard Westfall's monumental biography of Newton.[5] This work, besides being an impressive distillation of decades of research by Westfall and others on the development of Newton, provides a sophisticated reformulation of the old positivist position.

Westfall admits—indeed, documents to a degree no one before ever has—that Newton was interested in an extraordinary variety of intellectual pursuits throughout his life, some scientific and some occult, some mathematical and some theological. Westfall does not try to present the simplistic picture of a great scientist in his decline doddering into theology. He admits that Newton in his maturity, if left to himself, might well have given up scientific pursuits entirely for the sake of his other interests. He might have, but—and here is Westfall's crucial move—the World intruded. The occult and the theological belonged, in Westfall's view, to the past; science and mathematics were forces of the future. Once the age, the progressive elements of the age, realized the extent of Newton's mathematical and scientific gifts they would not let him rest until he had shared them with the world.

Westfall's approach is subtler than the older positivist position because he displaces the positivism from Newton to the age. The modernity of the context, not the modernity of Newton himself as an

---

[5] Richard Westfall, *Never At Rest* (Cambridge, 1980).

individual, becomes the explanation of the contrast between public and private in Newton's work.

An alternative, but not necessarily incompatible, approach to that of Westfall might be called the psychological. Newton *was* a very strange man. His reluctance to publish, his sensitivity to criticism, his repeated camouflaging of his true intentions, and perhaps too his preoccupation with the millenarian and the occult—all these point to a neurotic behavior pattern that makes the nervous breakdown of 1693 far from surprising. This, of course, is the approach taken by Frank Manuel in his rival biographical study of Newton.[6] Not the full-scale biography that Westfall provides, Manuel's succeeds strikingly at what it attempts to be, a portrait of Newton. Whatever the psychoanalytic excesses of his attempted etiology (and they are easy to ridicule), Manuel has succeeded in making Newton come alive as an individual to a degree that no biographer has before or since. His work, like Westfall's, represents a watershed in Newton studies.

Nonetheless, as much as I have learned from Manuel and Westfall, I find myself dissatisfied with both their handlings of the relationship between Newton's scientific and non-scientific intellectual pursuits. I am in fact suspicious of both because they both seem to require a transcendental cocksureness about Reason. By way of explaining my prejudice I should confess that I read Richard Popkin's *History of Scepticism* at a formative age—and then made the mistake of reading the sources he had shown to be so important.[7] And so when I read a Newtonian scholar confidently distinguishing between Newton's methods and his metaphysics, between the forces of the past and the forces of the future, between the neurotic and the normal, I find involuntarily coming to my mind that all-purpose response of Montaigne: "If that is true, it is subject to a long interpretation."

I want to try today, using the millenarian tradition and the rhetorical method of analysis, to suggest another approach, less profound than the philosophical or psychological, but workable nonetheless. Popkin mentioned to me just last night an incident that dramatizes for me the usefulness of the millenarian tradition in suggesting a third approach.

---

[6] Frank Manuel, *A Portrait of Newton* (Cambridge, 1968). Manuel earlier produced the most detailed treatment of Newton's historical studies, *Isaac Newton, Historian* (Cambridge, 1963).

[7] Richard Popkin, *History of Scepticism* (Berkeley, 1979). This second edition contains significant new material.

John Dury told of having a serious discussion with René Descartes. They agreed that the profound crisis in the thought of their time had been caused by the emergence of skepticism. They also agreed that a way had to be found to challenge this skepticism directly. They disagreed only as to the most promising source of this response. Descartes thought mathematics was the most likely to succeed; Dury thought the study of Biblical prophecy. They wished each other well.

Within the context of the seventeenth century the study of prophetic history was as plausible a way to resolve the skeptical crisis as mathematics—this is what the episode seems to me to dramatize. Until we see them as more or less equally plausible alternatives, we are not seeing the crisis with seventeenth century eyes. Individuals at the time could reasonably disagree as to which of the two, mathematics or prophecy, was more promising. Many, understandably, would try to hedge their bets. And the greatest genius of the age, Isaac Newton, fully aware of his powers, would attempt a synthesis.

In so doing he had ample precedent. Trevor-Roper, himself no friend of the irrational in history, has emphasized precisely this point with regard to the early seventeenth century.[8]

> From our rationalist heights we might suppose that the new discoveries of science would tend to discredit the apocalyptic vaticinations of Scripture; but in fact this was not so. It is an interesting but undeniable fact that the most advanced scientists of the early seventeenth century included also the most learned and literal students of Biblical mathematics; and in their hands science and religion converged to pinpoint, between 1640 and 1660, the dissolution of society, the end of the world.

(History has a way of making us all descend from the rationalist heights to which we think we have climbed.)

What Trevor-Roper has said of the period of Napier and Mede is as true of the period of More and Newton, only that they were warier about pinpointing dates for the end of the world. If we then accept such an interest in millenarianism (and Scriptural vaticination) as reasonable behavior within the context, as I think we clearly should, then we can begin to reassess Manuel's portrait.

To what extent does this interest in millenarianism help explain Newton's admittedly peculiar behavior as an author? Obviously we will never be able to dispense entirely with his personal idiosyncracies,

---

[8] Hugh Trevor-Roper, "The General Crisis of the Seventeenth Century,' *Crisis in Europe, 1560–1660* (New York, 1965), ed. by Trevor Aston, pp. 59–95.

which can perhaps be tied to specific experiences in his childhood. But first—or so it seems to me—we ought to see how far these oft noted characteristics are themselves reasonable given Newton's millenarian convictions. Let me show how we might do this by way of analogy.

One of the classic questions in the interpretation of *Paradise Lost* is: why does the snake have all the good lines? Or, to put it more generally, why are the virtuous characters so dull, while the evil ones so interesting? Stanley Fish has suggested that we assume Milton knew what he was doing, that he intended these effects.[9] Why would Milton have done such a thing? Fish believes the answer is clear once we consider Milton's view of his audience. Milton believed his audience to be composed of fallen men—men, moreover, who because of their fallen nature were not inclined to admit their own fundamental depravity. In *Paradise Lost* Milton was recounting for his audience the epic of how they became depraved. An important part of this recounting was for Milton's audience to realize, to realize fully, that they were indeed the sons and daughters of Adam and Eve, that they were fallen men, weak to the temptations of the Arch-Tempter. So Milton gives his Devil the tools of his trade, fully expecting his audience to fall again and again to his charms, to fall only to be reminded again and again that they had been listening in admiration to the embodiment of all evil.

Let us take another example, far from Milton but closer to Professor Manuel's heart. Sigmund Freud tells us that men will offer tremendous resistance to the dredging up of the unconscious; yet his own work is primarily devoted to just such dredging. It stands to reason, therefore, that when Freud is addressing an audience which is not already committed to psychoanalysis, he must anticipate a very strong emotional resistance to his ideas, a resistance he must find a way to neutralize if he is ever to get a fair hearing.

Freud in his writings for a general audience deals with this problem in a variety of ways. He will, of course, often directly urge his audience to keep an open mind. In his work on Leonardo, for example, Freud will remind his readers that a Leonardo DaVinci would keep an open mind about a subject until all the evidence was in.[10] However,

---

[9] Stanley Fish, *Surprised By Sin* (Berkeley, 1967). See also his *Self-Consuming Artifacts* (Berkeley, 1972).
[10] Sigmund Freud, *Leonardo DaVinci* (New York, 1916).

he does not limit himself to such direct appeals; he must also use indirect means, just as Milton had to surprise his readers into recognizing their own sinfulness.

Such an indirect approach can most easily be seen in the way Freud presents one of his arguments in the Leonardo book. Freud believed that when Leonardo spoke of a childhood memory of a vulture, he was unconsciously speaking of his mother. How could one possibly establish a connection between vultures and mothers? In fact, it is not difficult, for culturally there was such a connection. The basis of it is not important for our purposes. It was a connection first made apparently by the Egyptians, picked up by classical writers like Plutarch, and widely cited by the Church fathers. In other words, it was, in Leonardo's time, a cultural commonplace. There would seem no particular difficulty in proposing that Leonardo probably was aware of it. What first appeared to be a difficult step in Freud's proof, actually, when the evidence is in, appears a rather easy one. Freud, however, sees more possibilities here; he sees an opportunity to expend some of his readers' energy, their defensive energy. It is an opportunity to wear down their resistance, so they will be able objectively to consider Freud's argument.

Therefore, Freud, when first proposing this connection, fails to mention the Church fathers or Plutarch. He rather introduces it as something which we have learned from Egyptian hieroglyphics. Immediately the readers, who have been looking for a way out all along, ask, "Did Leonardo know hieroglyphics?" (And, if they have not thought of that objection, Freud raises it for them). Yes, Freud sadly admits, you are right, Leonardo could not have known hieroglyphics. With the readers now feeling safe, Freud seems to shelve the subject, apparently goes on to something else, and two pages later, ever so politely pulls the rug. The readers feel then compelled to admit that a major objection to Freud's psychoanalysis has been overcome—an objection which they would never have made, if Freud had not led them to do so.

Whatever the intrinsic merits of my reading of Freud or Fish's of Milton, I think the general point is extremely important for the intellectual historian. When someone, genius or otherwise, has a definite view about either human nature in general or the specific state of humanity at the time he is writing, it is fruitful to ask how this view influences the discourse he produces. This is especially true of those who have deep commitments to their views, like Milton, Freud, or Newton.

And make no mistake about it. Newton was convinced that he and his contemporaries were entering into the last age, the very age prophesied in the Bible.[11] The rediscovery of the *prisca theologia* by Newton and his contemporaries was a crucial sign of the beginning of the end. Daniel had written, "Many shall run to and fro; and knowledge shall be increased." Columbus had begun the fulfillment of the first half of this prophecy; Newton was finishing the fulfillment of the second half. Understanding the prophecy itself was part of it. Every prophecy understood brought closer the time of the end. Hence it is easy to understand why Newton should have been so excited by the developments in Biblical interpretation of his own time. Witness Henry More's account in a letter to a friend of Newton's response to a recently published book of his that attempted to unravel the Apocalypse:

> I remember you either here at the time or at London before asked me about Mr. Newton and my agreement in Apocalyptical Notions. And I remember I told you both, how well we were agreed. For after his reading of the Exposition of the Apocalypse which I gave him, he came to my chamber where he seem'd to me not onely to approve my Exposition as coherent and perspicuous throughout from beginning to the end, but (by the manner of his countenance which is ordinarily melancholy and thoughtfull, but then mighty lightsome and chearfull, and by the free profession of what satisfaction he took therein) to be in manner transported.

This can help us explain Newton's peculiar attitude toward his own science. For instance, in 1676, Newton, after having threatened to do so before, withdrew from public philosophizing. He had in 1672 published a brilliant paper on the theory of colors, and had spent four years answering various objections to it. Finally he became fed up, and refused to discuss his theories any more, about colors or anything else. It would be almost a decade before Halley would coax the *Principia* from him, and it would be almost thirty years before his *Opticks* would see light.

This withdrawal is usually taken as a sign of Newton's incipient madness—or, if you prefer, a genius understandably impatient with

---

[11] The following account of the theological background to Newton's thought is based upon my *The Confidence of British Philosophers* (Leyden, 1976), chs. 1–2, with new citations from theological manuscripts published in Frank Manuel's *The Religion of Isaac Newton* (Oxford, 1974).

those of lesser gifts. Let me try to account for Newton's behavior differently.

In 1676 the first half of Ralph Cudworth's *True Intellectual System of the World* was published. This was to be the great Cambridge attempt to reconstruct systematically and publicly the *prisca theologia*—and in the process to provide a decisive refutation of materialism, atheism, and skepticism of other kinds. The public response to the book was disappointing in the extreme. Cudworth even found himself being attacked for covert atheism and materialism. Cudworth and his Cambridge associates had obviously made a similar mistake to that made by the early seventeenth century interpreters of apocalyptic vaticinations; the time of the end was not quite so close as they thought. And Cudworth had learned to his sorrow what happened when one spoke openly of prophetic truths to a fallen world.[12]

Cudworth himself never finished his system, or at least the second part of his system was never published. In that same year of 1676 Henry More, himself the other leader of the Cambridge Platonists, announced that he too was giving up philosophy to devote himself exclusively to theology; no longer would he speak to those who did not accept the Bible as revelation. More turned to a careful study of Biblical prophecy, and in the same year Newton did as well. This all seems to me more than just coincidence. And, placed in such a context, Newton's behavior is far from peculiar.

But you might ask what was Newton doing studying the theory of colors in the first place. Here I am going to indulge in speculation if only to work us back into the intellectual context, a context in some ways so different from our own. The Cambridge Platonists were preoccupied with showing the inadequacy of any materialistic physics. They were looking, in particular, for principles necessary to any adequate system of the physical world that would have to be recognized as manifestations of a spiritual being. It is well known that two of the candidates suggested by Henry More—absolute space and gravity (a force acting at a distance)—eventually became distinctive features of Newton's physics.[13] What is not often recognized is that there was a

---

[12] One of the treasures of the Clark Library is Newton's notes on Cudworth's *True Intellectual System*.

[13] It might be asked why if active forces were so important to Newton did he late in life entertain the possibility of an aether. Here it is important to keep in mind what

third candidate obvious to anyone who had read in the neoplatonic tradition: light. Pure white light, like pure space, could be interpreted as a manifestation of the spiritual.

The Cambridge Platonists as a group were alive to the suggestiveness of light considered figuratively. One of them, John Smith, had actually written a book entitled *Spiritual Opticks*. Henry More had interpreted a prophecy about "whiteness rising" as a reference to the moral purity of the Protestant Reformation. Newton in one of his theological manuscripts suggests that colored light represents our present fallen condition.

If white light is the action of spirit, then what is colored light? Obviously the theory of colors is quite important for this line of thought. One theory consistent with the matter/spirit dualism so dear to the Cambridge Platonists was the ancient one that regarded colored light as a mixture of white light with darkness. And in fact precisely this theory was revived by a fringe member of the Cambridge Platonists, Isaac Barrow, from whom Newton got both his Lucasian chair and the idea of absolute time.

What relevance do Newton's earliest optical papers have to such a speculative identification of white light with spirit? Quite simply, they prove that it is not possible. They claim to demonstrate that white light far from being "pure" is really a mixture of colored light. Pure light is not white but colored. The implication for a Cambridge Platonist was obvious: light was material, not spiritual.

However, those who responded to Newton's paper seemed oblivious to this implication. They were concerned with what possible material models for light Newton's experiments seemed to support. The experiments seemed to support a corpuscular theory, light as a stream of microscopic projectiles. Newton's refusal to discuss this, despite the fact that he obviously preferred such a theory, has been taken as a sign of duplicity, arrogance, or just plain bad manners.

But, just possibly, Newton was beginning to understand not only how advanced intellectually he was over the outside scientific community, but also how advanced spiritually. His critics had entirely failed to see the metaphyscial, the religious implications of what he had done. Hence there was no point in talking to such persons unless you

---

kind of aether it was. It was an aether that itself possessed an active power, a force of repulsion between its particles. In other words, Newton's aether was a way to unify the active principles of his system, not do away with them. Not atheism, but unitarianism.

were completely explicit. And the reception of Cudworth showed what happened when you were.

This does not mean that Newton's papers on light were intended to support materialism covertly; quite the contrary. His papers were intended to support covertly another Platonist candidate for proof of a spiritual presence in the physical world. Westfall himself has admitted that Newton, in his optical paper of 1675, had "disguised considerably" (Westfall's phrase) his real position in order to avoid any direct reference to "active Principles"—namely, those very forces which by acting at a distance show the inadequacy of mechanical explanations in optics and thereby necessitate the postulation of a spiritual power governing the light (The force of gravity would be another, more famous Active Principle.) When his *Opticks* were finally printed, Newton admitted his conviction that the phenomena of light, along with those of chemistry, argued for the existence of both attractive and repulsive forces acting at the atomic level. Typically, he did not argue for this conclusion in the main body of the *Opticks*, but in one of a series of Queries added to the end—moreover, this most important query was not to be found in the first edition of the *Opticks*, but was tucked into the first Latin edition published two years later. In short, he remained secretive even when he did publish his views.

The historical studies of religion which he was also pursuing throughout his career give ample explanation for this secretiveness, especially when we realize that his views in their general outlines were far from uncommon. He made a deep study of the Arian controversies of the fourth century, and concluded that the public debate had resulted in the Council of Nicea betraying the Christian tradition by adopting the trinitarian doctrine. Public dispute in that case had decisively failed to serve the Truth. He himself, as another of his manuscripts indicates, would have expected little better treatment if he made public the correct interpretations of Scripture.

> They will call thee it may be a hot headed fellow, a Bigot, a Fanatique, a Heretique. And tell thee of the uncertainty of these interpretations, and the vanity of attending to them . . . . The world loves to be deceived, they will not understand, they never consider equally but are wholly led by prejudice, interest, the praise of men, and the authority of the Church they live in . . . . This is the guise of the world, and therefore trust it not.

This distrust of the present did not lessen his faith in the future. In a manuscript tentatively dated by Manuel in the early 1680's, Newton describes with great enthusiasm the glories of the millennium when it finally occurs. The Blessed will be able to live wherever in the universe they choose. "Thus may the whole heavens or any part thereof whatever be the habitation of the Blessed, and at the same time the earth be subject to their domination." And in the same manuscript there is a passage that bears significantly on his attitude on the present world in which he finds himself. "To conceive that the children with the resurrection shall live among men and converse with them daily as Mortals do with one another and reign over them after the way of temporal kingdoms is very absurd and foolish. Do men converse with Beasts and Fishes?"

That time had not yet come, however soon Newton and many others of the elect thought its arrival. Therefore, insofar as one spoke publicly, one had to anticipate a divided audience, or rather an audience in the process of being divided into the elect and the fish. And they were not being separated simply by learning or intelligence. As Newton put it in yet another of his theological manuscripts, even among those who do carefully study religious matters almost all do it purely "for worldly ends."

Anyone with such views, anyone who looks forward to the time soon when he will have no more discourse with the bulk of humanity than he does at present with fishes, will, if he publishes at all, in all probability write rather differently from someone who thinks that life is just a bowl of cherries and readers are beings of good will. Newton, no more than Freud, could consistently address his readers as exclusively open-minded and rational. Newton's *Principia*, and other writings, had to be written in anticipation of readers both saved and damned, readers godly and atheistical, and even jesuitical. It would have been irresponsible of Newton, perhaps damnably irresponsible, to address such an audience candidly. He would have to try to write so that the wise might be purified, but also so that the wicked might be vexed.

In light of this we should see Newton's lack of candor about, for example, attraction as a physical principle neither as primarily a lamentable psychological quirk nor as an admirable epistemological perspicacity. We should not be surprised that some of the most important parts of the *Principia* should be found in the scholia—the scholium on space and time, the General Scholium of the second edition on God. Or indeed that important parts of the *Principia* should appear in drafts which were never published—the claims concerning the *prisca theologia*, or the corollary once intended for the second edition: "There exists an infinite and omnipresent spirit in which matter is moved according to mathematical laws." Or even be surprised that Newton, as the time for publication came close, almost suppressed the whole third book of the *Principia* in which his mathematical principles were applied to the physical world.

In Newton we may well be able to find our positivist distinction between procedures and metaphysics, our social distinction between progress and regress, even our psychological distinction between the normal and neurotic. But Newton would have us read his own work in terms of its role in the salvation history described in the Bible. He would have us read it as a challenge to be numbered not among the damned of the anti-Christ, but the elect of the millennium. And it is here with this reading, with Newton's own reading of his work, that we as historians should start.[14]

There, nonetheless, remains an objection from the Westfall side which must be addressed forthrightly. The objection, put somewhat impolitely, would be: who still reads Mr. Dury? In other words, Descartes and Dury might have faced a similar choice; but Descartes made it correctly and is still a living influence on our civilization; Dury made it wrongly and is justifiably forgotten. In Newton we admittedly have both elements, that which makes him one of the enduring intellects of Western Civilization, and that which makes him look all too human. Even so, a reading of the *Principia* which makes the latter as important as the former, the ephemeral as the enduring, is at best misconceived and at worst perverse.

The issue is more difficult than whether or not the millenarian tradition persists after Newton. If that were all, then one could quickly point to M.H. Abrams' magisterial interpretation of Romanticism, *Natural Supernaturalism*, which makes apocalypticism central to it—or Leszek Kolakowski's monumental study of Marxism, which sees this influential movement similarly.[15] The issue, rather, is whether millenarianism retains its importance for thinkers who would see themselves, and be recognized, as legitimate heirs to Newton. In short, I am assuming I will not be permitted to make my case with

---

[14] I have attempted to sketch such a reading in my *Confidence of British Philosophers*, ch. 3.

[15] M.H. Abrams, *Natural Supernaturalism* (New York, 1971); Leszek Kolakowski, *Main Currents of Marxism* (Oxford, 1978), 3 v.

respect to the likes of Blake or Lenin. So I will rather make it with respect to the beginnings of analytic philosophy itself, the very philosophy which gives rise to objections such as the one I am answering. But first I must say a few more words about skepticism for reasons which I hope will become clear.

Skeptics are commonly characterized as thinkers who reject or deny—deny the metaphysician's distinction between appearance and reality, reject the scientist's search after the deep structure in things. And yet if we look at this tradition only a little more closely, we discover examples of a somewhat more complex response to the search for knowledge. We need, in fact, only to turn to the earliest surviving work of the Pyrrhonist tradition—that of Sextus Empiricus. He begins his outlines of Pyrrhonism by observing that in the search for knowledge there are three possible outcomes: one can conclude that the truth has been discovered; one can conclude that it cannot be found; or one can go on searching. The skeptical position, according to Sextus Empiricus, is the decision to go on searching. To deny that knowledge can be found is to have a doctrine of a negative kind. He who denies that knowledge can be found is as much an epistemologist as he who claims to have found it. He knows what knowledge is because he knows he can never possess it. The true skeptic knows not even this, and hence must go on searching.[16]

Skepticism, as described by Sextus Empiricus, and sometimes practiced by others, is primarily not a doctrine, not a hypothesis, not an argument—but rather an attitude toward doctrines, hypotheses, arguments, even arguments, doctrines, hypotheses of a negative kind. As Hume so well put it, "The true skeptic must be as diffident of his doubts as he is of his certainties." If this is taken seriously, then it should transform the performance of the skeptical writer. The center of the discourse should radically shift away from the logos to what the ancient rhetoricians called the ethos, the character of the speaker. In the logos we must properly find the assertions and denials—in the ethos one specifically locates the tentativeness, the uncertainty toward both, that leads one to continue the search.

"I am myself the matter of this book," Montaigne writes in the

---

[16] A convenient selection from Sextus Empiricus has been edited by Philip Hallie under the title *Scepticism, God and Man* (Middletown, 1964). Hallie has also written perhaps the best evocation of a skeptic in his *The Scar of Montaigne* (Middletown, 1966).

preface to his *Essays*, "you would be unreasonable to spend your leisure on so vain and frivolous a subject." In the essay form, a genre virtually invented by Montaigne for this skeptical purpose, what is said becomes less important than the tone in which it is said, *ethos* characteristically taking precedence over *logos*.

What then would a skeptical history of philosophy look like? It would not be a polemical denunciation of the search for knowledge, for it would not be able to assert either that this search has certainly proved futile in the past, nor that it necessarily will do so in the future. Rather such a history would quietly shift its focus away from the arguments of the philosophers to the characters of the philosophers themselves, especially as that character was realized in their writings. It would be not a logical analysis of philosophy but a rhetorical analysis.

Let me read to you two sentences which say much the same thing but which rhetorically could not be farther apart. "Philosophy, from the earliest times, has made greater claims and achieved fewer results than any other branch of human learning." This is the first sentence from Bertrand Russell's *Our Knowledge of the External World*. Compare that with David Hume's first sentence in his essay "The Sceptic."[17] "I have long entertained a suspicion with regard to the decisions of philosophers upon all subjects, and found in myself a greater inclination to dispute than to assent to their conclusions." These are, I suggest, two versions of the assertion that all philosophy is bunk. But the doubt in Hume's version clearly applies to himself as well, to his own diffidence with respect to philosophy—"long entertain a *suspicion*," "*found* within myself," "a *greater* inclination to dispute than to assent." Each twist in the sentence further qualifies the assertion—and so the essay proceeds, taking away with one hand what it gives with another until at last, the whole essay has virtually dissolved before us, like the Cheshire cat, leaving behind only its grin of skepticism. It concludes, "To reduce life to exact rule and method is commonly a painful, oft a fruitless occupation: and is it not also a proof that we overvalue the prize for which we contend? Even to reason so carefully concerning it, and to fix with accuracy its just idea, would be overvaluing it, were it not that to some tempers, this occupation is one of the most amusing in which life could possibly be employed."

---

[17] Bertrand Russell, *Our Knowledge of the External World* (Chicago, 1914); David Hume, "The Sceptic," *Essays Moral Political and Literary* (Oxford, 1963), pp. 161–84.

This is far from the clarion call of cocky Russell's sweeping denunciation of all past philosophers. Russell has no diffidence about his doubts. And so we are scarcely surprised when a few sentences later we learn that Russell's philosophy is to be an exception to the centuries of futility. "I believe that the time has now come when this unsatisfactory state of things can be brought to an end." His work would be "an achievement surpassing all that has hitherto been accomplished by philosophers." Our intellectual hopes would be satisfied, Russell said, "more fully than former ages could have deemed possible for human minds." In Hume and Russell we have found the extremes of philosophical ethos—in Hume the skeptical extreme, in Russell what we might call the millenarian extreme.

The skeptic characteristically regards his work as the end or cure of philosophy, its dissolution—he will commonly be uncertain whether to regard his work as philosophy at all, or rather, in Wittgenstein's phrase, "an heir to philosophy." The millenarian, in contrast, regards his work as the beginning of true philosophy, all earlier philosophers being worthy of that title, if at all, only insofar as they were prophets of his coming.

We should, therefore, expect to find in the early history of analytic philosophy in England many of the characteristics of millenarianism. And in this expectation we are not disappointed.[18] Bertrand Russell and G.E. Moore believed that they had discovered, for the first time in all history, the true foundations of philosophy. Their earliest disciples—most fellow members of a semi-secret Cambridge society called the Apostles—experienced an enthusiasm of messianic proportions. For Maynard Keynes (the same Keynes who wrote a pioneering essay on Newton the alchemist) it was "exciting, exhilarating, the beginning of a renaissance, the opening of a new heaven on a new earth, we were the forerunners of a dispensation, we were not afraid of anything."

They were particularly excited because G.E. Moore had discovered the true nature of The Good, and thereby had given a foundation to ethics, a foundation of mathematical certainty. Lytton Strachey wrote to the master himself, "The truth, there can be no doubt, is really upon the march. I date from October 1903 the beginning of the age of reason." October 1903 is the date of publication for Moore's

---

[18] The following account of the movement is based upon my *Confidence of British Philosophers*, Part IV.

Principia Ethica. Moore's disciples had begun to describe him in terms worthy of Apollo. "What a brain the fellow has! It dessicates mine! Dries up my lakes and seas and leaves me merely an arid tract of sand. Not that he is arid—anything but: he's merely the sun." Strachey ranked him ahead of Jesus. Keynes thought him better than Plato. Nearer the divine no mortal may approach.

And the parallels with Newton were far from accidental. Moore and Russell believed that they were completing the mathematization of philosophy begun by Descartes, a mathematization the first enduring monument of which was Newton's *Principia*. Newton had his *Principia*, Moore and Russell would each have theirs. And the personal exaltation they received from their disciples, no less than that received by Newton from his, was both functional to their movement and profoundly connected to the specific doctrine they taught.

Moore and Russell were convinced that the true foundations of Reason were to be found in indefinable ideas that, in some sense or other, really existed. Philosophy, therefore, consists in, to quote Russell, "the endeavor to see clearly, and to make others see clearly, the entities concerned." Through a process of analysis the philosopher would bring his reader or listener to a state in which these ideas would be present in all their simplicity in his mind. Then would come the moment of truth. The moment for which the philosopher had prepared his disciple, the moment at which the disciple *saw* the ideas, saw them as the deepest indefinable reality. Russell and Moore apparently were the first people in all of history ever to see these ideas as such, to know them for what they were in themselves, the first who could simply be in their presence without attempting definition. Who could doubt that this could be the beginning of a new age?

This is not to say that these visions were easily gained, even by someone whose mind was like the sun. In particular, Moore at times would feel himself unequal to his task of making lesser minds see what he saw. Here he is at the conclusion of one of his most famous papers, "The Refutation of Idealism," in which he tries to make his readers see consciousness as indefinably distinct from all other things.

> The moment we try to fix our attention upon consciousness and to see *what*, distinctly, it is, it seems to vanish: it seems as if we had before us a mere emptiness. When we try to introspect the sensation of blue, all we can see is the blue: the other element is as if it were diaphanous. Yet it *can* be distinguished if we look attentively enough, and if we know that there is something to look for. My main object in this paragraph has

been to try to make the reader *see* it; but I fear I shall have succeeded very ill.

Of course, one must not overemphasize the humility in this passage, or rather one must see how functional that humility is. If Moore has succeeded ill, it is perhaps because of his own inadequacies, the difficulty of the subject, *or* the obtuseness of the reader—but it is *not* because there is nothing to see. Moore's conviction in the reality of his vision is as strong as ever. The reader who doesn't see should try harder or simply take the word of someone who had.

Moore, Russell and their early disciples did not expect universal assent to their truths, any more than Newton did to his. They, like any believers in a transcendental reason, knew that argument, analysis could only lead to the threshold of vision. Their writing would serve to divide the world between those who had eyes to see the true and the good, and those who did not. And they trusted that the forces governing history, the future, would assure the triumph of those who had vision, as these forces had assured the triumph of Newton in his age.

My point quite simply is that the fundamental division in intellectual history lies less between the Descartes's and the Dury's, than between them both and the Montaigne's. The Descartes's and the Dury's of this world have far more in common than they, at least in the twentieth century, like to admit.

This makes it all the more important that we attend to—no, more than that, *emphasize* the millenarianism of the single greatest figure in the development of the modern mind, Isaac Newton. In his millenarian science he was near its strange core. Through the incongruous agglomeration that was his mind we can confront the incongruous agglomeration that is our own.

HENRY LEWIS GATES

THE VOICE IN THE TEXT: MESSIANISM, MILLENARIANISM, AND THE DISCOURSE OF THE BLACK IN THE EIGHTEENTH-CENTURY

> [if one can establish] that the negro intellect is fully equal to that of the white race ... you not only take away the best argument for keeping him in subjection, but you take away the possibility of doing so. *Prima facie*, however, the fact that he *is* a slave, is conclusive against the argument for his freedom, as it is against his equality of claim in respect of intellect .... Whenever the negro shall be fully fit for freedom, he will make himself free, and no power on earth can prevent him.
>
> —William Gilmore Simms[1]

I

In January, 1925, at the annual dinner celebration of the New York Urban League, Heywood Brown, generally a rather sedate observer, argued that only through Art could the Negro gain fully equality among the world's races, a metaphysical manumission, or legislated civil rights before the law. "A supremely great negro artist," Brown told a hushed crowd, "who could catch the imagination of the world, would do more than any other agency to remove the disabilities against which the negro now labors." Brown continued, moreover, that this messianic artist-redeemer could come at virtually anytime, then asked his audience to remain silent for ten seconds to imagine his coming! The Black Christ would be a poetaster.[2]

The notion of the production of art as a millennial force, indeed as the only force sufficient to refurbish dramatically the image of "the race" in the Western imagination, assumed its fullest shape in black letters in the New Negro Renaissance of the nineteen-twenties. Even that ironic entitlement, characterized by its hauntingly belated adjective "new," represents a profoundly secular appropriation of an

---

[1] William Gilmore Simms, rev. of *The Key to Uncle Tom's Cabin*, by Harriet Beecher Stowe, *Southern Quarterly Review* (July, 1853), p. 221.
[2] New York *Times*, 26 Jan. 1925, p. 3.

evangelical messianism which, since the Great Awakening of the mid-eighteenth century, has stood in relation to black letters, if not precisely as a determining influence, then at the least as an antithetical, negated discourse, an ironic silent second text, as it were, against which the creation of black letters is (in)formed. I mean to say, by this grand and sweeping generalization, that the writing of persons of African descent in Latin and Dutch, French and English, Spanish and German, since the eighteenth-century, has to a remarkable degree been characterized both explicitly and implicitly, thematically and structurally, by the twin concepts of millenarianism and messianism, *or* the act of deliverance through the printed word.

Heywood Brown's admonition to his 1925 Urban League auditors, only stands as a convenient emblem of a pervasive idea with a curiously received history. We could just as readily have overheard W.E.B. Du Bois addressing the newly-incorporated American Negro Academy, in 1897, on "The Conversation of Races." Du Bois, attempting eloquently to invert the racist typology of turn-of-the-century pseudoscience, asked rhetorically if black people "in America [have] a distinct mission as a race—a distinct sphere of action and an opportunity for race development, or is self-obliteration the highest end to which Negro blood dare aspire?" Du Bois, as was his wont, answered unequivocally:

> We are Americans, not only by birth and by citizenship, but by our political ideals, our language, our religion. Farther than that, our Americanism does not go. At that point, we are Negroes, members of a vast historic race that from the very dawn of creation has slept, but half awakening in the dark forests of its African fatherland. We are the first fruits of this new nation, the harbinger of that black tomorrow which is yet destined to soften the whiteness of the Teutonic to-day.[3]

It is only the descendants of Africans, Du Bois continues, who have saved America from "its mad money-getting plutocracy" by giving to a largely imitative and derived American culture its only unique contributions to the world's collective traditions of music and mythology, a black difference at all points touched by "pathos and humor," Du Bois continues, the only salient traces of humanism to be found among the multivarious strands that comprise the weave of "American" culture. It is only this slender black thread, Du Bois concludes,

---

[3] W.E.B. Du Bois, "The Conservation of Races," *The American Negro Academy Occasional Papers*, no. 2, (Washington: American Negro Academy, 1879), pp. 11–12.

which saves America from its anti-humanist proclivities. To deliver the nation fully is the mission of "the race." A touch of the tar-brush makes the culture humane. More particularly, Du Bois draws upon the figure of inscription to make his clearest statement about the redemptive mission—the millennial impulse and mandate—of "the race":

> No people that laughs at itself, and ridicules itself, and wishes to God it was anything but itself ever wrote its name in history; it *must* be inspired with the Divine faith of our black mothers, that out of the blood and dust of battle will march a victorious host, a mighty nation, a peculiar people, to speak to the nations of earth a Divine truth that shall make them free.[4]

Here, Du Bois endows "the race," as a collective force, with a messianic function and a crucial millennial role in that vast and turbulent terrain of the creation of a humanistic—and humane—world culture. Black people deserved equality, he implies, because they alone are especially suited for an especial "mission," a mission destined to be realized and signified by those especial powers, racially-determined, which he would later call "the gift of black folk."

Du Bois's conflation of messianism and millenarianism is only an elegantly-structured sign of a pervasive idea within black letters at the turn-of-the-century and well beyond the New Negro Renaissance. Indeed, Du Bois's figuration of the race as millennial redeemer is only a summary of two hundred years of a curious dialectic between the representation of blacks in Western discourse as messianic forces, and the idea outlined above, nurtured by black people themselves, that by inscribing their "racial-self" in western discourse they could both liberate "the race" from racist aspersions upon the collective black intellect and perhaps fulfill the larger "mission" of restoring post-Renaissance Western culture's impulse toward a meaningful humanism. The (so-called) Western dissociation of sensibility, which Eric Auerbach, for example, attributes to the fratricide of the First World War, blacks attribute to the enslavement and bondage of the African by the European in the fifteen and sixteenth centuries, a transformation of human beings into commodities for barter and consumption as pernicious as cannibalism, and sufficiently lucrative to support in part those splendid movements of ideas, of the arts and sciences,

---

[4] Ibid., p. 12.

which we know as the Renaissance and, later, as the Enlightenment.

The discourse of the black—by which coinage I mean the black as subject *and* object in Western discourse (how blacks are *figured* in western languages, and how blacks *figure* western languages)—is as densely peopled with Black messiahs as it is informed by what we might, with some profit, think of as the millennial impulse implicit in the very *creation* of black letters themselves. This is not the place to undertake a foray into sources; nor, however, is this sort of collection and cataloguing of images necessary, since scholars of black literature have, at least since the Paris Exhibition, prepared with infectious zeal annotated lists of titles by and about black subjects. Most recently, Wilson Jeremiah Moses, in *Black Messiahs and Uncle Toms*, has explicated in wonderfully careful detail the social and figurative manifestations of messianism within black culture, essentially from the mid-nineteenth century to the post-Martin Luther King era. In the presence of such historical erudition, I have no need to rehearse, or could serve little purpose by rehearsing Professor Wilson's observations.[5]

Rather, I would like to point to a few examples of the black as messianic figure, which serve to demonstrate the various ways in which the ancient tradition of messianism has manifested itself within the discourse of the black between Du Bois and the Latin Middle Ages. Then, I wish to show how this theme of the black-as-redeemer became "internalized," as it were, within Anglo-African discourse in the eighteenth-century, becoming the very *structuring principle*, the silent second text, of black letters themselves, culminating in the ironic form of Heywood Brown's fantasy, of the Black Redeemer as a Black Dante, a Black Shakespeare. Figure, or *topos*, becomes structuring principle, and principle of structure, in its turn, again becomes theme.

Traditions of figuration are sometimes easier to trace retrospectively, just as Merlin moved through time. This, after all, is one import of T.S. Eliot's claim, in "Tradition and the Individual Talent," that a great new work of art revises remarkably that manner in which we formulate our textual notions of "tradition." Revised tropes teach us how to read key texts, again retrospectively; and the trope of the black

---

[5] Wilson Jeremiah Moses, *Black Messiahs and Uncle Toms: Social and Literary Manipulation of a Religious Myth* (University Park: The Pennsylvania State University Press, 1982).

as Messiah is both central and recurring in the discourse of the black, and in its discrete manifestations serves to reveal just how dynamic our tradition's received definitions of messianism splendidly are.

Black messiahs abound in the twentieth century, from Marcus Garvey to Martin Luther King, by way of Sweet Daddy Grace and Father Divine. I wish to mention here, however, only a few nineteenth-century fictional examples of this type to remind us just how pervasive this figure has been. Toussaint L'Ouverture and Nat Turner, both in deed and in legend, are the nineteenth-century's prototypical historical Black messiahs. In fiction, on the other hand, the crucial decade of the 1850's "opened," in a sense, with the ironic portrayal of the Christ-like Uncle Tom, and ended with Martin R. Delany's negation of the long-suffering Tom, a character called Henricus Blacus, whom Delany created to be the protagonist of his novel, *Blake*. While Uncle Tom needs little introduction, the figure of Henricus Blacus, perhaps, is somewhat less familiar.

The figures of Uncle Tom and Henricus Blacus are polar opposite Black messiahs, figured negations whose exaggerated extremes define the two types of Black Redeemer-as-personal savior, neither of whom seem to be too distant in Western discourse when the other appears. It is important to pause here a bit to consider these two figures, since we may read both as bifurcations of that late eighteenth-century Black Redeemer, who managed somehow to contain these warring aspects of personality within one princely demeanor. I am thinking here of Aphra Behn's Oroonoko, whom many scholars believe to be our first black noble savage, a maroon version of the great Prester John.

Uncle Tom descends from the eighteenth century "Dying Negro" genre of romantic poetry, as exemplified in Thomas Day and John Bicknell's well-known poem, aptly entitled *The Dying Negro, a Poetical Epistle, from a Black, Who Shot Himself on Board a Vessel in the River Thames, to His Intended Wife*, published at London in 1773. The Dying Negro genre of poetry, as well-intended as it was, sought, however, to convert foes to friends of abolition by arousing sentiment and tears, by a direct appeal not to empathy, but to sympathy. An epigraph to this mode of poetry could well be the following sentence about the Hottentots printed in *Gentleman's Magazine* in 1775: "But what signifies the mind's being vacant, if the heart be full, and the sweet emotions of nature agitate it?" The effectiveness of the Dying Negro poem meant that the black subjects depicted in these poems could not partake of the commanding strength and compelling presence of the European convention of the noble savage. We realize that with some clarity by considering the character of Uncle Tom.

In popular usage, an "Uncle Tom" is one who, in one of several forms, betrays his race. I say "his" race because, in the feminine, an Uncle Tom becomes an "Aunt Jane." Harriet Beecher Stowe's Uncle Tom, however, the figure of the black messiah as redeemer through silent suffering, would seem to bear little in common with his debased metaphorical heritage. Upon reflection, however, we realize that Uncle Tom's "crime" against the race, to subsequent generations of blacks, was precisely this silence in the face of relentless persecution. Tom's very failure to defend his self is a failure to defend the race, in a synechdochic relation of part-for-whole. No racial self-defense, most certainly results in racial suicide, a death for the whole as resoundingly final as the individual deaths of Uncle Tom and his antecedents who dwell in the Dying Negro poems.

Tom was the martyred Black messiah, sacrificed as a surrogate for the sins of the South. The collective messianism that we have explicated in the turn-of-the-century writings of Du Bois, Mrs. Stowe prefigures in the words of George Harris:

> I think that the African race has peculiarities yet to be unfolded in the light of civilization and Christianity, which, if not the same with those of the Anglo-Saxon, may prove to be, morally, of even a higher type .... If not a dominant and commanding race, they are, at least an affectionate, magnanimous, and forgiving one ....[6]

Although it may seem ironic to link George Harris's sentiment about affection, magnanimity, and forgiveness to the strident Du Bois, who stands for many of us today as an almost mythic figure of would-be redemption with the pen, rhetorically "dominant and commanding," we must not forget that even Du Bois's still resonant "Credo" includes the notion that "the Negro Race: in the beauty of its genius, the sweetness of its soul, and its strength in [its] meekness ... shall yet inherit this turbulent earth."[7] This despite the fact that Du Bois embodies in our own mythology the central example of the black, eternal-return, the black who, time, penance, and apprenticeship served dutifully in the wilderness, returns to mete out justice to the

---

[6] Harriet Beecher Stowe, *Uncle Tom's Cabin* (1852; New York: Dodd, Mead, 1952), p. 428.

[7] W.E.B. Du Bois, *Darkwater: Voices from Within the Veil* (New York: Harcourt, Brace, 1920), pp. 3–4.

oppressor with his own tools of domination: for Du Bois, the sword of redemption is the pen itself, and in the printed word is to be wielded the telling sword of redemption.

More closely related to Du Bois in the sense of the myth of messianic redemption as the eternal retributive return is Martin Delany's protagonist of his novel, *Blake*, Henricus Blacus. Delany's novel, serialized partially in the *Anglo-African Magazine* in 1859, then fully in *The Weekly Anglo-African* in 1861, is an explicit formal revision, indeed negation, of *Uncle Tom's Cabin*. Both texts were serialized before they were printed as books; and there their direct similarities end. The negative pastiche of *Blake*, or the formal signifying as I defined this sort of formal revision, begins with the two text's titles. Although Stowe's initial serialized subtitle was "The Man Who Was a Thing," her novel's title stresses Tom's *cabin* as her subject as much as the kindly Uncle Tom. Delany's subtitle, "The Huts of America," revises and critiques Stowe by a metaphorical substitution which inserts peasant connotations to the life of the slave. Delany also substitutes a revolutionary black for Stowe's mulatto George Harris, then critiques Stowe's representation of the personal messiah as masochistic martyr by figuring a hero who not only escapes and surreptitiously tours the South, sharing with other slaves his dream of a united insurrection against the slave-holders, but who then sails to Cuba, buys his wife's freedom, becomes General of a black revolutionary force, and, with the aid and poetry of Placido, the black Cuban poet, plots a revolution for Cuba that would free it from American colonization. *Blake*, in short, is *Uncle Tom* turned inside-out, a marvelous signifying riff upon Harriet Beecher Stowe (Delany even uses as epigraphs to the two parts of his novel stanzas from Stowe's poetry, transforming them thereby from expressions of piety, in their initial context, into battle-cries for black warriors). Harvard-trained Martin R. Delany stands Mrs. Stowe upon her pro-colonization, Protestant New England head!

Henricus Blacus, we are quick to see, is the fictional representation of black historical personages such as Toussiant and Nat Turner, Gabriel Prosser and Denmark Vesey. More relevant in this context, Henricus Blacus and Uncle Tom merely embody two salient aspects of Mrs. Aphra Behn's noble black messiah, Oroonoko, the stage versions of which proved to be so popular as to warrant frequent productions in England and in France between 1696 and 1800.

Long before Nat Turner's unsuccessful rebellion at Virginia in

1831, Europeans and Americans had both feared and predicted the coming of a Black Messiah, who, after demonstrating a remarkable degree of intelligence and Christian piety, would *turn* against the evil white enslavers, *returning* in kind the horrors of enslavement with redemptive, violent retributive justice. We recall Thomas Jefferson's fear of cataclysmic fall of the young Republic, recorded in his *Notes on the State of Virginia*, which because of its implicit equation of the "turn" of the wheel of fortune with the "return" of a nation's sins upon itself, here warrants citation:

> And can the liberties of a nation be thought secure when we have removed their only firm basis, a conviction in the minds of the people that these liberties are the gift of God? That they are not to be violated but with his wrath? Indeed I tremble for my country when I reflect that God is just; that his justice cannot sleep forever; that considering numbers, nature and natural means only, a revolution of the wheel of fortune, an exchange of situation is among possible events; that it may become probable by supernatural interference! The Almighty has no attribute which can take side with us in such a contest.[8]

Jefferson, of course, merely reiterates here the Abbé Raynal's call, published in his great *History* of 1770, for a rebellion of slaves, a cataclysmic upheaval, led by a "Black Spartacus," "who would be a vehicle for nature asserting her rights against the blind avarice of European and American colonists."[9] The millenary promise of America, the Abbé maintained, could only be fulfilled with the retributive, bloody return of the Black Messiah. Just as original sin was endemic to human beings, so too was human slavery endemic to America, preventing it from realizing its true state of bliss. Slavery and original sin were bound together in a synechdoche of part for whole in the discourse of millennial America.

II

We have been working steadily in reverse from the discourse of Afro-American messianism and millennialism, as conflated in W.E.B. Du Bois, to the turn of the eighteenth-century; to a period which for

---

[8] Thomas Jefferson, *Notes on the State of Virginia* (New York: Harper & Row, 1964), p. 156.
[9] David Brion Davis, *The Problem of Slavery in Western Culture* (Ithaca: Cornell University Press, 1966), p. 17.

our purposes here we can date from 1688, marked by the publication of *Oroonoko; or The Royal Slave*, to 1892, in which David Walker published his messianic *Appeal in Four Articles* and an anonymous author published *The Ethiopian Manifesto*. Since the *literacy* of the character, Oroonoko, is so crucial to an understanding of the subtle manner in which millennialism—the very black voice of individual deliverance which would, in turn, deliver America from slavery, truly, its original sin—I would like to discuss briefly two configurations of the black messianic myth, the myth of the eternal return, which even the most diligent scholars of millennialism tend to overlook. I refer here to the medieval myth of Prester John, and to the eighteenth-century Asante myth of Osei Tutu, and the sword-in-the-stone.

We know from visual evidence collected by Ladislas Bugner and the Menil Foundation that the great Ethiopian Emperor, Prester John, was depicted as a black African in visual and verbal late medieval and early Renaissance texts.[10] As the slave-trade increased, certain versions of the myth retained Ethiopia as the site of John's kingdom, peopled with black subjects, but transmuted John's color from black to white, approximately at the same time, paradoxically, in which a black magus first appeared in European representations of the nativity, as if in a displacement relationship. Nevertheless, Prester John was the first great black messianic figure in the European imagination, a direct prefiguration of "the noble slave," Oroonoko.

If the Christian Church often cast the black man in the part of the Devil, it also provided the source of a marvelous myth of a miraculous black king of Ethiopia whose power and dominion were so unequalled and so vast that European nations took to the seas to find this king and secure his allegiance in the Holy Crusades against the Saracen Muslims. This legendary king was called Prester John. The chronicler of Prince Henry the Navigator's pioneering voyages down the West Coast of Africa tells us that the search for Prester John was one of the main reasons the Portuguese Prince was determined to explore the then uncharted waters of Africa. These voyages of Prince Henry's, and the thousands of other voyages that followed, led to the enslavement of the black Africans for plantation labor in the New World. It is indeed a dark irony of history that the search for the black Christian king, Prester John, led not to his discovery in far-off Ethiopia, but

---

[10] *The Image of the Black in Western Art* Vol. II (New York: William Morrow, 1979).

to the discovery of a labor force of millions of black slaves. And indirectly, it was slavery which helped to produce the splendor that made the Renaissance possible, including the great works of Da Vinci, Michelangelo, and Raphael, among countless other master artists.

When we read of Prester John's splendor, it is not difficult to appreciate Prince Henry's zeal.[11] These splendors were recounted in a letter which appeared in Europe in the latter half of the twentieth century. In the letter, sent to various Christian kings and especially to the Emperor Manuel of Constantinople and the Roman Emperor Frederick, the fabulous Prester John declared himself to be a Christian ruler over a vast empire. The letter announced that Prester John was willing to liberate the Holy Sepulchre from the Muslim infidels against whom Christian Europe had launched the Crusades. Prester John extended an invitation to Western rulers to enter his service. In return, the great king promised high administrative offices and large estates to those who followed him. But more important, Prester John's letter described the river for which so many Spanish *conquistadores* sought in vain in the New World. That river was the Fountain of Youth, the miracle waters of which made it possible for the Apostle Thomas, though dead for over a millennium, to preach annually the wonders of Christian faith in one of the Prester's royal places.

The myth of an immortal black King of the Ethiopians reminds us of Homer's depiction of the ancient Aethiopians, the most blessed and favored of Zeus and all the gods. But there was no king on earth like the five hundred year old Prester John. Prester John, a descendant of the black magus who made the pilgrimage to the infant Jesus, wielded an emerald scepter, and an imaginative pen. John's kingdom included an enchanted palace, a magic looking-glass, dukes, counts, and knights who served as servants, bishops and archbishops who stood as his advisors. His army was comprised of more than one million troops, and no less than seventy-two kings paid him tribute. Where, then, was this remarkable country? "Our magnificence," he writes, "dominates the Three Indias, and extends to farther India, where the body of St. Thomas the Apostle rests. It reaches through the valley of deserted Babylon close by the Tower of Babel."

Neither south in the heart of Africa nor west in the New World did

---

[11] This summary of Prester John's Kingdom is derived from Ronald Sanders, *Lost Tribes and Promised Lands: The Origins of American Racism* (Boston: Little, Brown, 1978), pp. 40–43.

the Spanish, Portuguese, or English explorers ever find the magical kingdoms of Prester John. When a diplomatic mission finally reached Ethiopia in 1520, after many futile attempts, they found "not the jewel-studded realm of the Prester John legend, but the thatched roofs and rock of the kingdom of Lebna Dengel.[12] But European voyagers, as they discovered more and more black Africans along the coasts of Africa, brought back to Europe with them vivid and fantastic descriptions of black monsters and cannibals related much more closely in size and shape to the ape than to European human beings.

Even during the High Middle Ages, received knowledge retained a certain primacy, with almost disastrous consequences on the popular image of the black. As Europe lingered in this twilight of the mind, even the greater geographers and cosmographers of the fourteenth centuries were slow to correct the received correlation between blackness and monsters. Their maps of the world, the *mappae mundi*, teem with anthropophagi, homunculi, Troglodites, earless people, noseless people, headless races, gorgons, and sea monsters—a surprising number of whom happen to be black.

Lest we think that the medieval messianic expectations of Prester John had long since died by the seventeenth-century, let me recount a curious event. In 1634, an Ethiopian visitor arrived at Paris, and announced himself to be the Zaga Chrestos, or "Zaga Christ," the son of Emperor Jakub. According to contemporary accounts, this Ethiopian was received in court with considerable fanfare and embraced as the son of the long-sought deliverer, Prester John. Cardinal Richelieu, practical soul that he was, awarded the Zaga-Christ, a stipend, and kept him at Court for three years. But doubts about this messiah's credentials arose and persisted. Jean Dubois Fontannelle's *Anecdotes Africaines*, published in 1775, informs us that although the Zaga-Christ was thought to be an impostor, his name a fabrication, his epitaph was prepared to cover all possibilities: "Here lies the king of Ethiopia," its first line reads, "The original or the copy."[13]

One indigenous Black African messianic myth surrounds the life of Akomfo Anokye, the priest who helped Osei Tutu to found the Asante State in the late seventeenth century. The story has become an Akan topos. Akomfo Anokye was the priest who helped Osei

---

[12] Ibid., pp. 118–19.
[13] See Hans Werner Debrunner, *Presence and Prestige: Africans in Europe* (Basel: Basler Afrika Bibliographien, 1979), pp. 52–53.

Tutu, the first great Asante king, in the foundation of the Asante State at the turn of the eighteenth-century. He brought down the Golden Stool from heaven, according to tradition, and the Stool remains the most important item of the Asante Royal Paraphernalia. He also created a number of other magical symbols of the new unity of the Asante State: among them a bag containing many charms, which he said should never be opened, and of which he said its opening would lead to the dissolution of the State. Another symbol was a sword inserted in the earth, which he claimed also held the Asante nation magically together: its removal from the earth would also lead to the dissolution of the State. The bag, which is in the museum at the National Cultural Centre in Kumasi, Asante, has still not been opened, so far as anyone knows; and the sword is still in the ground in the gardens of the central hospital—Akomfo Anokye hospital—in Kumasi. Anthony Appiah can still remember Prince Philip and President Nkrumah both half-heartedly trying to pull it out of the ground on the Queen's visit to Ghana in 1962. The sword was a traditional Akan sword, with a wooden, carved handle and a metal blade, in length, I suppose, about 2 feet. It appears that at some point the sword's placement in the soil has been reinforced by the addition of concrete: a reflection of the seriousness with which Akomfo Anokye's predictions were taken. Akomfo Anokye is not supposed to have died. He went off into the forest, promising to return with the secret of eternal life, and saying that he would return if no one celebrated his funeral. Unfortunately, his enemies did celebrate his funeral: he returned to the ancestors.[14]

It would be irresponsible even to suggest connections between this Akan myth and eighteenth-century Anglo-African versions of the return. We can note in passing, nevertheless, that scores of eighteenth-century sources record the widely-held belief among Afro-Americans that death meant the "return to Guinea" for their souls, to be united, forever, with loved ones. Only death and the spiritual return dispelled the Black Diaspora. The physical return to Africa called for by a Black Messiah such as Marcus Garvey or maintained even today by the Jamaican Rastafarians is only the physical counterpart of an eighteenth century black metaphysical belief. Indeed, this

---

[14] See K. Yeboa Daaku, *Osei Tutu of Asante* (London: Heinemann, 1976). I am profoundly indebted to Anthony Appiah, Assistant Professor of Philosophy at Yale, for bringing this curious myth to my attention.

belief of the return to a millennial, post-White Africa is echoed in the refrain from a black spiritual, "O fly away home fly away," which in turn echoes the myth of the Georgia Sea Island blacks of "The Flying African," who could, while alive, simply spread his wings and return home. Versions of this myth were recorded as late as 1940 by the Savannah Unit of the Georgia Writer's Project. Robert Hayden's poem, "O Daedalus, Fly Away Home," prefigures a more familiar version of this myth, to be found in Toni Morrison's *Song of Solomon*.[15]

These popular mythic versions of messianism and millenarianism were well in place by the middle of the eighteenth-century, when Africans began to publish their works in English. We can begin to suggest the subtle manner by which these ideas of messianism and millenarianism, as exemplified by the myth of the eternal return and of individual and collective deliverance, informed eighteenth-century Anglo-African writing if we consider Aphra Behn's characterization of Oroonoko, the royal slave.

As I suggested earlier, the antithetical fictions of the Black Redeemer, as drawn in the figures of Uncle Tom and Henricus Blacus, are in fact subsequent bifurcations of a unity of opposites which seemed to dwell in repose in the "character" of Oroonoko. Published in 1688 as a short novel, adapted for the stage by Thomas Southerne and John Hawkesworth, and translated into French by Antoine de Laplace and the Abbe le Blanc, *Oroonoko* became one of the most popular tales of the eighteenth-century, and the prototype of many subsequent black noble savage figures. So popular and moving was the tale, that in 1749 two African princes, who had been betrayed, sold into slavery, ransomed by the British government, and presented to King George himself, attended a Covent Garden production of the play. The audience greeted their arrival warmly. One prince was so overcome at the suffering of Oroonoko that he had to leave the theatre at act four; the other remained, weeping openly.

I need not here recount the novel's plot. It is crucial to recall, however, that Oroonoko is an ironic African and an ironic noble savage, described as having a Roman nose, the body of a Greek god, and a face of "perfect Ebony, or polished jet," a princely contrast to his fellow black slaves, who "suffer'd not like men, who might find

---

[15] See Robert Hayden's account of this myth in "The Poet and His Art: A Conversation," in *How I Write*/1 (New York: Harcourt Brace Jovanovich, 1972), pp. 180–81.

a Glory and Fortitude in Oppression; but like Dogs, that lov'd the Whip and Bell, and fawn'd the more they were beaten." Despite his contempt for his ignoble and savage countrymen, Oroonoko at last leads a rebellion, becoming thereby the first great black Caesar, as he comes to be called, prefiguring Henricus Blacus, in fiction, and even Nat Turner, in real life. Mrs. Behn's description of his reaction to his brutal execution prefigures the patient martyrdom of Mrs. Stowe's Uncle Tom:

> And the Executioner came, and first cut off his Members, and threw them into the Fire; after that, with an ill-favour'd Knife, they cut off his Ears and his Nose, and burn'd them; he still smoak'd on, as if nothing had touch'd him; they hack'd off one of his Arms, and still he bore up and held his Pipe; but at the cutting off the other Arm, His Head sunk, and his Pipe dropt .... Thus died this great Man, worthy of a better Fate, and a more sublime Wit than mine to write his Praise: Yet, I hope, the Reputation of my Pen is considerable enough to make his glorious Name to survive to all Ages, with that of the brave, the beautiful and the constant *Imoinda*.[16]

More relevant to this discussion, however, is one crucial characteristic which Mrs. Behn attributes to Oroonoko, and which distinguishes him from the ignoble savages whom he leads as surely as do his aquiline features and his mysteriously straightened hair. I am referring here to his mastery of formal letters, of what the seventeenth and eighteenth centuries called "the arts and sciences." Indeed, Oroonoko's stellar literacy and capacity to interpret are as crucial to his characteristics as a Black Messiah as are his Roman nose and his straightened hair (He even comes to be called "Caesar" and studies Caesar's accounts of his war campaign.). Scholars often forget that the historical Nat Turner, like the fictional Oroonoko, was thought to have gained power and control over his fellow slaves and his slaveholding foes because of his ability to read and write, and because of the brilliance of his exegetical skills with even the darkest and most concealed passages of the Scriptures. The hallmark of superiority, in the eighteenth century, was mastery of the arts and sciences.

That Oroonoko would take the name of the author of text reminds us, of course of antebellum black naming practices after a bondsman escaped to freedom and the ex-slave became a man. Frederick

---

[16] Aphra Behn, *Oroonoko: or, the Royal Slave. A True History* (1688; New York: W.W. Norton, 1973), pp. 77–78.

Douglass's surname, for instance, a black man conferred upon him because of would-be similarities between Frederick and the character of *The Lady in the Lake*. Oroonoko is, in this sense, a prefiguration of naming practices in the tradition. But it is Oroonoko's *literacy*, inextricably bound with both his role as a Black Messiah and with the millennial thrust of his aborted revolution, which is of most import to the birth of the Anglo-African literary tradition in the eighteenth-century.

I could readily trace examples of the themes of messianism and millenarianism in the first writings of blacks in English. Both Phillis Wheatley and Jupiter Hammon, who published poems in the 1760's and the 1770's, freely admit their belief in the returning Christ and their joy at the Great Awakening. Wheatley so admired the Rev. George Whitefield that she published a moving tribute in his honor, the poem which was probably most frequently reprinted in her lifetime. Equiano, the great African master of narrative, makes Whitefield a character in his autobiography, whose sermon moved him deeply. Other black authors of the period are equally pious, and equally await both earthly deliverance and deliverance from slavery. It is this rather secular conception of deliverance, however, which came to be thematized in black texts, which also provided the motivational thrust of the enterprise of writing itself, and which reveals the curious manner in which the notion of a millennial-deliverance occupied the center of the black texts of the eighteenth-century. And that the first black slave narrative, Briton Hammon's *Narrative of the Uncommon Sufferings*, emphasizes the narrator's *Surprising Deliverance* in its title, serves as a convenient point of departure for us to trace this definition of literacy as a millennial force.

Anglo-African writing arose as a response to allegations of its absence, and claims that the African *could* not ever master the arts and sciences. Black people, we know, responded to these profoundly serious allegations about their "nature" as directly as they could: they wrote books; poetry, autobiographical narrative, political and philosophical discourse were the predominant forms of writing. Among these, autobiographical "deliverance" narratives were the most common, and the most accomplished. Accused of lacking a formal and collective history, blacks published individual histories which, taken together, were intended to narrate, in segments, the larger yet fragmented history of blacks in Africa, now dispersed throughout a cold New World. The narrated, descriptive "eye" was put into service as a literary form to posit both the individual "I" of the black author, as well as the collective "I" of the race. Text created author, and black authors, it was hoped, would create, or recreate, the image of the race in European discourse. The very *face* of the race, representations of the features of which are common in all sorts of writings about blacks at this time, was contingent upon the recording of the black *voice*. Voice presupposes a face, but also seems to have been thought to determine the contours of the black face.

The recordings of an authentic black voice, a voice of deliverance from the deafening discursive silence which an enlightened Europe cited as proof of the absence of the African's humanity, was the millenial instrument of transformation through which the African would become the human being. So central was this idea to the birth of the black literary tradition in the eighteenth-century that five of the first six eighteenth-century slave narratives draw upon the figure of the voice in the text as crucial "scenes of instruction" in the development of the slave on the road to freedom. James Gronniosaw, in 1770, John Marrant, in 1785, Otoobah Cugoano, in 1787, Olaudah Equiano, in 1789, and John Jea in 1806 all draw upon the figure of the voice in the text. Gronniosaw's usage bears citing here:

> My master used to read prayers in public to the ship's crew every Sabbath day; and when I first saw him read, I was never so surprised in my life, as when I saw the book talk to my master, for I thought it did, as I observed him to look upon it, and move his lips. I wished it would do so with me. As soon as my master had done reading, I followed him to the place where he put the book, being mightily delighted with it, and when nobody saw me, I opened it, and put my ear down close upon it, in great hope that it would say something to me; but I was very sorry, and greatly disappointed, when I found that it would not speak. This thought immediately presented itself to me, that every body and every thing despised me because I was black.[17]

That James Gronniosaw's figure of the talking book became the first and the fundamental *topos* of the Afro-American literary tradition attests to a degree of intertextuality, repetition, and difference in eighteenth-century black letters which scholars have not fully appreciated before.[18] More relevant to this context, however, is the fact

---

[17] James Albert Ukawsaw Gronniosaw, *A Narrative of the Most Remarkable Particulars in the Life of James Albert Ukawsaw Gronniosaw, an African Prince. Related by Himself* (1770; London: R. Groombridge, 1840), p. 8.

[18] I trace this relation of revisions in *The Signifying Monkey: A Theory of Literary History*, forthcoming.

that Gronniosaw's figure would seem to be an unwitting revision of a similar figure that Immanuel Kant used in his *Observations on the Feeling of the Beautiful and Sublime*, published in 1764.

In Section Four of his essay, Kant, revising Hume's opinions of the permanent inferiority of black people, as signified by their absence of "the arts and sciences,"[19] writes that

> The Negroes of Africa have by nature no feeling that rises above the trifling. Mr. Hume challenges anyone to cite a single example in which a Negro has shown talents, and asserts that among the hundreds of thousands of blacks who are transported elsewhere from their countries, although many of them have even been set free, still not a single one was ever found who presented anything great in art or science or any other praise-worthy quality, even though among the whites some continually rise aloft from the lowest rabble, and through superior gifts earn respect in the world. So fundamental is the difference between these two races of man, and it appears to be as great in regard to mental capacities as in color.[20]

Then, asserting that black men keep their women "always in a prison," because "a despairing man is always a strict master over anyone weaker," Kant repeats a quotation from a text of Father Labat's, which is a purported critique of European sexual relations rendered by an African. Kant's judgment upon the man's *capacity* for wisdom prefigures Gronniosaw's concluding sentence about the curse of his own blackness: "And it might be that there was something in this which perhaps deserved to be considered," Kant concludes, "but in short, this fellow was quite black from head to foot, a clear proof that what he said was stupid."[21] Clearly, as early as this, the curse of blackness could be eradicated only by the profound breaking of the silence of the African in Western letters.

That the figure of the talking book recurs in these five black eighteenth-century texts says much about the degree of presupposition and intertextuality in early black letters, more than we heretofore thought. Equally important, however, this figure itself underscores

---

[19] David Hume, "Of National Characters," *Essays and Treatises on Several Subjects*, 2 vols. (Edinburgh: Printed for Bell and Bradfate, and W. Blackwood; [etc.], 1825), I, pp. 521–22.
[20] Immanuel Kant, *Observations on the Feeling of the Beautiful and Sublime* trans. John T. Goldthwait (1764; Berkeley: University of California Press, 1960), pp. 110–11.
[21] Ibid., p. 113.

the received correlation between silence and blackness which we have been tracing, as well as the urgent need to make the text speak, the process by which the slave marked his distance from the master. The voice in the text was truly a millennial voice for the African person of letters in the eighteenth-century, for it was that very voice of deliverance and of redemption which would signify a new order for the black, and a degree of "freedom" larger than even "mere" manumission from slavery. It was to redress this enslavement of the mind that other writers in the black tradition, from Phillis Wheatley through the Harlem Renaissance, determined to produce black letters. The Black Messiah would, indeed, be a poetaster.